LESSONS OF THE
SPANISH REVOLUTION
1936-1939

Vernon Richards
Introduction by David Goodway

Lessons of the Spanish Revolution: 1936–1939
Vernon Richards
This edition © 2019 PM Press
All rights reserved. No part of this book may be transmitted by any means without
permission in writing from the publisher.

ISBN: 978-1-62963-647-4
Library of Congress Control Number: 2018949093

Cover by John Yates / www.stealworks.com

10 9 8 7 6 5 4 3 2 1

PM Press
PO Box 23912
Oakland, CA 94623
www.pmpress.org

Printed in the USA

Publisher's Note

This book began as a series of twenty-three weekly articles for the anarchist journal *Freedom* (July–December 1952). They were reprinted in volume form with an introduction (July 1953). A Japanese translation appeared the following year.

For an Italian edition in 1957 the author produced a considerably expanded version. Part I remained unchanged apart from minor corrections and some additions. Part II was all new material except for chapter 18 and the first part of the conclusions. A Spanish edition was published in Paris (Bellibaste, 1971).

For the second Freedom Press edition (1972) a bibliographical postscript was added to the Italian edition. This version has since been published in French (Paris: Editions 10/18, 1975), Italian (Pistoia: Edizioni "V. Vallera," 1974) and Spanish (Madrid: Campo Abierto Ediciones, 1977 [reprinted 1978]).

For the third Freedom Press edition (1983) the author added footnotes to a bibliographical postscript and also reprinted from *Freedom* (January 1978) a review of the third edition of Hugh Thomas's *The Spanish Civil War*.

This, the 2019 PM Press edition of Vernon Richards's classic analysis of the Spanish Civil War, is largely a reprint of the Freedom Press 1983 edition, with certain modernizations to spelling, hyphenation, capitalization, and punctuation. One brief section of approximately ten pages in the previous edition was removed—an overly arcane and largely redundant critique of the second edition of Hugh Thomas's *The Spanish Civil War*, a book already critically addressed at length elsewhere in the text.

CONTENTS

PART 2

INTRODUCTION
LESSONS OF THE SPANISH REVOLUTION AND VERNON RICHARDS

Lessons of the Spanish Revolution originated as twenty-three weekly articles published in *Freedom* between July and December 1952. In July 1953, these were reprinted as a book. A considerably expanded version was prepared for an Italian edition of 1957; and it was this text that was published as the second Freedom Press edition in 1972. A third Freedom Press edition appeared in 1983. In its various forms it has been one of Freedom Press's most influential and best-selling publications.

Lessons is a brutal, unrelenting and entirely unforgiving critique of the CNT-FAI's decision to enter the Popular Front government in October 1936, impressive in its documentation and irrefutable in its logic. On September 3, a clear-sighted editorial in *Solidaridad Obrera*, the CNT's daily newspaper, had argued: "The coordination of the forces of the Popular Front, of the organization of the supply of foodstuffs with an extensive collectivization of undertakings is of vital interest in achieving our objectives. . . . It has been achieved up to now in a non-governmental, decentralized, demilitarized manner." In contrast, it foresaw:

> A coalition government . . . with its base political struggles between majorities and minorities, its bureaucratization, based on chosen elites, and the fratricidal struggles in which the opposing political factions are engaged, [would] make it impossible for such a government to benefit our work of

liberation in Spain. It would lead to the rapid destruction of our capacity of action, of our will to unity and the beginning of an imminent debacle before a still fairly strong enemy.

Federica Montseny, who became one of the four anarchist ministers in the Madrid government, consulted her father, the veteran anarchist intellectual Federico Urales, before reaching her decision, and he had warned:

> You know what this means. In fact, it is the liquidation of anarchism of the CNT. Once in power you will not rid yourselves of Power.

Richards argues that the libertarian leadership made two fundamental errors, inexcusable since they were not errors of judgment but a deliberate abandonment of their principles. First was their belief that the war against authority could be waged more successfully within the framework of the state and by subordinating all else, including economic and social transformation, to winning the war. Second was their naive conviction that "it was essential, and possible, to collaborate with political parties—that is with politicians—honestly and sincerely," and this at a time when real power belonged to the CNT-FAI and the socialist UGT. As Montseny was to confess: "in politics we were quite ingenuous." From the outset the professional politicians ran rings around the libertarians, who were outwitted and outmanoeuvred on every issue. And whereas contact with the libertarians had no ideological impact on the politicians, some leading members of the CNT were converted to the principles of government and centralized authority, not just temporarily but permanently.

For Richards, the May Days of 1937 in Barcelona equate with Kronstadt in Russia in 1921, marking the suppression of the popular movement as it attempted to resuscitate the revolution. He concludes: "With the defeat of the revolution in May 1937 by the central authority the leaders of the CNT-FAI no longer represented a force to be reckoned with by the government, which proceeded to take over the militias, abolish the workers' patrols in the rearguard, and smash the collectives, thus pulling the teeth of the revolution; and it was left to the leaders of the CNT to break its heart."

Richards further considers that libertarians were misguided in voting for the Popular Front parties in the general election of February 1936. In 1933, the left had been routed in the first election under the new constitution of the Second Spanish Republic, largely on account of anarchist abstention. In consequence the *Bieno Negro* (Two Black Years) of reactionary rule followed, amassing thirty-three thousand political prisoners. The second *No Votar!* (Do Not Vote!) campaign was therefore half-hearted, and the Popular Front was able to form a government. Yet its victory was a disaster, Richards argues, since an effective military uprising now became inevitable. In contrast, had the right won, military conspiracy would have petered out. He insists, very salutarily given the customary loose language employed about "fascism," that there is "no real evidence to show that there was any significant development of a fascist movement in Spain along the lines of the regimes in Italy and Germany."

Richards also believes the CNT was remiss in making no attempt to seize the Spanish gold reserve, the second largest in the world. In the summer of 1936, the immediate need was for raw materials and arms. Catalonia was Spain's principal industrial and military centre, yet it was starved of funds by the Madrid government. For Catalan workers to produce arms it was necessary to re-equip and retool factories: the requisite machinery had to be bought abroad. Aircraft, motorized transport, rifles, guns, and ammunition also needed to be acquired outside of Spain—and for gold anything was available and from whatever source. Madrid's objection was that the war industry in Catalonia was controlled by its workers; and the CNT's response was pusillanimous.

★★★

Vernon Richards was born in London in 1915 as Vero Benvenuto Costantino Recchioni (and throughout his life was customarily called

"Vero"). His sister was named Vera. Their mother was Costanza (née Benericetti): on a couple of occasions he described her to me as "lovely," and my guess is that she spoiled him greatly. Their father, Emidio Recchioni (1864–1934), had been a railway worker and anarchist militant in Italy, becoming an admiring comrade of Malatesta. He was released in 1899 from the prison island of Pantelleria and emigrated to London, where in Old Compton Street he opened a grocer's shop that was to become known as "King Bomba." It was there that Richards grew up, but he was impervious to Colin Ward's repeated urging to write a memoir to be entitled *A Soho Childhood*. Educated at the Emmanuel School, Wandsworth, he then studied civil engineering at King's College, London. The family was following Malatesta's advice that an anarchist should acquire a practical occupation which could provide a livelihood during a lifetime of militancy.

He would visit France with his father, an inveterate conspirator in plots to assassinate Mussolini. The son was later to criticize him as just a "bourgeois terrorist" (and also an authoritarian in family relationships). In 1935, Richards himself was expelled from France and returned to London to edit the short-lived *Free Italy/Italia Libre* in collaboration with the outstanding anarchist Camillo Berneri. Berneri, a philosopher who had fled the Fascist regime, was living in exile with his family in Paris.

From December 1936, Richards, still a student, began to edit a fortnightly newspaper, *Spain and the World*, very necessary as a solitary advocate in England for Spanish anarchism attempting to counter the enthusiasm on the left for the Popular Front and its Communist partners, while documenting the social reconstruction of the Spanish Revolution from firsthand information. Yet, as he observes in the introduction to *Lessons of the Spanish Revolution*, he wasn't being wise after the event in his criticisms of the CNT-FAI, for most had first been aired fifteen years earlier in *Spain and the World*.

British anarchism had dwindled to almost nothing during the 1920s. *Freedom*, launched in 1886 by Kropotkin and others, had been suspended in 1927. Tom Keell, its editor, and his somewhat younger companion Lilian Wolfe withdrew with the stock of Freedom Press publications to the Whiteway Colony near Stroud, Gloucestershire. From Whiteway Keell produced fifteen irregular issues of a *Freedom Bulletin* until 1932, but thereafter nothing. He commented: "The *Bulletin* has just faded out of existence. . . . I feel the loss of a link with old comrades, but without money it had to be broken." Events in Spain, along with the appearance of *Spain and the World*, were responsible for a modest revival of anarchism in Britain. Keell proceeded to anoint *Spain and the World* as the true successor to *Freedom* (a dissident group had been publishing a rival *Freedom*). With the Nationalist victory early in 1939 *Spain and the World* was for six issues renamed *Revolt!*—becoming *War Commentary* for the duration of the World War II and finally, in 1945, taking the famous title of *Freedom* (initially as *Freedom through Anarchism*).

Richards had been joined in London in 1937 by the nineteen-year-old Marie Louise Berneri (originally Maria Luisa), daughter of Camillo Berneri, recently assassinated in Barcelona, almost certainly by the Communists. The couple married so that she could acquire the protection of a British passport. The Freedom Press Group that gathered around them was young, energetic, and gifted. It included John Hewetson, Tony Gibson, Philip Sansom, George Woodcock, and, lastly, Colin Ward—it was they who wrote the bulk of the papers—but Herbert Read (until his notorious acceptance of a knighthood in 1953), Alex Comfort, and later Geoffrey Ostergaard could be called upon to contribute articles. The brilliantly gifted Berneri was said by Hewetson to have been "the principal theoretical influence" behind *War Commentary* and *Freedom*. She gave birth to a stillborn baby at the end of 1948, and then in April 1949, aged only thirty-one, she died unexpectedly from viral pneumonia.

It was in 1945 that Freedom Press attracted national attention unparalleled in the rest of its existence, with the trial at the Old Bailey of the editors of *War Commentary* on the charge of conspiracy: "to seduce from duty persons in the Forces and to cause disaffection." Special Branch had belatedly begun to harry the few anti-war journals. John Olday, *War Commentary*'s cartoonist, had been imprisoned for twelve months in November 1944 for "stealing by finding an identity card"; two months previously a reader from Kingston upon Thames was jailed for fifteen months for distributing "seditious" leaflets. Then in December Special Branch officers raided the Freedom Press office (in Belsize Park) and the homes of the editors and some sympathizers, armed with search warrants issued under Defence Regulations 39b and 88a. In Orkney, Ward, still a mere reader of *War Commentary*, had his belongings searched, and Detective Inspector Whitehead, the man behind the persecution, travelled from London to examine him. *War Commentary* had been printing articles drawing attention to the revolutionary aftermath of the World War I and the establishment of soldiers' councils in Russia and Germany, as well as the way in which the European resistance movements were being urged to hand over their weapons to governments being set up under military auspices. One article proclaimed "All Power to the Soviets," another demanded "Hang on to Your Arms!" (although this was addressed to the Belgian underground). *War Commentary* had also circulated a duplicated "Freedom Press Forces Letter" along these lines to servicemen subscribers, of whom Ward was one.

So it was that in April 1945 Richards, Hewetson, Sansom, and Berneri were subjected to a four-day trial, with each man being found guilty and sentenced to nine months in prison. Berneri, to her fury, was acquitted on the technicality that under English law a wife cannot commit conspiracy with her husband, a married couple being legally one person. It was she who, with Woodcock, edited *War Commentary* while the men were in prison. Ward was one of four servicemen called to give evidence for the prosecution—they all testified that they had not been disaffected. This was his first personal contact with the Freedom Press Group and, as he was to comment, his "marginal part in the proceedings brought . . . a rich reward": "The defendants became my closest and dearest friends." For Comfort, the end of the war in Europe marked "The Beginning of a War," the title in his next collection, *The Signal to Engage*, for a group of poems dedicated to Hewetson, Richards, Sansom, and Olday, "Prisoners on Victory Day."

One consequence of the trial was that, the Communist-dominated National Council for Civil Liberties being indifferent to this anarchist cause célèbre, a Freedom Press Defence Committee was organized by the surrealist Simon Watson Taylor. Its starry sponsors included Aneurin Bevan, Harold Laski, Michael Foot, Bertrand Russell, E.M. Forster, J.B. Priestley, Julian Huxley, Henry Moore, Sybil Thorndike, Benjamin Britten, and Michael Tippett. After the trial it was enlarged and renamed the Freedom Defence Committee to uphold the civil liberties of libertarians, dissident leftists, pacifists, deserters, and other hard cases. George Orwell became vice-chairman and participated fully in this, the only voluntary body in which he was ever active, until its dissolution in 1949.

Vernon Richards had qualified as a civil engineer—during the war he worked on the last significant stretch of rail track to be constructed in the British Isles at March, in Cambridgeshire—but another consequence of the trial was the realization that his imprisonment would serve to blacklist him in his profession. In contrast, Malatesta had been safe as a working electrician. Richards and Berneri decided therefore to attempt to earn a living as photographers. They began by taking many images of their anarchist literary comrades: Read, Comfort, and Woodcock. They moved on to Orwell, who, though notoriously averse to being photographed, allowed the couple to take a remarkable series of shots of him and his infant son at his flat and theirs and also in the street: published in their entirety in 1998 as *George Orwell at Home (and among the Anarchists)*. As a reader of the Penguin editions of Orwell's works in the 1950s and 1960s I became very familiar with portraits attributed to "Vernon Richards." When I enquired how he knew which photographs had been taken by him and which by Berneri, he replied that he didn't! So we must conclude that Berneri was responsible for much of this excellent joint output (which may go far to account for Orwell's apparent ease, given that men were inevitably smitten by her).

The photography business, however, failed to take off, despite the talent displayed in the three volumes—in addition to *George Orwell at Home*—that Richards brought out at the end of his life. He had several photographs published in *Lilliput*, the "pocket magazine" that served not only to entertain its readers but also to introduce the British to photography as fine art. He now took over the running of the family shop, until its sale in the 1950s, as well as working a travel courier in Spain and Russia; while Berneri was responsible, with Lilian Wolfe, for the first proper Freedom Bookshop, which opened in 1945 in Red Lion Street.

A vicious split had occurred towards the end of the war between syndicalists, supported by Spanish exiles belonging to the CNT, and the anarchist communists gathered around Berneri and Richards, who had inherited Malatesta's scepticism of the revolutionary potential of syndicalism. The Spaniards seem not only to have supported the CNT's collaborationism but to have spoken ill of Berneri's father, to her immense annoyance. Camillo Berneri had been a major critic of the CNT-FAI leadership, publishing while in Spain an Italian-language weekly, *Guerra di Classe* (Class War), and advocating that agitators be dispatched to Morocco with the promise of autonomy in order to neutralize a key element upon which the military rebels had relied. In *Lessons* Richards quotes Malatesta's "profound understanding" of the incompatibility of anarchism and syndicalism: "Every fusion or confusion of the anarchist and revolutionary movements with the syndicalist movement ends either by reducing the syndicates to impotence, so far as their specific tasks are concerned, or by diminishing, diverting, or destroying the anarchist spirit." He comments that "Malatesta did not foresee that the result might in fact be the mutual destruction of these organizations." Richards was to publish several collections of his *Freedom* editorials, yet his most important book after *Lessons* was *Errico Malatesta: His Life and Ideas* (London: Freedom Press, 1965), the first work to introduce Anglophone readers to a substantial anthology of Malatesta's writings, with a short account of his revolutionary career. This was supplemented in 1995 by a further selection: *The Anarchist Revolution: Polemical Articles 1924–1931*. And during the 1950s the Malatesta Club, patronized by the *Freedom* anarchists, flourished in Holborn, and then Fitzrovia. Meanwhile their rivals worked through the Anarchist Federation of Britain, which was to become the Syndicalist Workers' Federation (forerunner of the contemporary Solidarity Federation) and its magazine *Direct Action*.

War Commentary had fared relatively well in wartime on account of the solidarity and intercourse between the small anti-war groups, principally *Peace News* but also the Independent Labour Party (ILP), with its *New Leader*. With the end of the war and Labour's electoral triumph in 1945, the anarchists were to become very isolated indeed, Freedom Press being unswervingly hostile to the Labour governments and their nationalization and welfare legislation. Berneri considered, very reasonably, in the late 1940s: "The paper gets better and better, and fewer and fewer people read it." In a review of the fifties, Ward was to observe:

> The anarchist movement throughout the world can hardly be
> said to have increased its influence during the decade. . . . Yet
> the relevance of anarchist ideas was never so great. . . . For
> the anarchists the problem of the nineteen-sixties is simply
> that of how to put anarchism back into the intellectual blood-
> stream, into the field of ideas which are taken seriously.

During the 1940s, *War Commentary*, followed by *Freedom*, had been fortnightly, but from 1951 the paper went weekly (until 1975, when fortnightly production was resumed). Richards's hope was always for a daily newspaper—after all *Solidaridad Obrera* in Barcelona and *Umanità Nova* in first Milan, and then Rome, had both been dailies! It was to break from the treadmill of weekly production that Ward began to urge the case for a monthly, more reflective *Freedom*; and eventually his fellow editors responded by giving him his head with the monthly *Anarchy* in 1961, while they continued to bring out *Freedom* for the other three weeks of each month. *Anarchy* ran for 118 issues, culminating in 1970. Sales never exceeded 2,800 per issue, no advance on *Freedom*'s 2,000 to 3,000.

Yet as editor of *Anarchy* Ward had some success in putting anarchist ideas "back into the intellectual bloodstream," largely because of propitious political and social changes. The rise of the

New Left and the nuclear disarmament movement in the late fifties, culminating in the student radicalism and general libertarianism of the sixties, meant that a new audience receptive to anarchist attitudes came into existence. My own case offers an illustration of the trend. In October 1961, in London again to appear at Bow Street after my arrest in Trafalgar Square during the Committee of 100 mass sit-down of September 17 against nuclear weapons, I bought a copy of *Anarchy* 8 at Collet's bookshop in Charing Cross Road. I had just turned nineteen, and thereafter was hooked, several weeks later beginning to read *Freedom* (and becoming a continuous subscriber the following year). When I went up to Oxford University twelve months later, I co-founded the Oxford Anarchist Group, and one of the first speakers invited was Colin Ward. By 1968, Ward himself could say in a radio interview: "I think that social attitudes have changed. . . . Anarchism perhaps is becoming almost modish. I think that there is a certain anarchy in the air today."

I am told that in Oxford during the 1970s members of the then anarchist group had no interest in *Freedom*, none reading it. It had been quite different ten to fifteen years earlier. We were conscious of being part of an anarchist revival; admired Freedom Press especially for *Anarchy* but also for *Freedom* and the books and pamphlets it published; and *Freedom* afforded a connection with the remnants of the old workers' movement scattered throughout two hemispheres. I was always fascinated by the repeated donations to the "Deficit Fund" raised by anarchist picnics in various parts of the USA: the family backgrounds of Richards and Berneri induced fierce loyalty among anarchists of Italian origin. And at the bookshop in Maxwell Road, Fulham, one would meet none other than Lilian Wolfe, by then living in Cheltenham but spending the week working for *Freedom* in London.

I can see, though, that *Freedom*'s lack of interest in good graphics and artwork (unlike the New Left publications, as well as *International Socialism*, Pluto Press, and *Black Dwarf*) might be especially off-putting to post-sixties anarchists—Rufus Segar's talents were only employed on the covers of *Anarchy*. In fact, I also became very critical of this visual philistinism. When in the late eighties Peter Marshall, then writing his major history of anarchism, *Demanding the Impossible*, and I were negotiating with Richards about a quarterly successor to *Anarchy* and insisting on the need for good design, we were told very firmly that it didn't matter how tatty the production was since it was the words alone that were important. Peter and I were not involved with the resulting *Raven*, the first seven numbers of which were edited with considerable distinction by Heiner Becker and Nicolas Walter. Heiner was to tell me with great bitterness, though, that he and Nicolas had received no word of praise or even thanks from Richards.

It was Richards who, for both good and ill, was the principal force behind *Freedom* following Berneri's death. He withdrew in the mid-sixties from editing the paper, moving to Golden Pightle, an organic market garden on the border of Essex with Suffolk; but he continued to take a close interest in the running of *Freedom*, intervening directly whenever he thought essential—until his official retirement from Freedom Press's affairs in 1995–1996. On the other hand, until the day before his death in 2001, he would still travel from East Anglia most Thursdays to work on the accounts in the office (where on my visits to London I looked forward to meeting him for a chat in the afternoon).

There was for several decades an acrimonious dispute with Albert Meltzer, originally a loyal member of the Freedom Press Group in the late forties and early fifties, who brought out the cantankerously militant *Black Flag* from 1970 in opposition to *Freedom*. After Meltzer's death in 1995 and Richards's six years later the supporters of the opposing papers reached a very welcome rapprochement, yet this did not provide *Freedom* with a necessary fillip and, ironically, *Black Flag* expired as a monthly several years before its rival folded as a hard copy publication in 2014.

It was, then, the passing of Vernon Richards which contributed decisively to *Freedom*'s decline. To the end there was usually in each issue at least one article or report well worth reading. For many years (until his death in 2000) this might be by Nicolas Walter, whose name always signified quality, or Ward's "Anarchist Notebook" column. The nurturing of Colin Ward's talent was possibly the greatest success of the Freedom Press Group, Freedom Press bringing out no fewer than nine of his books.

Richards's achievement was then considerable. *Spain and the World* in itself was remarkable, but it led to the excellent *War Commentary* and a revived *Freedom*. This *Freedom* was notable for its inclusiveness, its pages open not merely to Malatestan communists but to anarchists of all kinds: syndicalists, individualists, pacifists, even Buddhists. Freedom Press published an impressive range of diverse books and pamphlets, both anarchist classics and new titles. His own *Lessons of the Spanish Revolution* and *Errico Malatesta: His Life and Ideas* were two of the latter.

Then there are the matters of buildings and their ownership and of the printing press. In 1942, Freedom Press acquired Express Printers at 84a Whitechapel High Street. Both 84a and the ramshackle three-storey structure on the other side of Angel Alley at 84b Whitechapel High Street were, in 1968, purchased by Richards in his own name, and the bookshop was moved there from Fulham. By the early seventies the necessary change from letterpress printing to offset litho led to its closure of Express Printers. 84a was sold to the Whitechapel Art Gallery in 1982; and Aldgate Press was launched, initially on the ground floor of 84b, as an independent printing co-op. The stipulation was that Aldgate, after five years, would print *Freedom* and Freedom Press books, as well as other anarchist publications (which would include *Black Flag*!) as cheaply as possible at no additional charge. Also, in 1982, freehold ownership of the premises was vested in the Friends of Freedom Press, Ltd., a non-trading limited company with the responsibility of assisting the publication of *Freedom* and the publishing programme of Freedom Press and of safeguarding the continuance of anarchist publication and propaganda. This all amounts to an impressive record over Richards's long and vigorous life.

David Goodway
February 2019

INTRODUCTION
TO THE FIRST ENGLISH
EDITION (1953)

The struggle in Spain (1936–1939) which was provoked by the rising of the military, aided and abetted by wealthy landowners and industrialists, as well as by the Church, has generally been regarded in progressive circles outside Spain as a struggle between fascism and democracy, democracy being represented by the Popular Front government which had been victorious in the general elections of February 1936.

Such an interpretation of the situation may have served a purpose at the time as a means of obtaining support from the democracies (though in fact it did no more than gain popular sympathy, the democratic governments hastily sealing off Republican Spain from Europe by their policy of non-intervention). But such a simplification of the issues hardly bears examination in the light of facts. There is abundant evidence to show that, left to its own devices, the Popular Front government would have offered no resistance to Franco. Indeed, its first reaction to the insurrection was to seek to "make a deal" with Franco, and when this was refused outright the government preferred defeat to the arming of the people. If, then, in those first days of the struggle, Franco was defeated in two-thirds of the Peninsula we must seek the reasons elsewhere.

It was the revolutionary movement in Spain—the syndicalist organisation CNT (National Confederation of Labour) and some sections of the Socialist UGT (General Union of Workers)—which took up Franco's challenge on July 19, 1936, not as supporters of the Popular Front government but in the name of the social revolution. How far they were able to proceed in putting their social and economic concepts into practice while engaging Franco in the armed struggle is a study in itself, and the chapters in which I have dealt with the agricultural and industrial collectives are intended to do no more than hint at this important and neglected aspect of the Spanish Revolution. Perhaps one day the extensive documentation on the subject will be collected together and published.

In the present study I am more interested in seeking the reasons for the defeat of the revolution than for Franco's military victory. For a revolution can be defeated by internal disruption as well as by the enemy's superior armament. Franco's victory, it is true, was in part the result of German and Italian intervention on his side, coupled with the policy of non-intervention which adversely affected only the republican forces. It is also true that the disruption of the "republican" forces was the result of the application of Moscow-inspired tactics in return for Russian armament. But again, this is only part of the truth. For there is the inescapable reality that during the first weeks of the struggle no Italian, German, or Russian intervention had affected the issue in the decisive way that was to be the case a few months later.

To what extent, then, was the revolutionary movement responsible for its own defeat? Was it too weak to carry through the revolution? To what extent was the purchase of arms and raw materials outside dependent on the maintenance of an appearance of a constitutional government inside Republican Spain? What chances had an improvised army of "guerrillas" against a regular fighting force? These were some of the "practical" problems facing the revolutionary movement and its leaders. But in seeking to solve these problems, the anarchists and revolutionary syndicalists were also confronted with other questions which were fundamental to the whole theoretical and moral bases of their organisations. To what extent could they collaborate with the political parties and the UGT (the Socialist counterpart of the CNT to which half of the organised workers of Spain adhered)? In the circumstances was one form of government to be supported against another? Should the revolutionary impetus of the first days of resistance be halted in the "interests" of the armed struggle against Franco or be allowed to develop as far as the workers were able and prepared to take it? Was the situation such that the social revolution could triumph, and, if not, what was to be the role of the revolutionary workers?

With the passing of the years these have not become simply academic questions. For the Spanish workers who have continued the struggle against Franco both inside Spain and in exile, they are very real and controversial questions. And yet it will be many years before a complete and objective history of the Spanish Revolution will be written. Vast quantities of documents are either buried in the organisations' archives or dispersed, and the individual testimonies of those who played leading roles still remain to be recorded. Not least among the difficulties is the deep division in outlook, both in Spain and in exile, between those Spanish militants who would guide the revolutionary movement back to its traditional anti-governmental, anti-collaborationist position and those in whom the experience of 1936–1939 has strengthened the view that the revolutionary movement must collaborate in government and governmental institutions or disappear. The present study is therefore offered as a very modest attempt at unravelling and interpreting some of the many issues in the Spanish Revolution.

For my facts I have relied on official documents. Considerations of space made it quite impossible to reproduce them in full, but I have done my best not to distort the sense by quoting out of context. And in fairness to critics among my Spanish comrades, I accept full responsibility for the opinions expressed here. Some have criticised me for being wise after the event and for writing on events of which I was but a spectator from afar. I mention these criticisms as a warning to the reader of my limited qualifications for dealing with such a complex subject. But I feel I should in my defence also point out that most of the criticisms I have made in this book were expressed by me in 1936–1939 in the columns of the journal *Spain and the World*. This did not, and still does not, prevent me from identifying myself with the Spanish workers' heroic struggle against Franco's regime.

It has also been suggested to me that this study provides ammunition for the political enemies of anarchism. Apart from the fact that the cause of anarchy surely cannot be harmed by an attempt to establish the truth, the basis of my criticism is not that anarchist ideas were proved unworkable by the Spanish experience, but that the Spanish anarchists and syndicalists failed to put their theories to the test, adopting instead the tactics of the enemy. I fail to see, therefore, how believers in the enemy, i.e., government and political parties, can use this criticism against anarchism without it rebounding on themselves.

★★★

This book would never have been written but for the publication in Toulouse of the first two volumes of *La CNT en la Revolución Española*. This work contains hundreds of documents relating to the CNT's role in the Spanish struggle, and I wish to acknowledge here my indebtedness both to the editor, José Peirats, and to the publishers, the majority section of the CNT in exile. Of the many other sources which I have consulted, special mention must be made of Diego Abad de Santillán's frank and provocative work *Por qué perdimos la guerra* and Gerald Brenan's *Spanish Labyrinth*. For the reader who is unfamiliar with the political and social background in Spain and, in particular, the important role of revolutionary syndicalism and anarchism, Mr. Brenan's scholarly and eminently readable book cannot be too strongly recommended.

Vernon Richards
London
July 1953

GLOSSARY OF ACRONYMS

The following abbreviations have been used in the text to identify organisations and political parties.

CNT   (*Confederación Nacional del Trabajo*—National Confederation of Labour). The revolutionary syndicalist organisation influenced by the anarchists.

FAI   (*Federación Anarquista Iberica*—Anarchist Federation of Iberia).

FIJL   (*Federación Iberica de Juventudes Libertarias*—Iberian Federation of Libertarian Youth).

MLE   (*Movimiento Libertario Español*—Spanish Libertarian Movement). The combined CNT-FAI and FIJL.

PCE   (*Partido Comunista Español*—Spanish Communist Party).

PSO   (*Partido Socialista Obrero*—Workers' Socialist Party).

POUM   (*Partido Obrero de Unificación Marxista*). Dissident revolutionary Communist Party.

PSUC   (*Partido Socialista Unificat de Catalunya*—Catalan Unified Socialist Party). The combined Socialist and Communist Parties of Catalonia.

UGT   (*Union General de Trabajadores*—General Workers' Union). Reformist trade union controlled by the socialists.

PART I

CHAPTER I
THE ELECTIONS OF FEBRUARY 1936

By its constitution the CNT was independent of all the political parties in Spain and abstained from taking part in parliamentary and other elections. Its objectives were to bring together the exploited masses in the struggle for day-to-day improvements of working and economic conditions and for the revolutionary destruction of capitalism and the state. Its ends were libertarian communism, a social system based on the free commune federated at local, regional, and national levels. Complete autonomy was the basis of this federation, the only ties with the whole being the agreements of a general nature adopted by ordinary or extraordinary national congresses.

On January 6, 1936, the Regional Committee of the CNT in Catalonia called a regional conference to discuss two questions: the first, "What must the position of the CNT be with regard to organisations which, though not sharing our objectives, have a working-class basis?"; the second, "What definite and concrete attitude must the CNT adopt in the coming elections?" Owing to its hurried summoning as well as the fact that most of the syndicates were still illegal, the conference was hardly representative, and certain delegates went so far as to attribute to the Regional Committee a personal interest in discussing these questions. Nevertheless, the majority of the delegations, among whom prevailed the view that the anti-electoral position of the CNT was more one of tactics than of principle, were in favour of discussing the questions.

We are not told by the historiographer of the CNT in exile how the discussion developed,[1] but he reproduces a document from the secretariat of the IWMA (the International Working Men's Association, to which the CNT had been affiliated since 1922) headed "The IWMA and the Crisis of Democracy, the Elections and the Danger of the Lesser Evil." It is a closely reasoned defence of the CNT's traditional abstentionism and an exposure of the ineffectuality of the political Popular Front as an answer to the fascist and reactionary menace. It created a deep impression on the conference, and a reply was sent to the IWMA reaffirming the CNT's abstentionist position and a resolution drafted advising an anti-political and abstentionist campaign at the coming elections.

When the elections were held the following month, "the CNT had concluded an anti-electoral campaign unnoticed by reason of its timidity."[2] Peirats does not add that, in fact, the members of the CNT voted at the elections of 1936 in large numbers. Gerald Brenan maintains that the increase of a million and a quarter votes polled by the left compared with the 1933 figures, "can to a great extent be put down to the Anarchist vote."[3]

The socialist leader, Largo Caballero, in a speech he delivered in Valencia in October 1937, justifying his governmental collaboration with the anarchists, and replying to those critics in his

---

1   José Peirats, *La CNT en la Revolución Española*, vol. 1 (Toulouse: Ediciones CNT, 1951).

2   According to the delegate from *Hospitalet de Llobregat* at the CNT congress in Saragossa in May 1936: "In Catalonia the CNT collaborated with the Esquerra in the recent elections simply by keeping silent, and *Solidaridad Obrera* justified the triumph of the left-wing parties, thereby attaching importance to the vote which we have always denied, knowing this to be a fact. A confusionist position was adopted in the propaganda campaign that preceded the elections, so much so that we might as well have come out in favour of everybody voting. This carries with it such a grave responsibility that it must not happen again. We must also point to the fact that the decisions taken by the Conference were not implemented, since the recommendations of the Ponencia were a reconfirmation of the anti-electoral campaign of 1933, and this was not carried out."

3   Gerald Brenan, *The Spanish Labyrinth* (London: Cambridge University Press, 1943).

own party who had been largely responsible for his resignation as premier, drew attention to the importance of the anarchist vote in the February elections:

> And then come the elections, and when we see the left-wing list of candidates in danger [of defeat], then we have no scruples in calling the Confederation [CNT] and the anarchists and saying to them: "Come and vote for us." But when they have voted us in and we are in parliament and set up our government departments, we say to them: "You now cannot take part in political life; you have fulfilled your obligations."

For Santillán, the anarchist, there was no doubt that the anarchists voted, and in his opinion rightly so. According to him,[4] the masses voted with their "usual sure instinct" for certain definite objectives: to dislodge the political forces of fascist reaction from the government and to obtain the liberation of the thirty-three thousand political prisoners (victims of the savage repression following the Asturias rising in October 1934). He justifies this position with the added comment that "Without the electoral victory of February 16, we should never have had a July 19." "We gave power to the left parties, convinced that in the circumstances, they represented a lesser evil."[5] Santillán, it must be stated, was a leading member of the FAI, organiser of the anti-fascist militias in Catalonia and later one of the "anarchist" ministers in the Catalan government.

Having justified anarchist intervention in the elections, Santillán then goes on to say that "the left-wing parties having been returned to power, thanks to us, we then watched them carry on with that same lack of understanding and the same blindness towards us. Neither the workers in industry nor the peasants had any reasons to feel more satisfied than before. The real power remained in the hands of a rebellious capitalism, of the Church and of the military caste," and the military proceeded with preparations for their coup

---

4   Diego Abad de Santillán, *Por qué perdimos la guerra* (Buenos Aires: Imán, 1940).
5   Ibid., 37.

d'état "to deprive the republican parliamentarians of what they had gained legally at the elections of February 16." The victory of the left resulted in the opening of the prisons in February 1936 and the release of most of the political enemies of the right.[6]

Four months later, on July 20, when the workers of Barcelona had defeated the rebellion, their first task was to open the gates of the Barcelona prison, which, in Santillán's words, was "overflowing with our comrades"—this time victims not of the right parties but of the left! Santillán further admits that a change of government did not in fact transfer the "real power," and we know from documentary evidence that the generals had started preparing their coup before the elections of February. The CNT issued a manifesto before the elections in which they warned the Spanish people of the preparations being made by the generals—naming Spanish Morocco as the centre of activities—and calling on the revolutionary workers to be on their guard and ready for action. "Either fascism or the social revolution" was the keynote of this historic manifesto.[7]

The Popular Front government dismissed these warnings. In the words of the minister of war, they were "rumours" which could be described as "false and without any foundation" calculated to foment "public anxiety, to sow ill-feeling against the military and to undermine, if not to destroy, the discipline which is fundamental to the Army. The minister of war is honoured to be able to declare publicly that all ranks of the Spanish Army, from the highest to the lowest are keeping within the limits of the strictest discipline, ever ready to carry out their orders to the letter. . . . The Spanish Army, a model of self-sacrifice and loyalty, deserve from their fellow citizens the respect, affection, and gratitude that are due to those who, in the service and defence of their country and the Republic, have

---

6   The new premier, Azaña, "at once issued a decree releasing the 15,000 or so prisoners that remained from the October rising. *In many places the prisons had already been opened without the local authorities daring to oppose it*" (emphasis added); Brenan, *The Spanish Labyrinth*, 301.

7   A reproduction of the manifesto appears in Peirats, *La CNT en la Revolución Española*, vol. 1.

offered their lives if security and national honour so demand," and so on, ad nauseam.

During those few months, from the time of the February elections to the military rising in July, the whole of Spain was seething with unrest. One hundred and thirteen general strikes and 228 local strikes took place, many as protests against rightist outrages. In the struggle with the forces of "public order" and between political factions, 1,287 people were injured and 269 killed. And as we pointed out earlier, the prisons were filled with anarchist militants.

Spanish history—and recent history at that—was simply repeating itself. In 1931, with the proclamation of the Republic, a socialist-republican government was formed. It was politically impotent except, as Santillán puts it, in being used by the old politicians of the monarchy to carry out the usual repression of the revolutionary movement.[8] In the 1933 elections the left government was defeated by the right, largely as a result of mass abstentions by the workers for which the CNT was mainly responsible. Peirats describes this "electoral strike" by the CNT in these terms:

> The campaign was intense and was continued throughout the electoral period and ended with a monster meeting in the Plaza de Toros Monumental in Barcelona, at which the speakers of the CNT, Pavón, Germinal, Durruti, and Orobon Fernández launched the watchword: *Frente a las urnas, la revolución social.* [that is, that the alternative to the polling booth was the social revolution]. The CNT and the FAI, aware of the repercussions and the transcendence of their position, declared at that meeting that if the defeat of the left-wing parties was coupled with a victory for the right they would release the forces of the social revolution.

---

8   Victor Alba describes the position after eighteen months of the Republic: "the provocations of the right and the vacillation of the left resulted in the death of 400 people of whom 20 belonged to the police. Three thousand people were injured, 9,000 imprisoned, 160 deported; 30 general strikes and 3,600 local strikes; 161 periodicals were suspended of which four were right-wing publications"; Victor Alba, *Histoire des Républiques Espagnoles* (Vincennes: Nord-Sud, 1948).

Compare this position with that adopted by the CNT in 1936, and there can be no doubt that while paying lip service to the principle of abstention in the February elections, the leadership of the CNT was working behind the scenes, offering the left politicians the *potential* vote the Confederation represented in return, perhaps, for guarantees that the political prisoners would be released in the event of a Popular Front victory. These are far from being wild speculations. What is certain is that within the CNT there have always been strong personalities who, as is always the case with those who would ride roughshod over basic principles, declared themselves to be the practical men, the realists of the movement. And just as they used the potential vote of the CNT as a bargaining weapon in their discussions with the politicians (often without any mandate from the organisation), so they used the thousands of CNT political prisoners as an argument to justify their reformist and clearly anti-CNT policies and to blackmail the membership into accepting them.[9]

It might perhaps be said that we have made too much of the vacillating attitude of the CNT leadership in the elections of February 1936 in view of the general contempt in which all governments have been held by the Spanish workers, who would presumably approve of the participation by the CNT if it resulted in the release of the political prisoners without considering that such action would in any way compromise the revolutionary principles of the Confederation. If the issue could be isolated in this way, the human element involved might easily overcome objections of

---

9   Peirats, *La CNT en la Revolución Española*, vol. 1, reproduces a speech made by Juan Peiró, a leading member of the CNT, at a congress of the CNT held in 1931, in which the role of the Confederation in the political events leading up to the proclamation of the Republic was debated. Peiró in that speech revealed the most fantastic "behind the scenes" negotiations that had taken place with the politicians *and* justified them all. Peiró was among the scissionist syndicalists (the Treintistas) who were later readmitted to the CNT at the congress of May 1936. He became a minister in the Caballero government. After the defeat he was in France; was arrested by the Gestapo during the occupation and handed over to Franco's police. He was offered a job by the government, which he refused, and was executed.

principle. But this is not the case. Tactics are like the game of chess which demands that each move shall be viewed not only in the light of its immediate results but in all its implications several moves ahead. The moment the CNT leadership was prepared to abandon principles for tactics (and, as we shall see, it was neither the first nor last occasion that they did so) new factors besides the original one of liberating the political prisoners would have to be considered.

For instance, by ensuring the Popular Front victory as a result of their participation at the elections, the CNT had to take into account that such a victory made certain that the preparations for the military putsch would proceed unchecked. On the other hand, a victory of the right, which was almost certain if the CNT abstained, would mean the end of the military conspiracy and the coming to power of a reactionary but ineffectual government, which, like its predecessor, would hold out for not more than a year or two. There is no real evidence to show that there was any significant development of a fascist movement in Spain along the lines of the regimes in Italy and Germany. The right-wing parties were much the same as they had always been.

The CNT in taking part in the Popular Front campaign should therefore have taken into account the effect of a military uprising. Who would resist the generals? And the question fundamental to the CNT's very existence as a revolutionary organisation: Can such a situation as will arise be converted to the advantage of the social revolution? To the first question it was clear to them that no effective resistance could be expected from the government, which would prefer to perish rather than arm the Spanish people. Therefore, once more, all the sacrifices would have to be made by the workers who were without weapons and needed time to coordinate and to reorganise their forces just emerging from years of illegality against a trained and well-armed and financed army which had the advantage of initiative in attack on its side.[10] Could

---

10 Santillán, who was an active supporter of the Popular Front as the only means of resisting "the enemy" writes: "For the effective struggle in the streets, to use the weapons and win or die, clearly, our movement was practically the only one

the workers in the circumstances defeat the militarists' coup d'état? For failure to do so would mean wholesale reprisals, and once more the prisons would be filled with political prisoners, quite apart from the internal disruption in the revolutionary ranks that would result from the repression.

Such, as we see it, are some of the considerations and consequences resulting from the acceptance by a revolutionary movement of political tactics at the expense of principles.

The months before the militarist uprising were characterised, as we have already pointed out, by widespread political unrest and armed provocation from the right. So far as Peirats's account goes it would appear that the revolutionary movements took no steps to counteract the preparations being made by the military for their putsch, and even at the national congress of the CNT held in Saragossa in May 1936 there appears to have been no discussion on this question.

This was one of the most important congresses in the history of the CNT both because it was representative of the whole movement (it was attended by 649 delegates representing 982 syndicates with a total of 550,595 members) and because it discussed such important questions as the internal crisis and revolutionary alliances and examined the revolutionary activity of the movement in the

---

to rely on [he was of course referring to Catalonia where the CNT were unchallenged by the UGT or the political parties—V.R.]. A committee for coordination with the Generalitat [the Catalan government] was formed, in which I took part with other friends well-known for their determination and heroism. Besides advocating possible collaboration, we thought that in view of our attitude and activity, arms and ammunition would not be denied us, since the best part of our reserves and small deposits of munitions had disappeared after December 1933 (in the uprising following the elections of November 1933) and during the *bienio negro* of the Lerroux-Gil Robles dictatorship." But in spite of continued and laborious negotiations the government refused arms to the people. The reply given was that the government had no arms! And Santillán adds later, "Direct action gained what we had failed to obtain in our negotiations with the Generalitat." Here the author is referring to a daring action by members of the CNT who boarded a number of boats anchored in the port of Barcelona and seized rifles and ammunition from the ships' armouries; see Santillán, *Por qué perdimos la guerra*.

uprisings of January and December 1933 and of October 1934. At the same time the congress undertook to define the Confederation's concept of libertarian communism in its post-revolutionary applications to the important problems of the life of the community, as well as to study what was to be the organisation's position in regard to the government's programme of agrarian reform.

The internal crisis was soon resolved with the readmission to the CNT of the so-called scissionists (the Treintistas) and the 60,621 members they represented. On the question of a critical analysis of past struggles, the discussion of which was to determine any modification in the organisation's immediate and future activities and aspirations, Peirats does no more than reproduce in full the speech made by one of the delegates as an example of the high level of the debate. One would, indeed, be tempted to reproduce many paragraphs from this revolutionary and anarchist contribution, but to do so might lead one to a wrong evaluation of the general spirit of the congress.[11]

One of the "most significant results of the debates" was, according to Peirats, the resolution on revolutionary alliances, which is also significant when viewed in the light of later events. This resolution declared:

During the period of the Primo de Rivera dictatorship, many were the attempts at revolt by the people, resulting in efforts

---

11   When the above was written, the minutes of the congress published in *Solidaridad Obrera* nos. 1265–1283 (Barcelona, May 3–24, 1936) were not accessible. They were, however, published week by week in the journal *CNT* (Toulouse, 1954) and in book form as *El Congresso Confederal de Zaragoza* (Toulouse: Ediciones CNT, 1955). It is clear that opinions were strongly divided, broadly speaking between the anarchist and syndicalist interpretations. On the struggle in Asturias, in October 1934, agreement could not even be reached on the facts of the situation. In reading these minutes one is conscious of a deep division in the CNT and of much criticism of the political and revisionist development of the Confederation, yet at the same time a widespread desire to seek common ground and unity in the struggle before them. Nevertheless, a careful analysis of the discussions at this congress would go far to explain the collaborationist role of the CNT in July 1936.

by the high-level politicians to direct the revolutionary feelings of the workers into the reformist channels of democracy. This was made possible by the agreement of the UGT workers' organisms to enrol in the convocation of elections which resulted in the political triumph of the Republic. With the defeat of the monarchy, the UGT and the party which acts as its orientator have become the servants of republican democracy and have been able to verify by direct experience the uselessness of political and parliamentary collaboration. Thanks to this collaboration, the proletariat in general, feeling itself divided, lost a part of the revolutionary strength which was its characteristic in other times. The events of Asturias demonstrate that, once the proletariat recovers this feeling of its own revolutionary strength, it is almost impossible to crush it. In the light of the revolutionary period through which Spain has lived and is living, this congress considers it an inevitable necessity to unify in a revolutionary sense the two organisations UGT and CNT.

The conditions for realising such a pact were, as was the case at the regional conference in Catalonia earlier that year, so revolutionary as to be unacceptable to the politicians of the UGT. And only in April 1938, eighteen months after the military rising, was agreement reached between the two workers' organisations.[12] But by then the revolution had been crushed and the workers were engaged in a heroic but hopeless military struggle.

Space considerations prevent any detailed reference here to the congress's statement of principles and objectives. This long document can be described as an undogmatic exposé of anarchist ideas in which an attempt has been made to incorporate the many

---

12 *The Programme of Unity of Action between the UGT and CNT* was published in translation in *Spain and the World* no. 33, April 8, 1938. An earlier issue of the same journal (no. 31, March 4, 1938) published the texts of the original proposals for such unity put forward by the UGT and CNT respectively, as well as critical appraisals of these by the anarchist militant Emma Goldman and by the Spanish Anarchist Federation.

shades of interpretation of the libertarian society—from the syndicalist to the individual anarchist points of view. In the preamble, it is interesting to note that the CNT justified the discussion of the post-revolutionary society because it considered that the period through which Spain was passing could easily result in a revolutionary situation from the libertarian point of view. This attitude makes all the more surprising the lack of any discussion of the problems that might face the organisation during the revolutionary period. Or more specifically, what was to be the attitude of the organisation on the morrow of the defeat of the military putsch when it found itself suddenly at the head of the revolutionary movement. Such a possibility could easily be envisaged in Catalonia, if not in the provinces under the central government. Perhaps for the rank and file the answer was a simple one: the social revolution. But in the light of subsequent actions, for the leadership of the CNT it was not as simple as all that. Yet these problems and doubts were not faced at the congress, and for these serious omissions of foresight, or perhaps of revolutionary democracy in the organisation, the revolutionary workers paid dearly in the months that followed.

CHAPTER II
THE MILITARISTS' UPRISING OF JULY 1936

On July 11, 1936, a group of Phalangists seized the broadcasting station of Valencia and issued the following proclamation: "This is Radio Valencia! The Spanish Phalange has seized the broadcasting station by force of arms. Tomorrow the same will happen to broadcasting stations throughout Spain." Only a few hours earlier the prime minister, Casares Quiroga, had been confidentially warned that the military uprising was a fact. To which the political leader of Spain replied: "By which you mean you are sure that the military will *rise?* Very well then, but for my part, I am going to have a *lie-down.*" The joke was in bad taste for, in fact, in that sentence is summed up the whole attitude of the Quiroga and subsequent Spanish governments.

The generals launched their first attack in Morocco six days later. The army, headed by the forces of the Legion, occupied the towns, ports, aerodromes, and strategic places in the Protectorate, seizing and killing militant workers and prominent personalities of the left. The government's reply was to declare that "thanks to action previously taken by the government it can be said that a widespread anti-republican movement has miscarried. The government's action will be sufficient to re-establish normal conditions." But the following day, July 18, that same government had to admit that Seville was in the hands of General Queipo de Llano.

Faced with the accomplished fact, the reactions of the political parties and of the CNT to the situation are particularly interesting.

The Socialist and Communist Parties issued the following joint note:

> The moment is a difficult one. The government is sure that it possesses sufficient means to crush this criminal attempt. In the event that these means are insufficient the Republic has the solemn promise of the Popular Front, which is decided on intervention in the struggle the moment its help is called for. The government orders and the Popular Front obeys.

On the night of July 18, the National Committee of the CNT, from the broadcasting station (Union Radio) of Madrid, declared the revolutionary general strike, inviting all committees and militants not to lose contact and to be on guard, their arms to hand at their local meeting places. That same night the National Committee sent delegates to all the Regional Committees of the Confederation with detailed instructions.

On the morning of July 19, a large proportion of the soldiers of the Barcelona garrison left their quarters to occupy all the strategic buildings and centre of the city, linking up with other elements involved in the uprising. Some writers on the civil war in Spain have attempted to create the impression that both sides were so incompetent that the rising and the popular reaction were somewhat of a farce, and Ruritanian in character. Nothing could be further from the truth. The military putsch was without doubt a very carefully planned and timed military action and this must continually be stressed, because only then does one fully appreciate the magnitude and heroism of the popular resistance which in those first days triumphed in two-thirds of the Spanish peninsula.[1]

---

1   Even Professor Allison Peers, who by implication if not in so many words preferred Franco to the anarchists and the social revolution, writes in *Catalonia Infelix* (London: Methuen, 1937): "At 3:50 a.m. on July 19 the first of the Barcelona garrisons revolted. Leaving the Caserna del Bruc, in the district of Pedralbes, the troops advanced rapidly down the Gran via Diagonal. One contingent branched off down Urgell, past the industrial college, into the long street named after the Catalonian Cortes, and occupied the University, part of

To do so also reveals the impotence of the armed forces when faced by the determined resistance of the masses[2]—even when they are as poorly equipped as were the Spanish workers in the early days of the struggle.

In Barcelona it was the revolutionary workers of the CNT, with small sections of the Assault Guards and Civil Guards (implacable enemies of the anarchists in normal times) which had not gone over to the military who, within twenty-four hours, succeeded in forcing General Goded and his troops to surrender. Without losing any time the CNT and the FAI entered the barracks seizing the remaining armament which was then distributed to groups of workers who were sent to all the villages and towns of the region, thereby succeeding in preventing similar risings in Tarragona, Lerida, and Gerona. In Madrid, as in Barcelona, what appeared a hopeless situation for the workers was converted into victory, thanks to their heroism and initiative, as well as their revolutionary enthusiasm. But in other towns valuable time was lost through the indecision of government officials, as well as by the supporters of the Popular Front.

In Valencia the barracks were surrounded by the workers before the troops could take up strategic positions in the city. This situation lasted a fortnight, the government refusing to arm the people and declaring that the troops imprisoned in the barracks were "loyal." They also ordered the workers to end the general strike declared

---

the Plaça de Catalunya, and a number of the surrounding streets and squares. Another contingent went on until it joined forces with rebel troops from the Girona Barracks in the Gracia district and the Artillery Barracks of Sant Andreu farther north. Meanwhile, the soldiers in the barracks of Numancia occupied the Plaça d'Espanya, at the foot of Montjuic, and marching on towards the sea, joined up with various contingents which had come from the Icaria Barracks, in the harbour, and the Comandancia General, near the Columbus Monument. *It was all excellently planned, and considering the large number of soldiers, guards, and police involved in it, one would have thought its success certain*" (243–44). [emphasis added—V.R.]

2   Peirats points out that in the hand-to-hand fighting in the streets of Barcelona the discipline of the military was broken, and the soldiers once in contact with the people were soon influenced by them; many were those who used their arms against their officers.

on the first day by the CNT-FAI and to disband the executive committee which had taken over from the provincial governor whom
all were unanimous in considering incompetent.[3] But the government existed in name only and its authority (assuming that it was
"loyal") anyway was imprisoned in the barracks! Meanwhile the
CNT had made contact with the Confederation in Catalonia and
Madrid, and arrangements were made for rifles and machine-guns
to be sent to Valencia. It was then that the CNT took the decision
to launch an assault on the barracks, and so ended a fortnight of
struggle "in which heroism and temerity went hand in hand with
lameness and concubinage."[4]

In Saragossa, where the whole garrison joined the uprising, the
workers, in spite of their numerical strength (thirty thousand in the
two organisations, UGT and CNT) were unable to crush the rebellion. They lacked arms, and in the words of a leading militant of the
CNT, "we have to recognise that we were very ingenuous. We lost
too much time having interviews with the civil governor; we even
believed in his promises. . . . Could we have done more than we
did? Possibly. We relied exclusively on the promises of the governor
and expected too much from our numerical strength," not realising
that something more than thirty thousand organised workers was
required to face a violent rising of this order.

In Asturias, another revolutionary centre of the Peninsula, the
indecision of the authorities and of the Popular Front created grave
complications in the situation there, and only at the cost of many
lives was the uprising finally quelled.

But according to Peirats, it was the speed with which the
generals carried out their plan of linking up their two main forces
across Andalusia and Extremadura, using as intermediary bases
Seville, Cadiz, Algeciras, Jerez, etc. that constituted the key to all
their future military successes. We would, however, add that the

---

3   Curiously enough the CNT and UGT leaders ordered the return to work of
    all except the transport workers. The Valencia proletariat, however, refused to
    comply until the barracks had been attacked and the soldiers disarmed.
4   Juan López, quoted by Peirats, *La CNT en la Revolución Española*, vol. I,
    (Toulouse: Ediciones CNT, 1951).

real key to the rebels' military success was Morocco, which served "as the principal base for the fascists as a source of manpower and as a centre for provisioning, and the disposition, distribution and reorganisation of forces in their struggle against the heroic Spanish people. . . . Well can it be said that Morocco placed the Republic in mortal peril."[5] Peirats passes over in silence the question of Morocco. Yet the one that immediately comes to mind is: What was the attitude of the CNT-FAI to Morocco both before and after the uprising? By their actions, it is clear that they had no revolutionary programme which could have transformed Morocco from an enemy to an ally of the popular movement, and at no time did the leaders take notice of those anarchist militants in their midst, such as Camillo Berneri, who urged that they should send agitators to North Africa and conduct a large-scale propaganda campaign among the Arabs in favour of autonomy. This negative attitude of the CNT to Moroccan independence will be discussed later at greater length.

---

5   Carlos de Baraibar, "Ayer, hoy y siempre: Marruecos," *Timón* no. 2, (July 1938), published in Barcelona by Diego Abad de Santillán.

CHAPTER III

THE REVOLUTION AT THE CROSSROADS

Because the CNT in Catalonia was numerically the strongest section of the organisation in Spain; because Catalonia was the first region to liquidate the military uprising; and last, but not least, because in Catalonia the CNT represented the overwhelming majority both in the victorious battle of the streets in Barcelona and among the organised workers, its appraisal of the situation on the morrow of victory was bound to have far-reaching consequences throughout the country including, we would suggest, the areas under Franco's domination.

Luis Companys, president of the Generalitat summoned the CNT-FAI to his office in the presidency as soon as the uprising had been defeated in Catalonia.[1] The delegation included Santillán and García Oliver, both influential members of the organisations and both, later, ministers in the Generalitat and central government respectively. García Oliver has put on record the interview that took place and which, because of its historic importance, and as the key to all that followed so far as the revolutionary movement is concerned, must be reproduced in extenso:

---

1   To avoid confusion for some readers it should be explained that there were two governments in Spain: the central government with its seat in Madrid, later to be transferred to Valencia, and the Generalitat which was the government of the autonomous province of Catalonia. Under the Franco regime Catalan autonomy was abolished.

Companys received us standing up and was visibly moved by the occasion. He shook hands, and would have embraced us but for the fact that his personal dignity, deeply affected by what he had to say to us, prevented him from so doing. The introductions were brief. We sat down, each of us with his rifle between his knees. In substance what Companys told us was this: "First of all, I have to say to you that the CNT and the FAI have never been accorded the treatment to which their real importance entitled them. You have always been harshly persecuted, and I with much sorrow, but forced by political realities, I who before was with you, afterwards found myself obliged to oppose you and persecute you. Today you are the masters of the city and of Catalonia because you have defeated the fascist militarists, and I hope that you will not take offence if at this moment I remind you that you did not lack the help of the few or many loyal members of my party and of the guards and *mozos . . .*" He paused for a moment and continued slowly: "But the truth is that, persecuted until the day before yesterday, today you have defeated the military and the fascists. I cannot then, knowing what, and who, you are, speak to you other than with sincerity. You have won, and everything is in your hands; if you do not need me nor wish me to remain as president of Catalonia, tell me now, and I will become one soldier more in the struggle against fascism. If, on the other hand, you believe that in this position, which only as a dead man would I have abandoned if the fascists had triumphed, I, with the men of my party, my name, and my prestige, can be of use in this struggle, which has ended so well today in the city [Barcelona] but which will end we know not how in the rest of Spain, you can count on me and on my loyalty as a man and as a politician who is convinced that today a whole past of shame is dead and who desires sincerely that Catalonia should place herself at the head of the most progressive countries in social matters."

On this masterpiece of political oratory and cunning García Oliver comments:

The CNT and the FAI decided on collaboration and democracy, renouncing revolutionary totalitarianism which would lead to the strangulation of the revolution by the anarchist and confederal dictatorship. We had confidence in the word and in the person of a Catalan democrat, and retained and supported Companys as president of the Generalitat. The CNT-FAI accepted the Committee of Militias and established a proportional representation of forces to give it integrity, and though not equitable—equal representation with the CNT and the triumphant anarchists was given to the UGT and Socialist Party, both minority organisations in Catalonia—was intended as a sacrifice with a view to leading the authoritarian parties along a path of loyal collaboration which would not be upset by suicidal competition.[2]

If July 19, 1936, is a day when the revolutionary workers of Spain wrote a chapter in the history of the struggle by the world's oppressed for their liberation, July 20 will, we think, be regarded as the beginning of the betrayal of the workers' aspirations by their representatives. Harsh words, but no words can be too harsh to describe the actions of a group of men who usurp their functions,

---

2 Quoted in Peirats, *La CNT en la Revolución Española*, vol. 1, (Toulouse: Ediciones CNT, 1951), 162–63. Santillán's version of the interview is substantially the same so far as the conclusions are concerned, but he does not quote any of Companys's remarks. In the interests of accuracy it must be pointed out that Peirats does not quote García Oliver's account in full. The complete text can be found in *De Julio a Julio: Un año de Lucha* (Barcelona: Tierra y Libertad, 1937), 193–96. An important omission from Peirats's extracts is García Oliver's statement: "We had been called (by Companys) to listen. *We could not commit ourselves to anything. It was for our organisations to make the decisions. We told Companys this.* The fate of Spain—and no one will appreciate the real magnitude of the role played by Companys and our organisations in that historic meeting—was decided in Catalonia, between libertarian communism, which meant an anarchist dictatorship, and democracy, which meant collaboration." [emphasis added—V.R.] However, we have seen no documentary evidence to show that the "decisions" to which Oliver refers were in fact taken by the "organisations." All the evidence points to these decisions having been taken by the "superior" committees of the CNT-FAI without prior consultation with the syndicates and groups.

and in so doing jeopardise the lives and the future of millions of their fellows.

Peirats asks whether the dilemma of social revolution or collaboration had been thoroughly discussed by the confederal and anarchist militants; whether the consequences of such a decision had been considered and the pros and cons examined. Or again whether the lessons from past experience and from the history of past revolutions had been taken into consideration. All he can say is that

> what is beyond any doubt is that the majority of the influential militants interpreted the situation in the same way. A few dissenting voices among them were lost in thin air; the silence of others was really enigmatic. Between those who protested in vain and those who remained silent through lack of determination, the collaborationist solution paved a way for itself.

But what was the opinion of the organisation, of the men who had spilled their blood in the unequal, yet victorious, struggle in the streets of Barcelona; of those in the Asturias double-crossed by Colonel Aranda and the government who assured everyone he was "loyal"; of those in Valencia who were refused arms by the government to storm the barracks? They were not consulted, though their actions eloquently expressed better than words their true feelings. "We trusted in the word and in the person of a Catalan democrat," wrote García Oliver, the "influential" member of the CNT, of President Companys. And he should have added, "but not in the revolutionary workers of Spain."

On July 20, the Madrid government and the Generalitat of Catalonia existed in name only. The armed forces, the Civil Guard and Assault Guards were either with the mutinous generals or had joined the people. The armed workers had no interest in bolstering the government which only two days previously had been reshuffled to include right-wing elements in order to facilitate a "deal" with the military insurgents.

All that nominally remained in the hands of the central government was the gold reserve, the second largest in the world, worth 2,259 million gold pesetas. No attempt was made by the CNT to seize it. They were repeating the mistakes made by the revolutionaries at the time of the Paris Commune who respected the property of the banks. "From July 20—writes Santillán—we placed improvised guards in banks, safe deposits, and pawnbrokers, etc." How obliged the central government must have been to the anarchists for their oversight, or short-sightedness! And how astutely they used the gold to fight the revolutionary forces! For instance, the withholding of funds from Catalonia, which was much too revolutionary for their liking, almost paralysed Spain's principal industrial and military centre. That it also affected the successful prosecution of the armed struggle against Franco mattered little to these men who, as we have already said, had preferred Franco to arming the people. Indeed, during the first seven weeks and before the non-intervention pact came into force, the Giral government failed to purchase any arms abroad, though there was ample gold to pay for them and no shortage of willing vendors.

In those July days, then, there was only one authority in "Republican" Spain: that of the armed workers, most of whom belonged either to the CNT or the UGT. In Catalonia the Committee of Anti-Fascist Militias had been formed representing the workers' organisations as well as the various political parties. The government of the Generalitat simply acted as the rubber stamp for the committee, but, as we shall see, an astute politician such as Companys would not for long tolerate a situation of inferiority. The initiative and revolutionary drive, however, were with the workers. They created the armed columns which were to engage Franco's forces (four days after the victory in Barcelona the first column of 10,000 volunteers left for the Saragossa area) and in a matter of days—according to Santillán—more than 150,000 volunteers were available and willing to fight in whichever sector they were most needed. In the industrial districts the workers were taking over the factories and, where possible, converting them to the production of arms, armoured cars, and other weapons for the struggle.

Meanwhile the peasants were taking over the landed estates. In the large towns the public services were reorganised under workers' control, and the distribution of food was guaranteed by the workers' organisations.

But as each day passed the gulf between the revolutionary workers and their representatives became greater. And understandably so: for from being their representatives they had virtually formed themselves into an executive body, responsible to the Committee of Anti-Fascist Militias and not to the members of the CNT. We are once more faced with the situation of the revolutionary masses pushing ahead and consolidating their gains while the leadership lags behind paralysed with apprehension at its inability to control the situation, and appealing, cajoling, threatening, and always counselling moderation. In the first manifesto broadcast on July 26, by the Peninsular Committee of the FAI, the most extravagant language is used to describe the struggle "against the fascist hydra," but not a word about the social revolution.

On the other hand, a most violent and threatening attitude was adopted by the leaders of the CNT-FAI to stamp out the relatively minor wave of looting and the settling of personal scores that took place in those early days of the revolution. Yet considering the magnitude of the social upheaval, the disorganisation of the economy, the breakdown of public services, and the total absence of the forces of "law and order," the looting and shooting and the burning of churches were insignificant compared with the deep sense of responsibility and the initiative shown by the workers in reorganising the life of the country, not along the old lines, but inspired by their concepts of social justice and equity.

They organised security patrols; they replaced the customs officials at the frontier to prevent any rearguard activity by Franco's friends; they controlled the telephone exchanges so as to be in a position to check on any political intrigues between Barcelona and Madrid. In a word, they were showing plain common sense and foresight in the revolutionary period, while their leaders were absorbed in questions of a strategic, diplomatic, or political character and losing every time. The tragedy, however, was that the forces of government, by manoeuvring the political parties into a bloc against the CNT, were rapidly gaining ground. Indeed, within two months the problem of the duality of power between the Committee of Anti-Fascist Militias and the government of the Generalitat was resolved with the abolition of the former. Having learned nothing from their earlier experience of collaboration in a revolutionary committee with the political parties, the CNT-FAI leadership, obsessed by the idea that the revolution must wait until the war was won, joined the government of the Generalitat.

CHAPTER IV
ANARCHIST DICTATORSHIP OR COLLABORATION AND DEMOCRACY

The dilemma of the "anarchist and confederal dictatorship" or "collaboration and democracy" existed only for those "influential militants" of the CNT-FAI who, wrongly interpreting their functions as delegates, took upon themselves the task of *directing* the popular movement. One does not question their integrity and courage as men and as members of long-standing in the revolutionary movement in Spain. But as leaders—not in the sense that Durruti or Ascaso were leaders but as *directors* who in their wisdom guide the "masses"—they suffered from the diseases of leadership: caution, fear of the uncontrolled masses, remoteness from the aspirations of these masses, and a messianic feeling that all wisdom and initiative flow from above and that all the masses need do is carry out unquestioningly the orders of these supermen. Santillán, for instance, expects us to believe that the Committee of the Anti-Fascist Militias, a group composed of representatives of all the political parties and the UGT and CNT (in which he played a prominent part), was responsible for establishing revolutionary order in the rearguard, the organisation of the armed militias, and the training of specialists; victualling and clothing, economic organisation, legislative and judicial action. "The Committee of Militias," he writes, "was all this and attended to all this and the transformation of civilian industries to war requirements, propaganda, relations with the Madrid government, help to all the centres of struggle, the cultivation of all available land, hygiene, guarding the coasts and frontiers, a thousand tasks of all kinds," and so on until he reaches a point where he writes: "It was needful to strengthen and support the Committee so that it might the better fulfil its task, *for salvation depended on its strength.*" (emphasis added) Is it surprising that with such a mentality— and it smacks of that contempt which all politicians have for the toiling masses—the CNT-FAI leaders should have continued to participate in, and thereby strengthen, the state institutions and be completely blinded to the real revolutionary potentialities of the working people?

"Either libertarian communism, which means the anarchist dictatorship, or democracy, which means collaboration" was the way García Oliver and the "most influential militants" interpreted the "realities of the moment." We shall be more bold than Peirats who writes: "We shall not examine here the correctness of that appreciation." None of the foreign anarchists who criticised the course taken by the CNT-FAI ever suggested that the Spanish revolutionaries should impose the social revolution on the population by *force.* Assuming the moment was not ripe for such a complete social transformation, does it follow that the only alternative was collaboration with political parties which, when they had power, had always persecuted the CNT-FAI? If that were the case, why had the CNT-FAI never collaborated with them in past struggles when the chances of establishing libertarian communism had been much more doubtful than on July 19? We can already hear the answer: "Because this time Spain was fighting international fascism, and we had first to win the war and then proceed to the social revolution. And to win the war it was necessary to collaborate with all the parties opposed to Franco."

This argument contains, in our opinion, two fundamental mistakes, which many of the leaders of the CNT-FAI have since recognised, but for which there can be no excuse, since they were not mistakes of judgment but the deliberate abandonment of the principles of the CNT. Firstly, that an armed struggle against fascism or any other form of reaction, could be waged more successfully within the framework of the state and by subordinating all else, including the transformation of the economic and social structure of the country, to winning the war. Secondly, that it was essential, and possible, to collaborate with political parties—that is with politicians—honestly and sincerely, and at a time when power was in the hands of the two workers' organisations.

It was, for instance, abundantly clear from the beginning that the Communists who were such a small minority in Spain (and non-existent in Catalonia) would use the breathing space offered by collaboration to worm their way into the Socialist ranks, by political alliances, and by playing on the politicians' fears of the threat to any future political hegemony represented by a thoroughgoing social revolution. To this end the Communists from the outset abandoned all revolutionary slogans and declared themselves the champions of "democracy."

The first mistake, it should be remembered, was made in the early days of the struggle, when an ill-armed people were halting a carefully prepared military operation carried out by a trained and well-equipped army, which no one, not even some of the "influential members" of the CNT-FAI, imagined could be resisted. And these same workers showed their determination by volunteering in large numbers for the armed columns setting out to liberate the occupied areas. All the initiative—and we have said this before and will repeat it again and again—was in the hands of the workers. The politicians instead were like generals without armies floundering in a desert of futility. Collaboration with them could not, by any stretch of the imagination, strengthen resistance to Franco. On the contrary, it was clear that collaboration with the political parties meant the re-creation of governmental institutions and the transferring of initiative from the armed workers to a central body with executive powers. By removing the initiative from the workers, the responsibility for the conduct of the struggle and its objectives were also transferred to a governing hierarchy, and this could not have other than an adverse effect on the morale of the revolutionary fighters. The slogan of the CNT-FAI leadership—"the war first, the revolution after"—was the greatest blunder that could have been made.

Santillán realised the enormity of the mistake only when it was too late:

> We knew that it was not possible to triumph in the revolution if we were not victorious in the war. We even sacrificed the revolution without noticing that that sacrifice also implied the sacrifice of the objectives of the war.

"The social revolution or democracy," "the anarchist dictatorship or democratic government" were the alternatives only for revolutionaries who had lost faith with their people and in the rightness of the basic principles of the CNT-FAI.

Such alternatives are contrary to the most elementary principles of anarchism and revolutionary syndicalism. In the first place, an "anarchist dictatorship" is a contradiction in terms (in the same way as the "dictatorship of the proletariat" is), for the moment anarchists impose their social ideas on the people by force, they cease to be anarchists. We believe that all men and women should be free to live their own lives. To oblige them to be free against their will, apart from being a self-contradicting proposition, is as much an imposition on their freedom as that of the authoritarians who use force to keep the people in subjection! Since the anarchist society will never be established by force, the arms the CNT-FAI held could be of no use for imposing libertarian communism on the whole of Catalonia, much less in the rest of Spain where they were in a minority in the working-class organisations. To do so would have been disastrous not only in the struggle against the armed forces of reaction represented by Franco, but also in making certain that the social revolution would be stifled at birth.

The power of the people in arms can only be used in the defence of the revolution and the freedoms won by their militancy and their sacrifices. We do not for one moment assume that all social revolutions are necessarily anarchist. But whatever form the revolution against authority takes, the role of the anarchists is clear: that of inciting the people to abolish capitalistic property and the institutions through which it exercises its power for the exploitation of the majority by a minority.

From these general considerations of the role of the anarchists we will attempt to examine its application to the Spanish situation.

From the outset we have to recognise that the insurrection was not initiated by the people. It came from a group of generals, with the moral support of some reactionary politicians and the financial backing of Spanish industrialists, landowners, and of the Church. Their rebellion was directed against the revolutionary workers' organisations as well as against the government in power, from which they aimed to seize the whole apparatus of government and operate it in their interests with utter ruthlessness. That the Popular Front government was weak is not, in fact, a reflection on the liberal-mindedness or progressiveness of the men that composed it, though let us concede that they were not of the same calibre of ruthlessness as the generals and their allies. The Popular Front government was weak because there existed in Spain a public opinion generally hostile and sceptical of the abilities of any government to find solutions to the economic problems of the country and armed forces whose loyalty to the government was all along a doubtful factor.

The military rebellion was launched on July 17. The government's immediate reaction was to reshuffle the cabinet with a view to coming to terms with the generals. Had the generals doubted their ability to seize power they would have agreed to this. By refusing to do so they revealed the strength behind the coup d'état. There were two courses open to the government: the demobilisation of the armed forces (which would have given the legal and moral authority to soldiers and officers who were not in sympathy with Franco to desert or even in some cases to disarm the leaders of the military revolt) and the arming of the people. Neither of these was taken, and the government thereby clearly showed its lack of determination in face of the uprising and its lack of confidence in the armed people (by which we mean its fear of being unable to exercise any control on the people in arms). Any initiative to resist was torn from the hands of the government by the people and in a matter of days they had succeeded in frustrating the generals' intentions. At the same time, and as a result of this swift action, the governments in Madrid and Barcelona ceased to exist either de jure or de facto.

The people in arms were the workers—the producers—and it was a natural consequence of the defeat of the rebellion and of government authority that they should view their status as workers in a new light; no longer as that of employees or serfs but as human beings freed from the tyranny of the boss and with all the means of production in their hands. And without hesitation they proceeded with the task of reorganising the economic life of the country with more or less intensity and success, depending on their ideological and technical preparation and revolutionary initiative in the different regions. We shall deal with these problems at some length later.

We cannot develop our argument clearly unless the reader understands the relationship between the CNT and the FAI. The CNT was a revolutionary workers' organisation existing for the purpose of bringing together all the exploited masses in the struggle for better working and economic conditions and for the eventual destruction of capitalism and the state. Its ends were libertarian communism, its means direct action independent of all party politics. As a mass movement (not only in name, since it had a million members in July 1936, and more than two and a half million in 1938) it was not surprising that the CNT should include in its ranks those who supported its determined and uncompromising defence of workers' demands, but who did not necessarily share its final objectives, looking to the political parties for the introduction and legalisation of social reforms. In other words, though almost all the anarchists of the FAI were members of the CNT, not all members of the CNT were anarchists. It follows therefore that if in considering whether the anarchist social revolution was a possibility in Spain or even only in Catalonia in July 1936 we rely on numbers alone, we must recognise that the numerical strength of the CNT could not be simply taken as a necessarily true picture of anarchist influence. And apart from Catalonia, where the workers were in an overwhelming majority in the CNT, the fact is that half of the organised Spanish workers were in the ranks of the Socialist Party–controlled UGT.

It is clear then that though the anarchist social revolution was not generally acceptable, the workers had demonstrated their determination to carry through a deep and thorough social revolution along lines which must in the end lead to a society based on anarchistic principles. And in such a situation, as we see it, the role of anarchists was to support, to incite and encourage the development of the social revolution, and to frustrate any attempts by the bourgeois capitalist state to reorganise itself, which it would seek to do by reviving its means of expression: the government apparatus and all its parasitic institutions.

The power of government rests on three main assumptions: that it has armed strength at its command, that it controls directly or indirectly the channels of information (press, radio, telephones, etc.), and that it controls the economy of the nation. During those eventful days of July 1936 in the unoccupied zone of Spain, it commanded no armed forces and controlled no information channels. The economy of the country was in the hands of the workers, except that the government still controlled de jure the financial reserves. We have already briefly mentioned the question of the gold reserves. The more one studies the history of the Spanish struggle the more is one shocked by the gravity of the error committed by the revolutionary workers' organisations in not seizing the gold reserves during the first days when they were strongest and the forces of government weakest.[1] Examples have already been given of the ways

---

[1] Are we justified in saying that if the social revolution is to succeed it is necessary to abolish every vestige of propertied capitalism and bourgeois power? If that is conceded then it is the height of revolutionary naivety to leave hundreds of tons of gold in the hands of an otherwise powerless government or ruling class. It is, however, only an *error* if, having the possibilities to seize this gold, no action is taken. Were the revolutionary workers in Spain in a position to do so? José Peirats, *La CNT en la Revolución Española*, vol. 1 (Toulouse: Ediciones CNT, 1951), devotes some four pages to the gold reserves—not to tell us what the CNT did about it but to lament that behind everybody's backs the Caballero government had sent five hundred tons of gold to Russia! Diego Abad de

in which this error in elementary revolutionary tactics was used by the politicians to creep back to power; many more will emerge in the course of this study.

By the end of July 1936, the attempted coup d'état by the generals had been crushed in half of Spain, but elsewhere Franco's armies by mass executions and terror had established themselves and were preparing for the offensive against the remainder of the peninsula. The success of the social revolution was therefore directly linked with the ability first to defend the territory freed from Franco's forces and then to proceed to the offensive against

---

Santillán is more informative in *Por qué perdimos la guerra* (Buenos Aires: Imán, 1940) when he writes in connection with the refusal of Madrid to supply funds to Catalonia: "Was ours to be the first war to be lost through lack of arms when the necessary funds with which to buy them were in the national bank? Meanwhile the enemy, after the disaster of Talavera, was advancing on Madrid in a dangerous manner. The plan was conceived to seize Catalonia's share. The treasure in the Bank of Spain could not be left to the mercy of a government which never did anything right and which was losing the war. Would we also fail in the purchase of arms? At any rate, we were sure of not failing in the purchase of raw materials and machinery for our war industry, and we could then ourselves manufacture the arms. With very few accomplices, the idea was mooted to transfer to Catalonia at least a part of the gold in the Bank of Spain. We knew beforehand that it would be necessary to have recourse to violence and three thousand trusted men were posted in Madrid and surrounding districts and all details settled for transporting the gold in special trains. The operation would take only a short time if properly carried out and, in less time than would be required by the government to take the measure of the situation, we would be on our way to Catalonia with part of the nation's gold, the best guarantee that the war might take a new course. Only, when it came to action, the instigators of the plan did not wish to take upon themselves a responsibility which was to have a great historic repercussion. The proposals were communicated to the National Committee of the CNT and to some of the best-known comrades. The plan made the friends shudder with fright; the principal argument that was used to oppose the plan . . . was that it would only increase the existing hostility directed against Catalonia [by Madrid]. What could be done? It was impossible to also oppose one's own organisations and the matter was dropped. Some weeks later, the gold left Madrid, not for Catalonia but for Russia; more than five hundred tons." We have nowhere read a denial of this statement by Santillán, which, if true, is a reflection on the caution as well as the lack of foresight of the leaders of the CNT. Here we must leave the question until documents or further information are forthcoming which will confirm or refute our conclusions.

the regions occupied by Franco. As to how this struggle was to be organised most effectively was of the utmost importance to the leaders of the CNT-FAI, and whatever criticism one may have to make of the decisions they took in this respect, one cannot doubt their sincerity in thinking that the concessions they made would ensure the victory over Franco.

The first problem that faced them was that the armed struggle could not be carried on exclusively by the CNT-FAI. That in any case there were large numbers of workers in the UGT and in some of the political parties who had taken part in the struggle in the streets and who were just as determined as they were to defeat Franco's armies. Clearly there was common ground between the CNT-FAI and other organisations in the struggle against Franco. But it was equally clear that the methods and the reasons for the struggle were different. So far as the political parties were concerned, their objectives in opposing Franco were, firstly, to prevent the establishment of his dictatorship over the country (with which the anarchists could not but agree) but with victory the creation of a government, the nature of which would depend on the political views of the party or parties which would emerge triumphant: from the federalism professed by some, to the out-and-out dictatorship of the Communists.

In a speech made on January 3, 1937, Federica Montseny, a leading "anarchist" and at that time minister of health in the Madrid government, referred to a problem compared with which that of the war is an easy one. For the war, a common cause against a common enemy, made it possible to have and to maintain the unity of all the anti-fascist forces—republicans, Socialists, Communists, and anarchists. But imagine the situation once the war is over with the different ideological forces that will attempt to impose themselves, one over the other. The war ended, the problem will arise in Spain with the same characteristics as in France and Russia. We must prepare ourselves now. We must declare our point of view so that the other organisations will know what to expect. . . . We must look for the platform, for the point of contact which will permit us with the greatest measure of freedom, and with a minimum plan of economic demands, to continue on the road until we reach our goal.[2]

We do not think Federica Montseny was being frank when she declared that the common cause—the war—had made it possible to "have and maintain the unity of all the anti-fascist forces." There was already too much evidence to the contrary. However, what she states in no uncertain terms is that a struggle for power in the anti-Franco camp was inevitable once armed victory was achieved. This concern with the "post-war" problems was even more forcibly expressed by another "anarchist" minister, Juan Peiró. In his opinion:

> The danger of the Spanish people being subjected to a fascist regime will be infinitely greater at the end of the war than it is now when we are at the height of the war.[3]

For the social revolution to succeed, therefore, it was necessary for the workers to emerge from the armed struggle against Franco *stronger* than when they entered it, and to make sure that the political parties emerged *weaker*. This implies that in the course of the "war" the workers' organisations had to go on strengthening their control over the economic life of the country; that is, as producers of the economic wealth of the country they should consolidate their control over the means of production. And at the same time making sure that control of the armed struggle, in which they were both the fighters and the producers in the arms factories, did not develop in such a way as to allow any strengthening of the institutions of government by permitting control of the armed forces to pass into the hands of the politicians.

Collaboration by the CNT-FAI in the government, so far as we can judge from the evidence, did not result in any improvement in

---

2   Federica Montseny, *Militant Anarchism and the Reality in Spain* (Glasgow: Anti-Parliamentary Communist Federation, 1937). Max Nettlau, "Reflections on Federica Montseny's Address," *Spain and the World* 1, no. 6, February 19, 1937.

3   Juan Peiró, *Problemas y Cintarazos* (Rennes: Imprimerie Réunies, 1946). This work was first published in Barcelona on January 26, 1939, the day the city fell to Franco's forces, and all but two copies of that edition were destroyed.

the military situation. But it certainly added prestige to the government and weakened the CNT-FAI as a revolutionary organisation in the eyes of the workers. In this connection Peiró's position is not without interest. Again and again in *Problemas y Cintarazos* he defends the anti-collaborationist view:

> Those who believe that without co-participation in governmental responsibility the CNT would have lost positions which were fully legalised are mistaken. The reality of strength has not its roots in force itself but in moral authority, and so far as the moral authority of the CNT is concerned it would have been immensely greater by having collaborated nobly and disinterestedly, as it always did, without hankering after, or accepting, portfolios, council posts, or official jobs. . . . It is by such conduct that the CNT has greater personality and has to be taken into account by everybody, much more than has been the case on important occasions during these past two years of war.

To understand what was at the back of Peiró's mind, we must add that in contrast with this anti-collaborationist position during the struggle against Franco, he nevertheless considered that it was *after the victory,* when, as we have quoted him as saying, the "danger of the Spanish people being subjected to a fascist regime" was greatest that he "esteemed it necessary to have unconditional collaboration, as direct as possible, in the government of the Republic."

Peiró's anti-collaborationism is therefore revealed in its true light: not as a question of principle but of tactics. The importance of this to us is not to expose Peiró for the revisionist that he was, since he makes no attempt to hide the fact, but that his anti-collaborationist tactic is an admission that the struggle against fascism could not be fought by the CNT *at any price,* but that on the contrary with victory the Confederation should emerge with a personality stronger than ever (*demasiada personalidad*) in order to be in a powerful position vis-à-vis the post-war government.

This was not, however, the attitude of the leaders of the CNT, hypnotised by the slogan: *Sacrificamos a todo menos a la victoria* (Let us sacrifice all except victory). And, in our opinion, they were also mistaken in orientating their propaganda with the slogan of "anti-fascist war" and even to suggest, as did Federica Montseny, in the meeting already referred to, that "the struggle is so great that the triumph over fascism alone is worth the sacrifice of our lives." Surely the enemy of the revolutionary workers is as much the system of which fascism is an expression.

But the consequences of such an attitude as adopted by the leadership resulted in a one-sided "unity," in which the CNT-FAI made all the concessions, and from which the political parties reaped the benefits. The "war" went from bad to worse and, later, when the forces of government, virtually controlled by the Communists, were strong enough, they declared war on the social revolution.

CHAPTER V

THE CNT AND THE UGT

The only unity which could strengthen the resistance to Franco without jeopardising the social revolution was between the CNT and the other workers' organisation, the UGT. We do not say that this was a simple task. The very fact that militant workers were in two rival organisations was itself proof of a deep ideological cleavage, but whereas all previous attempts had failed, the heroic struggle by the people, irrespective of factions, on July 19, undoubtedly created possibilities of co-operation at least among the rank and file of these two organisations.

Just as the million members of the CNT were not all anarchists, similarly it would be a mistake to assume a homogeneity in the ranks of the Socialist UGT; and if we examine the reasons for its meteoric increase in membership from the time of the fall of the dictatorship, when it had less than three hundred thousand members, to the million and a quarter members it boasted in 1934, we shall see what possibilities there were in 1936 for the organised workers in the CNT and the UGT to find a common objective in the armed struggle and the social revolution. The increased membership of the UGT in the years before 1936 did not come from the miners, factory workers, and railwaymen who were already either in the CNT or the UGT but from the small peasants, landless labourers, and shop employees who had hopes that the new legislation and the presence of the Socialists in the government would bring improvements of their conditions. With nearly half their membership among the rural workers, the UGT leaders were for obvious reasons most concerned that some attempt should be made at agrarian reform.

From the point of view of the CNT, therefore, any revolutionary programme which included taking over the large estates would be bound to have the support and co-operation of the landless labourers in the ranks of the UGT. The moral strength of the CNT, even before July 1936, is another factor which cannot be discounted. It was this strength, coupled with the failure of the Socialists to do anything in the way of agrarian reform during three years in office that created a revolutionary wing in the ranks of the UGT, which, for fifty years, had followed a course of strict reformism. And it was Largo Caballero, president of the UGT, who in February 1934, had declared that "the only hope of the masses is now in social revolution. It alone can save Spain from fascism."

Gerald Brenan has pointed out that at the root of the Socialists' disillusion with the Republic was the refusal of the republican parties to treat agrarian reform seriously.

> It was a feeling that welled up from below, affecting the young more than the old, the recently joined rather than the confirmed party men. That it was especially strong in Madrid was perhaps due to the small but energetic Anarchist nucleus in that city. (Generally speaking, a small but well-organised group of Anarchists in a Socialist area drove the Socialists to the Left, whereas in predominantly Anarchist areas, Socialists were outstandingly reformist.)[1]

The obstacles to joint action or fusion between the UGT and the CNT were not of recent origin. At the second congress of the CNT, which was held in Madrid in 1919, the delegates rejected outright a proposal of unity with the UGT and instead proposed the absorption of its members into the ranks of the CNT on the somewhat curious grounds that the CNT membership was three

---

[1] Gerald Brenan, *The Spanish Labyrinth* (London: Cambridge University Press, 1943), 273.

times as large as that of the UGT, and that since the representatives of the UGT had not accepted the invitation to be present at the congress it was clear that they could not accept the CNT position or share its desire for unification. The congress then proposed that the Confederation should draft a manifesto directed to all the Spanish workers giving them three months in which to join the CNT, adding that those who did not would be considered as *amarillos* (blacklegs) and outside the workers' movement. However, the repression at that time was such that in spite of this rigid attitude, Salvador Seguí, an outstanding militant of the CNT, later murdered by gunmen in the pay of Martinez Anido (the civil governor of Barcelona), negotiated a pact with the UGT which was unanimously condemned by a plenum of the CNT held at the end of 1920.

But since the pact was a fait accompli it was decided by the CNT to put the good faith of the Socialist leaders to the test. On the issue of the strike of the Rio Tinto miners, the UGT backed out from taking part in a general strike, proposing conciliatory solutions, which resulted in the defeat of the strike. Later, the UGT refused to take part in a general strike to protest against the wave of assassinations of leading militants of the CNT (including Salvador Seguí). With this further proof of the lack of revolutionary spirit in the UGT the pact was broken between the two workers' organisations.

During the years that followed, the problem of workers' unity came up again for discussion but without solution, except partially in the Asturias where a revolutionary pact was signed by the CNT-UGT in March 1934 which declared that the only possible action in face of the political-economic situation was the joint action of the workers with "the exclusive objective of inciting and bringing about the social revolution." This pact of alliance was put to the test some months later, on October 6, 1934, with the rising of the workers of Asturias. In practice, it was not altogether satisfactory, for a number of reasons outside the scope of the present study, but in Peirats's words, "it leaves no doubt as to its revolutionary importance."

At the Saragossa Congress of May 1936, the resolution on revolutionary alliances was so revolutionary and intransigent as to be clearly unacceptable to the UGT. Why was it that the CNT, which made compromise after compromise with the political parties and the government from the first day of the struggle against Franco, adopted such an intransigent attitude to the UGT that no official pact of unity emerged until April 1938,[2] when the struggle had degenerated into a fratricidal war and final defeat was only a question of time? And to what extent did unity in fact exist among the workers in industry and on the land from the moment these were taken over by the workers? Was it possible for two workers' organisations jointly to direct the revolutionary economy and the armed struggle against Franco?

We believe that the determination and initiative that existed in the workers' ranks during July 1936 could have made possible a revolutionary alliance between the CNT and the UGT with fewer compromises and concessions than were made to the political parties; that such an alliance would have permitted effective control by the syndicates, thus neutralising any attempts by the politicians to gain control and with it the consequent centralisation—and concentration of power in a few hands.

If we bear in mind that between them the CNT and the UGT comprised the majority of the working classes, not excluding black-coated and professional workers, it seems inconceivable that they should have entered governments or joined in alliances with political parties which had ceased to have any real influence or power. Under CNT-UGT control, those political parties with a class basis would have still been represented through their members who were also members of either the CNT or the UGT and only the professional politicians would find themselves isolated and without a voice

---

2   It would, for instance, be interesting to know the CNT's objections to Largo Caballero's proposals in 1934 for a Workers' Alliance *(Alianza Obrera)* which Gerald Brenan describes as "a sort of Popular Front, confined to working-class parties and organised locally." Mr. Brenan explains the CNT refusal as follows: "Feeling between the two great unions was very bitter and the Anarcho-syndicalists refused to believe that the Socialists could change their skin so suddenly and after fifty years of domesticity develop revolutionary instincts. They also had a deep distrust of Caballero who had always displayed a strong hostility to them. They got on better with the right wing, with Prieto"; *The Spanish Labyrinth*, 274.

in the conduct of the struggle. And one can hardly believe that this would have been a matter for concern, and certainly of no consequence in the successful prosecution of the struggle.

The confused thinking that reigned among the leaders of the CNT-FAI, so evident in the contradicting statements, manifestos, and decisions taken by them, springs from many causes, often equally contradictory. They felt that an alliance with all the anti-Franco parties and organisations on a basis of loyalty was essential for victory; yet, at the same time, in their hearts they knew that such loyalty would be one-sided—on their side only. They felt that some central authority was necessary to maintain international political and economic relations, yet fundamentally they distrusted governments. They were tempted by the idea that to fight a disciplined well-equipped army such as Franco's demanded an equally centralised, disciplined army, yet at bottom they realised the superior strength of the people in arms. ("The government of Madrid thinks that one can proceed with the creation of an army to fight fascism which has no revolutionary spirit. The army can have no other expression than that which emanates from the voice of the people and must be 100 per cent proletarian," we quote García Oliver, on August 10, 1936.) They hoped for the solidarity of the international proletariat, yet at the same time were so obsessed by the possible reactions of the British and French governments and their inability to buy materials abroad that they encouraged the facade of a struggle between a legal government and a rebellious army. They were afraid of imposing the "anarchist dictatorship" yet were in favour of conscription.[3]

---

3   Not only did the CNT-FAI by participating in the Generalitat of Catalonia subscribe to its political declaration which includes this phrase, "creation of conscript militias (*militias obligatorias*) and strengthening of discipline," but in September 1936, at a national plenum of Regional Committees, presided over by the National Committee of the CNT, a resolution on the Constitution of a National Council for Defence included a demand for the "creation of a Militia of War based on conscription (*con caracter obligatorio*)." There can be no doubt but that the CNT leaders, who were unwilling, to the point of self-effacement, to oblige the Spanish people to have anarchism forced on them, were, however, quite prepared to oblige them to fight against Franco on behalf of the government!

They proclaimed that the war must be won at all costs, even at the expense of the revolution, yet they knew in their hearts that the war and the revolution were inseparable.

This mental confusion in the face of realities is, we submit, the result of a further confusion: between principles and ideals. None of the anarchist "critics" of the CNT-FAI have ever suggested that it was possible in 1936 to establish the anarchist society overnight or that because this was not possible the anarchists had to withdraw from the struggle. Concessions so far as our ideals are concerned is quite another matter to concessions of our principles. Faced with a powerful enemy, we believe it was necessary that every effort and every compromise of our ideals should have been made to bring about an immediate and effective alliance between the two workers' organisations in Spain. For they represented the real forces and the only effective basis for waging battle against Franco and reorganising the economy of Spain and at the same time having control of the means of production and the arms for the struggle. Instead, to draw these two organisations into a government, a Generalitat, Anti-Fascist Committee or Defence Council—which were all governments except in name—as *minorities,* was simply to transfer power from the syndicates to a central body, in which the politicians were in a majority. This could have no other effect but that of encouraging the politicians to rebuild the institutions of government, with their own armed forces and laws, law courts, judges, prisons, jailers, and so on. The anarchists and the CNT could have no part in such a conspiracy. For then the revolution would be faced with two enemies: Franco and a once more powerful republican government. This is in fact what happened, with the result that every excess perpetrated directly or indirectly by that government (militarisation, the May Days of 1937, the armed attacks on the workers' collectives, *carte blanche* to the Communist minority to control the army and to assassinate militant workers, trumped-up trials of the POUM—the opposition Communist Party—etc.) to which in normal times the CNT-FAI would have replied with general strikes and more, was condoned by them because not to do so "would open the fronts to Franco."

May we sum up in two sentences: an alliance between the two workers' organisations, which were the spearhead of the struggle, justified concessions in ideals (final objectives) without abandonment of principles (e.g., workers' control). Alliance with political parties in governments was the abandonment of principles and ideals (final objectives) as well as of immediate objectives (defeat of Franco).

Because this was not the view of the leaders of the CNT-FAI, and is still not the view of some of them, we must pass on to examine the reasons which prompted the CNT's acceptance of portfolios in the governments, the results achieved, and the price paid.

CHAPTER VI
THE CNT JOINS THE CATALAN AND CENTRAL GOVERNMENTS

The social revolution and the armed struggle against Franco at no time suffered from a shortage of men or from a spirit of self-sacrifice and a determination to win the struggle and reconstruct a Spain based on new concepts of freedom and equity. What the Spanish workers lacked were weapons, both in quantity as well as quality, raw materials for their industries, fertilisers and modern equipment for their agriculture, food, and, last but not least, experience both in organising the new economy and in waging a prolonged armed struggle. But it was only the political leaders and some of the most representative members of the workers' organisations who were so horrified by the situation and, not knowing which way to turn, sought refuge in the institutions of the state. Instead, the workers, with their usual good sense, faced the situation with the available materials and the knowledge at their command.

Their method of taking over the public services and the distribution of food may have been chaotic, but no critic has yet told us that anyone died of starvation; their improvised defence of Barcelona, Madrid, Valencia may have been unorganised but, just the same, they defeated the well-organised and armed military formations which had expected to be masters of all Spain on July 19; their (badly) armed columns may not have taken Saragossa and other key towns, but they nevertheless contained the enemy for many weeks. They may have been chaotic, but, as a professional soldier (Colonel Jiménez de la Beraza) so succinctly put it when asked what he thought of those improvised columns: "From a military point of view it is chaos, but it is chaos which works. Don't disturb it!"[1]

Let us forestall criticism by saying that we are fully aware of the disadvantages of this "chaos"; of the fact, as García Oliver has told us, that transport was so chaotic that militiamen at the front stayed sometimes four days without food; that no medical services had been organised to tend the wounded militiamen; and even the extreme case of those militiamen defending Madrid, who at seven o'clock in the evenings would leave their places in the front line to go and see their sweethearts in Madrid! All we have said is that the Spanish workers were able, in a situation which had paralysed the government (except for its ability to publish unheeded and useless decrees in the *Gazette*) and the politicians, to improvise and organise beyond anyone's expectations. And if further resistance to Franco's armies was possible it is thanks to this glorious "chaos" in the first weeks of the struggle.

The role of the anarchists it seems to us was to seek to support this vast mass of goodwill and energy, and to work for its consolidation and coordination by explaining the problems to their fellow workers, suggesting solutions, and at all times encouraging the idea that all power and initiative had to remain with the workers. And not only to the workers of the CNT but to those of the UGT as well, who, disillusioned with "socialist" governments, which had proved no different from others, would have lent a more receptive ear to such arguments than to the weak and timorous counsels of most of their leaders.

"Without disorder, the Revolution is impossible," wrote Kropotkin.[2] So preoccupied instead were many of the influential members of the revolutionary organisations with the struggle against Franco that their exhortations to the workers were, from the

---

1   Quoted in Diego Abad de Santillán, *Por qué perdimos la guerra* (Buenos Aires: Imán, 1940).

2   From a letter to a friend during the Russian Revolution; quoted in George Woodcock and Ivan Avakumovic, *The Anarchist Prince* (London: T.V. Boardman & Co., 1950).

outset, for order, a return to work, longer working hours to supply the needs of the armed struggle. This attitude can be summed up in two sentences contained in an article by Juan Peiró in which he opposes the idea of a reduction of the working day for factory workers in Catalonia: "Napoleon's celebrated phrase is too often forgotten. Wars and their success always depend on money, because wars in all times have rested on an economic basis." How true this was in the case of Spain in August 1936! But, instead of telling the workers that their first step should therefore be to make sure that the banks and the gold reserve were securely in their hands, he exhorts the workers in the rearguard to work more and more hours in order to produce more. Not that what he wrote was not true. But it was also a fact that who controlled the gold reserves would also control the direction of the war and the economy of Spain.

In those early days of the struggle the immediate need was for arms and raw materials. For the Catalan workers to produce arms it was necessary to re-equip and retool factories; machinery had to be bought outside Spain with gold. Similarly, for aeroplanes, motorised transport, rifles, guns, and munitions; and for gold, even German and Italian armament could be obtained. The gold reserve was the key to the armed workers being able to pass from the defensive to the attack. For, while it is true that they lacked training and there was a need for coordination of the militias, yet without adequate armament and transport these problems were of secondary consequence.

To add to the confusion in financial matters was the rivalry between the governments of Catalonia and Madrid, a rivalry which ignored the common enemy at the gates and gave to the Madrid government, controlling the gold, the whip hand. An advantage which it used in its attempt to stifle the revolution in Catalonia and to sabotage the Aragon front and the campaign for the Balearic Islands—all of which were initiatives taken by the CNT. According to Santillán, the same attitude prevailed when Caballero took over from the Giral government in September 1936.

Let us observe further the evil that was wreaked by the gold remaining in the wrong hands.

On September 24, 1936, a regional plenum of syndicates was held in Barcelona at which were present 505 delegates representing 327 syndicates. At that plenum, Juan P. Fábregas, CNT delegate in the Economic Council, after outlining the activity of the syndicates, dealt with Catalonia's financial difficulties created by the Madrid government's refusal to "give any assistance in economic and financial questions, presumably because it has little sympathy with the work of a practical order which is being carried out in Catalonia. . . . There was a change of government, but we continue to come up against the same difficulties." Fábregas went on to recount that a commission which went to Madrid to ask for credits to purchase war materials and raw materials, offering one thousand million pesetas in securities lodged in the Bank of Spain, met with a blank refusal. It was sufficient that the new war industry in Catalonia was controlled by the workers of the CNT for the Madrid government to refuse any unconditional aid. Only in exchange for government control would they give financial assistance.

What this open sabotage by the central government signifies in terms of production of armaments is revealed in a report of the conversations which took place on September 1, 1937, between Eugenio Vallejo representing the CNT-controlled Catalan war industry, and the sub-secretariat of munitions and armament attached to the central government, during which the latter, before witnesses, admitted that

> the war industry of Catalonia had produced ten times more than the rest of Spanish industry put together and agreed with Vallejo that this output could have been quadrupled as from the beginning of September if Catalonia had had access to the necessary means for purchasing raw materials that were unobtainable in Spanish territory.[3]

---

3   *De Companys a Indalecio Prieto: Documentación sobre las Industrias de Guerra en Cataluña* (Buenos Aires: Servicio de Propaganda España, 1939). This ninety-page volume contains a number of documents including a letter from Companys (President of Catalonia) to Indalecio Prieto (minister of national defence in the central government) in which he demonstrates with figures what Catalonia's

But to return to September 1936. The regional plenum of syndicates completed its deliberations on September 26. On the following day, the press announced the entry of the CNT into the government of Catalonia. In a press statement the CNT denies it is a government insisting that it has joined a Regional Defence Council! Who took this decision? Neither Peirats nor Santillán enlighten us. There is not even an indication that the matter was discussed at the regional plenum. A national plenum of Regional Committees presided over by the National Committee of the CNT was held, however, on about September 20, following the formation of the Caballero government, the object of which was to seek a face-saving formula whereby "collaboration" might be possible. It was resolved that a "National Defence Council" should be formed and that the existing ministries should be transformed into departments. Various decisions regarding the militias, the banks, Church properties, etc. are included in the resolution. But the document has no real importance since the use of the term National Defence Council was only a less terrifying word for CNT ears than "government."

This the political parties understood so well that they paid no attention to the proposals and called the CNT bluff, so that when ten days later a further plenum was held, the CNT could only lament that their proposals had not been accepted. At the end of this document they imply, however, that the formation of the Regional Defence Council (as they euphemistically call the government of Catalonia with CNT participation) was the result of the prevailing plenum, and add that they will continue to agitate for a National Defence Council. But since the Regional Defence Council *was* the government of Catalonia, it is not surprising that

---

war industry had contributed to the armed struggle, pointing out that much more could have been achieved had the means for expanding the industry not been denied them by the central government. Other documents deal with the achievements of the CNT in Catalonia's war industry, statistics show quantities produced and draw attention to the fact that during this period Catalonia had produced articles which had never before been manufactured in Spain. Finally, there is the report on *Tentativos de acuerdo entre Cataluna y Madrid* (Attempts at agreement between Catalonia and Madrid) from which our quotation is taken.

in November the CNT capitulated and four members entered the Caballero government in Madrid.

The formation of a government in Catalonia with CNT participation ended the duality of power between the Anti-Fascist Militias Committee and the government of the Generalitat, by the elimination of the Militias Committee. With all its shortcomings, the Committee was more representative of the aspirations of the revolution than the government; and it had no real powers to impose its decisions. It need hardly be added that in the new government the workers' organisations were a minority and the political parties the majority. So, in a matter of some two months, the humble Companys of July 20, who had offered to "become one soldier more in the struggle" if the CNT so desired, now held the reins of political power in his hands. The next step was to see whether he could also crack the whip!

In what way would the struggle against Franco benefit by this change? Santillán offers the following explanation:

> If it had been simply a question of the revolution, the very existence of the government would have been not only an unfavourable factor but an obstacle to be destroyed; but we were faced with the demands of a fierce war, international ramifications, and being forcibly tied to international markets, to relations with a statal world. And for the organisation and direction of this war, and in the conditions in which we found ourselves, we did not possess the instrument that could have replaced the old governmental apparatus.

Santillán goes on to point out that "a modern war" required a vast war industry, and this presupposes, in the case of countries that are not entirely self-dependent, political, industrial, and commercial relations with the centres of world capitalism which hold a monopoly of raw materials. And the outside world was hostile to the revolution and might refuse to supply raw materials if there were no semblance of government. The dissolution of the Committee of Militias was not the last sacrifice that was made to "demonstrate our good faith and our overriding desire to win the war. But the more we have given in for the common interest the more have we found ourselves trampled on by the counter-revolution, in the person of the central power." "With what results?" asks Santillán. "Certainly not to the benefit of the war, or at least not to the benefit of victory over the enemy."

By this time, Moscow had entered the fray, and the handful of Communists in Catalonia who had started by absorbing the various Socialist groups into a single party[4]—the PSUC, were emboldened by the growing control exercised by Russian agents and technicians in all departments of the state. It was Moscow's intention to destroy Revolutionary Catalonia by starving the region of armament and by direct assault. But the time was not yet ripe for this, and it is therefore not surprising to see that the Communists were prepared, on October 25, 1936, to sign a pact of Unity of Action between the CNT-FAI-UGT and PSUC. The pact represented yet another step towards the complete concentration of power in the hands of the Catalan government. The points of agreement include collectivisation of the means of production and expropriation without compensation *but* with the proviso:

> We agree that this collectivisation would not give the results desired if not directed and coordinated by a genuinely representative organism of the collectivity which in this case can be no other than the Council of the Generalitat in which all the social forces are represented.

Agreement also on the municipalisation of housing in general, and the fixing of maximum rents by the municipalities. Agreement

---

4   The Communists claimed to have thirty thousand members at the end of 1935. Most observers, such as Borkenau and Brenan, give three thousand as a more likely figure. This is also the view of General Krivitsky who was closely connected with the party's activities during the struggle against Franco. Frank Jellinek in his pro-Communist *The Spanish Civil War* (London: Victor Gollancz, 1938) gives one an idea of the weakness of the Spanish Communist Party: "It had to be recognised that the Communists, although they were even yet (October 1934) insignificant, *had increased their membership five hundredfold.*" (emphasis added) But what were they before they were "insignificant"?

on a single command to coordinate the action of all the fighting forces; creation of conscript militias converted into a vast popular army and the strengthening of discipline. Agreement on the nationalisation of banks and workers' control, through the committees of employees, of all banking transactions effected by the chancellory of finances of the council of the Generalitat. Agreement on "common action to liquidate the harmful activities of uncontrollable groups which, through lack of understanding or dishonesty, imperil the implementing of this programme."

Two days later, a large public meeting was held to celebrate this new victory of the counter-revolution. The speakers included the regional secretary of the CNT, Mariano Vázquez, the future anarchist minister of health, Federica Montseny, that sinister figure of Catalan Socialism, Joan Comorera . . . and the Russian consul general in Barcelona, Antonov Ovseenko!

The Pact of Unity was simply a stepping-stone for the Communists in their plan to seize power. From the beginning, the petit bourgeoisie had been a stumbling block in bringing about the social revolution. The CNT had respected their interests and now the Communists were directing their attention to winning over these supporters of Companys. The crisis that occurred in the Catalan government in December 1936 was ostensibly over the indiscretions of the dissident Communist organisation POUM (with one representative in the government) in exposing Russia's international policy. However the occasion was also used by the Communists to discredit the CNT by asking in its press why no offensive was taking place on the Aragon front (which was chiefly manned by the anarchists).[5] Two days later, the crisis was "resolved" with the removal of the POUM minister.

---

5   This propaganda about the inactivity of the Aragon front was used by the Communists throughout the world to discredit the anarchists. It will be found in this country in the Communist Party's pamphlet by J.R. Campbell, *Spain's Left Critics* (London: Communist Party of Great Britain, 1937). It follows in every detail the Spanish Communist Party's campaign against the POUM, which, it was alleged, was driving a wedge between the anarchists and Communists. At the same time, Campbell makes the disparaging reference to the Aragon front!

What a tragic balance sheet of defeats faced the CNT in Catalonia by the end of 1936. They were not defeats for the work of collectivisation, in which the workers had extended and consolidated their early victories. The defeats for the workers were the successes of the politicians in transferring to themselves, step by step, all those powers which, so long as they remained in the hands of the workers, made it impossible for the government to re-emerge from its deserved obscurity. By the end of 1936, Companys was literally in control, but he too would have to pay a price for this victory: to the Communists. And from such a new situation the CNT, had it remained outside the political struggle, might have drawn advantage. But it was floundering in a sea of compromise and facing away from the land. What could be more disastrous to the revolutionary movement than leaders so blind that they could say, with García Oliver, "The Committees of Anti-Fascist Militias have been dissolved because now the Generalitat represents all of us"!

Meanwhile, in Madrid, Largo Caballero, who succeeded Giral as prime minister, had as his first mission that of creating a government that would function. During the previous weeks, to quote Peirats, "the masses had gravitated to the workers' organisations, dazzled by their revolutionary achievements, or to the front line to face the common enemy," and he adds:

> To save the government, the principle of government, it is necessary to give it prestige with watchwords and with a man. The watchwords can be improvised, and the man, once the situation is saved, removed from office. What is important is to find a formula which will permit the reconstruction of the state apparatus, place the reins in the hands of any government which will carry out the task of disarming the people and reducing them to a state of obedience. In a word, to put the revolution in a straitjacket. For this, Largo Caballero was the man sent by providence.

He was the leader of the Socialist-dominated UGT and an "extremist" of the Socialist Party who was held in esteem by the

CNT.[6] His immediate task would be to give prestige to the badly battered republican institutions and new life to the state, thereby making it possible to achieve what the previous governments had been impotent to do: militarisation of the militias, reorganisation of the armed corps, and the control of these by the government, with the simultaneous disarming of the rearguard. The watchword was not difficult to find: the need for discipline and a single command as a reply to the reverses of the war; the necessity of carrying on and winning the war above all else.

The CNT's reply to the Caballero government was the national plenum of Regional Committees held in the middle of September 1936, in which they proposed the constitution in Madrid of a National Defence Council which they described as "a national organism empowered to take over the tasks in matters of direction, defence, and consolidation in the political and economic fields." As we have already stated, this Council would have powers to "create a conscript War Militia." In other words, this "Council" was a government in disguise, albeit a revolutionary government.

On November 4, 1936, four members of the CNT entered the Caballero government: Juan López and Juan Peiró as ministers of commerce and industry respectively; Federica Montseny as health minister; and the portfolio of justice was entrusted to García Oliver. None of these ministers has been able to say of his six months' tenure of office that the presence in the government of representatives of

---

6   According to Peirats. The reader will recall that in an earlier reference to Caballero's relations with the CNT, quoted from Gerald Brenan, *The Spanish Labyrinth* (London: Cambridge University Press, 1943), the contrary view was put forward. We believe that both Peirats and Brenan express the situation as it existed at the times they were describing (i.e., 1936 and 1934 respectively). The attitude of the CNT-FAI leaders to the politicians sheds interesting light on their outlook to politics. Both Caballero and Companys had been responsible at some time or other for sending anarchists to jail, but neither side views this with disgust or shame respectively. It appears to be accepted as part of the political game, with neither side bearing any grudge against the other. So that in July 1936 the CNT in Catalonia could declare their faith in "the word of a Catalan democrat (Companys)" and in the cabinet crisis of May 1937 refuse to join a central government in which Caballero was not prime minister. One cannot help feeling that the CNT-FAI leaders were politicians at heart.

the CNT in any way contributed to an improvement in the military situation. Juan López has pointed to the impossibility of achieving anything in the economic sphere when the portfolios of commerce and industry were in the hands of syndicalists, and agriculture and finances in the hands of a Communist and right-wing Socialist respectively. Federica Montseny has publicly admitted that the CNT's participation in the government was a failure, and only García Oliver was ecstatic in describing his achievements as the legislator for justice. He might perhaps have shown less enthusiasm for his "revolutionary" discoveries in the field of penology had he been acquainted with the work of even such cautious, though well-meaning, bodies as the Howard League for Penal Reform in capitalist Britain![7]

The acceptance of government posts by the CNT was described in their daily paper, *Solidaridad Obrera,* as "the most transcendental day in the political history of our country." It goes on to explain that

the government in this hour, as a regulating instrument of the organisms of the state, has ceased to be an oppressive force against the working class, just as the state no longer represents the organism which divides society into classes. And both will tend even less to oppress the people as a result of the intervention of the CNT [in the government]. The functions of state will become reduced, by agreement with

---

7   All four CNT ministers in the Caballero government gave an account of their activities in their respective ministries at huge public meetings. These were published in pamphlet form. The CNT-FAI ministers in the Catalan government do not appear to have made similar statements, but we have found two references by Santillán published in the magazine *Timón* (Barcelona, August 1938) which we think of considerable interest. "Simply as governors," writes Santillán, "we are no better than anybody else and we have already proved that our intervention in governments serves only to reinforce governmentalism and in no way to uphold the rights of labour against its parasitic economic and political enemies." Elsewhere he declares that one must trust and serve the people. "But one cannot serve two masters at the same time. If we are with the people we cannot also be with the state, which is the enemy of the people. And at the moment we are on the side of the state, which is the same as saying that we are against the people."

the workers' organisations, to those of regularising the development of the economic and social life of the country. And the government's only preoccupation will be to ably direct the war and to coordinate the revolutionary task according to a general plan. Our comrades will bring to the government the collective and majority will of the working masses previously gathered in vast general assemblies. They will defend no personal or capricious criterion but the freely determined wishes of the hundreds of thousands of workers organised in the CNT. It is an historic fatality which falls on everyone. And the CNT accepts this fatality to serve the country by its determination to win the war quickly and to see the revolution is not disfigured.

Compare this opportunistic nonsense with the views they expressed two months earlier in their *Information Bulletin* (no. 41, September 3, 1936) and reproduced in the very *Solidaridad Obrera* from whose editorial we have just quoted. With the significant title, "The Uselessness of the Government," the CNT-FAI pointed out that

The existence of a Popular Front government, far from being an indispensable element in the anti-fascist struggle, is qualitatively a cheap imitation of this very struggle.

It is useless to recall that, faced with the fascist putsch, the governments of the Generalitat and of Madrid did absolutely nothing. Authority has only been used to hide the manoeuvres being carried out by the reactionary elements and by those of which the government was consciously or unconsciously the instrument.

The war that is being successfully waged in Spain is a social war. The importance of the moderating power, based on stability and the maintenance of classes, will not know how to impose a definite attitude in this struggle in which the foundations of the state are vacillating and which is itself without any security. It is, then, true to say that the government of the Popular Front in Spain is no more than the reflection of a compromise between the petty bourgeoisie and international capital . . .

. . .The idea of replacing these governments, feeble guardians of the *status quo*, of property, and of foreign capital, by a strong government based on an ideology and on a "revolutionary" political organisation would only serve to postpone the revolutionary uprising.

It is not a question, therefore, of Marxism seizing power, nor of the self-limitation of popular action for reasons of political opportunism. The "workers' state" is the end result of a revolutionary activity and the beginning of a new political slavery.

The coordination of the forces of the Popular Front, of organisation of food supplies with an extensive collectivisation of undertakings is of vital interest in achieving our objectives. This is clearly what matters at this hour. It has been achieved up to now in a non-governmental, decentralised, demilitarised manner. . . . Many improvements remain to be made to meet these necessities. Greater use could be made by the syndicates of the CNT and UGT of their forces to bring about these improvements. A coalition government, on the contrary, with its base political struggles between majorities and minorities, its bureaucratisation, based on chosen elites, and the fratricidal struggles in which the opposing political factions are engaged, make it impossible for such a government to benefit our work of liberation in Spain. It would lead to the rapid destruction of our capacity of action, of our will to unity, and the beginning of an imminent debacle before a still fairly strong enemy.

We hope that Spanish and foreign workers will understand the justice of the decisions taken in this sense by the CNT-FAI. To discredit the state is the final objective of socialism. Events demonstrate that the liquidation of the bourgeois state, weakened by suffocation, is the result of economic expropriation and not necessarily by a spontaneous orientation of the "socialist" bourgeoisie. Russia and Spain are living examples.

This important statement contains all the arguments we would have wished to put forward in order to demonstrate that collaboration with governments and political parties was a mistake from all points of view: from that of the social revolution and the armed struggle, of revolutionary tactics and principles.

Whatever the apologists of collaboration may say to the contrary, events—from the time of the "war" government of Largo Caballero to the Negrín "Government of Victory," ending in the ignominious surrender of Catalonia and the liquidation of the Communists and the Negrín government in Central Spain prior to final capitulation—confirm in every detail the analysis contained in the historic document we have reproduced.

What caused this somersault which landed the CNT-FAI in ministerial armchairs only a few weeks later? And to what extent was the rank and file of the organisation responsible for this complete abandonment of anarchist principles and revolutionary tactics?

CHAPTER VII

THE CNT AND POLITICAL ACTION

The CNT since its inception has never been without its politicians, its political demagogues and its internal "ideological" crises. That they have harmed the Confederation there can be little doubt, but not to the extent that any other organisation would have suffered. Indeed, the greatness of the CNT is that of its rank-and-file militants. Though the organisation did not succeed in preventing political leaders from rising in its midst it always retained a spirit of independence, as a result of its decentralised structure, and a revolutionary spirit which successfully resisted the efforts of the reformists and politicians in its ranks.

Internal "crises" in a revolutionary movement are not necessarily bad. Any movement, and especially a mass movement that is not ossified, must be continuously subjecting its ideas and tactics to discussion. A movement that is always unanimous is generally one in which there are only sheep and shepherds. Not that the CNT did not also have its would-be shepherds, and especially since July 19, 1936, but it is significant that though (because of the peculiar circumstances through which Spain was passing) they did much harm to the revolutionary cause and the struggle against Franco, they never succeeded in converting the rank-and-file militants of the CNT into sheep.

As one firsthand observer of the Spanish scene has put it:

An orator in a plenum might get away with a decision in favour of collaboration; but, left to themselves again, all our comrades returned to their deeper convictions and went on with the tasks of the revolution. These men were as capable of taking up arms as of running a collective, of tilling the soil and wielding a hammer as of guiding a local meeting or a meeting of the syndicate with their sensible opinions on the practical problems that needed a solution. And thanks to this strength and to the visible activity of the rank and file of the Spanish libertarian movement—particularly those among the militants who had gained their experience through long years of struggle in the syndicates of the CNT—the libertarian organisations were able to develop, in spite of the rebirth, or, rather, the consolidation of the state and the development of governmental political parties.[1]

Elsewhere the same writer, dealing with the entry of the CNT into the Caballero government, points out that

some anarchist delegates, who had become ministers or official personages in different capacities, took their tasks seriously: the poison of power took effect immediately. But what was saved was the potential of the Spanish anarchist movement. It had thousands of seasoned militants in all or almost all the villages of Aragon, the Levante, and Andalusia. Almost all the militants of the CNT had a solid experience of practical organisation in their own trades or in the life of a village and enjoyed an indisputable moral ascendancy. Furthermore, they were gifted with a strong spirit of initiative.

The gulf that existed between the leaders and the rank and file of the CNT-FAI can be explained simply by two complementary references, one from Gaston Leval's work, the other from Peirats's. In drawing the conclusions in his book, which deals with the Spanish

---

1   Gaston Leval, *Né Franco né Stalin: Le collettivita anarchiche spanuole nella lotta contra Franco e la reazione staliniana.* (Milan: Milano Istituto editoriale italiano, 1952).

Collectives, Leval points out that the outstanding militants such as
Federica Montseny

> played no part in the work of the collectives. From the begin-
> ning they were absorbed in official posts which they accepted
> in spite of their traditional repugnance for governmental
> functions. Anti-fascist unity determined their attitude. *It
> was necessary to silence their principles and to make provisional
> concessions.* This prevented them from continuing to carry
> out their tasks as guides. They remained outside this great
> reconstructive undertaking, which offers workers valuable
> lessons for the future.[2]

Peirats, in dealing with the political orientation of the CNT
from the beginning of the struggle, refers to the almost complete
unanimity among the "influential militants" for a policy of collaboration with the politicians, but adds that

> a large part of the militants and the immense majority of the
> confederal rank and file were only interested in the problems
> that confronted them in the armed struggle at the fronts, the
> routing out of hidden fascists, and the expropriation and
> canalisation of the new revolutionary economy.[3]

The reader cannot avoid noting in this extract the references
to "influential militants" and to the "rank and file." Perhaps in a
mass movement which accepts all workers in its ranks irrespective of their political affiliations, though its objectives are those of
libertarian communism, it may be inevitable that to protect these
objectives it must have recourse to behind the scenes manoeuvres
and take decisions at a "higher level," i.e., by the "militants" or by
the "influential militants." Though it may be inevitable, clearly it

---

2   Leval, *Né Franco né Stalin*, 307. (emphasis added)
3   José Peirats, *La CNT en la Revolución Española*, vol. 1, (Toulouse: Ediciones
    CNT, 1951), 161–62.

must provoke resentment as well among the militants and rank and file. Such a problem existed in the CNT from its foundation and had resulted in more than one internal crisis. There can be no doubt that many decisions taken and tactics adopted by the CNT during the struggle against Franco were not discussed in the syndicates, and only too often were fundamental questions decided by the "influential militants" and accepted as a fait accompli by the delegates at plenums and not even discussed by the rank and file in the syndicates.

The abandonment by the CNT of its traditional method for taking decisions was justified by the necessity of acting with a minimum of delay. There might be questions in which such a position could be justified, but on fundamental questions of principle and revolutionary tactics there could be no excuse for not consulting the syndicates. The fact that the CNT-FAI did not enter the governments of Catalonia and Madrid until the end of September and November, that is more than two months and three months, respectively, after the July uprising, makes nonsense of any claim that there was no time to consult the organisation before the decisions were taken. Many local and regional plenums had by then been held, but so far as we have been able to ascertain no discussion took place on the subject of governmental collaboration. The problem was one discussed only at the "highest level" of the organisation, and when it was finally decided to have CNT ministers in the Caballero government, the Confederation was not even consulted as to who would be their representatives in that government.

In a speech made by Federica Montseny in Toulouse in 1945 (quoted in the *Internal Bulletin of the MLE-CNT in France*, September–October 1945) she is reported as saying:

> By agreement between Largo Caballero and Horacio Prieto the latter came to Catalonia and explained the position reached in the negotiations, which had resulted in the nomination of Juan López, Peiró, García Oliver, and myself as members of the government. I refused to accept. Horacio

Prieto and Mariano Vázquez insisted.[4] I asked for twenty-four hours to think over the matter. I consulted my father who, thoughtfully, said: "You know what this means. In fact, it is the liquidation of anarchism and of the CNT. Once in power you will not rid yourselves of power."

Yet Federica Montseny and the others entered the government as *representatives* of the organisation. We are told that, though the CNT was not consulted, its leaders were, in fact, representing the wishes of the overwhelming majority by joining the government. Such a method for determining the opinion of an organisation may be in order under a dictatorship but is inadmissible in an organisation such as the CNT. One cannot, in attempting to establish the real position of the organisation as a whole to collaboration, accept the view of the leaders that they were representing the wishes of the overwhelming majority of the organisation, without asking whether this same "overwhelming majority" was also opposed to collaboration as late as September when the anti-collaboration article, from which we have quoted above, appeared in the *CNT-FAI Information Bulletin*. And, again, after six months of collaboration was once more opposed to it when in May 1937 the CNT leaders refused to enter the Negrín government. Such somersaults are typical of politicians; the rank and file thinks more slowly and also generally changes opinions less frequently.

It is significant that while the leaders of the CNT were vainly attempting to pit their political wits against those of the professional politicians, the rank and file and the militants in the syndicates were consolidating their victories in the economic field, functioning completely independently and outside the reach of government control. Indeed, how could it be said that they would support the strengthening of government by the participation of their representatives, when they were aware that the government would never permit such radical reorganisation of the country's economy if it had the power to prevent it?

---

4   Horacio Prieto was at the time national secretary of the CNT and Mariano Vázquez regional secretary of that organisation.

Furthermore, it was obvious to everyone (and even the "influential militants" have admitted it on more than one occasion) that the government was much more concerned with strengthening the rearguard than in strengthening the fronts manned by the militias and thereby hastening the defeat of Franco. One can substantiate with facts the assertion that it was not in the interests of the government to hasten the defeat of Franco during the first months when the best chances of doing so existed. A victory over Franco before the government had consolidated its power was an unthinkable situation for the politicians, since their position would have become even more precarious than on the morrow of the partial defeat of Franco on July 19. Only in this way can one explain how, for example, there was such a shortage of arms on the Aragon front that it was impossible to launch an offensive in the direction of Saragossa,[5] yet in the rearguard there were sixty thousand rifles and more ammunition than at the front.

In the rearguard the arms were held not only by the government's police and Assault Guards but by the political parties and the workers' organisations. It was a kind of armed camp, each faction being on the lookout against any attempt by another to impose its will by force of arms. Such a situation was a clear indication of the impossibility of any effective unity between the revolutionary workers' organisations and the political parties and government forces. There existed among the armed workers in the rearguard the preoccupation of defending the social revolution from growing encroachments by the government forces. For all arms to be sent to the front therefore it was necessary not to strengthen the government by committing the CNT to its decisions but, on the contrary, to weaken it by removing the armed forces at its command. The workers realised this in spite of their "influential" leaders.

---

5   This front, largely manned by members of the CNT-FAI, was considered of great strategic importance by the anarchists, having as its ultimate objective the linking of Catalonia with the Basque country and Asturias, i.e., a linking of the industrial region with an important source of raw materials.

In October 1936, a serious incident occurred which deserves to be mentioned here because it gives an idea of the attitude and temper of the anarchist militiamen at a time when their "leaders" were negotiating with Caballero and allocating ministerial portfolios among themselves. We refer to the Columna de Hierro (The Iron Column), at the time a garrison force on the Teruel front, which made an armed incursion on the rearguard in Valencia, which it realised was being armed, not for the benefit of the men fighting at the fronts but in order to strengthen the power of the government. A manifesto issued by the Column afterwards pointed out that they had previously sent the following demands to the "interested parties": the total disbanding of the Civil Guard and sending to the front of all the armed forces in the service of the state. They also called for the destruction of the archives and dossiers of all the capitalist and state institutions. They declared:

> We based this petition on revolutionary and ideological points of view. As anarchists and revolutionaries, we understood the danger represented by the continued existence of a purely reactionary body such as the Civil Guard, which at all times and particularly during this period has quite openly displayed its true spirit and its methods. The Civil Guard was unbearable to us and we did not wish to see it continue in existence because for overwhelming reasons we distrusted it. For that reason, we asked that it should be disarmed and for that reason we disarmed it.
>
> We asked that all the armed corps should be at the front, because there is a shortage of men and arms at the front, and the fact of remaining in the city, in view of the present situation, was and is a hindrance. We have achieved this only partially and will not give way until it is complete.
>
> Finally, we asked for the destruction of all those documents which represented a complete tyrannical and oppressive past against which our free consciences rebelled. We destroyed the papers . . .

These objectives brought us to Valencia, and we carried them out, using the methods which seemed to us most suitable.

There was no question of a coup d'état by the Columna de Hierro. It was an act of defence by men who were prepared to sacrifice their lives at the front but who could not stand by indifferently while preparations were being made in the rearguard to stab them in the back at the appropriate moment. Such a clear awareness of the duplicity of all governments cannot have been an isolated phenomenon in a movement which, after all, owed its existence, unlike the other workers' organisation—the UGT—to such an awareness and to its determination to achieve its ends by other methods. There is reason to assume, therefore, that had the question of collaboration been debated by the CNT-FAI in the syndicates and the groups and with full knowledge of the facts, the good sense of the rank-and-file militants would have prevailed against the politico-legal arguments of the "influential militants."

CHAPTER VIII

THE CORRUPTION OF POWER

It is thought by some critics that anarchists exaggerate the corrupting effect that power has on individuals. They also maintain that those anarchists who look upon all governments in the same light are being unrealistic. The argument always advanced is that from the anarchist point of view, a government which permits freedom of speech and of the press is to be preferred and supported against one that crushes the elementary freedoms and demands that all should speak with a single voice. This may be true in a sense, but it is nevertheless a choice between evils and ignores the fact that the government which can permit the people to criticise it and to attack it with words is in reality a stronger and more secure government than one which denies all criticism of the social system and the men in power, and perhaps, therefore, from a revolutionary point of view, a greater obstacle to overcome.

Many anarchists have been influenced by these criticisms and by those people who, while sympathising with the anarchist philosophy, nevertheless, consider it utopian and beyond the realms of practical application. "Perhaps in a thousand years," they say as they return to the problems of the hour. And these anarchists, stung by the accusation that they are "dreamers," seek to put forward "practical solutions" capable of realisation in the present. But for these solutions to be "practical" they must inevitably be effected through the existing governmental and state institutions, and this can only mean one thing: a recognition that the problems of our time can be solved by governmental action. And to admit this is to destroy the whole anarchist criticism of government—a criticism not based on emotion or prejudice but on the accumulated knowledge of the purpose and function of governments and the state.

The recognition that anarchists and revolutionary syndicalists cannot usefully advance their social ideas within the framework of state institutions does not, to our mind, imply that they must therefore be condemned to impotence and silence. What made of the CNT in Spain such a vital force compared with the UGT—numerically its equal—was just the fact that it was from the outset in opposition to the state and all governments and its organisation diametrically opposed to that of government, control being exercised by the members of the organisation and not by permanent officials with executive powers. The UGT, on the other hand, was controlled by the Socialist Party leaders and therefore subject to all the political vicissitudes of that party, which used the numerical strength of the UGT as a political weapon, with consequences similar to those with which we are only too familiar in the trade unions of France and Italy (where we find Catholic-, Socialist-, and Communist-dominated unions), Britain (where they are virtually an integral part of the state machine), and Russia (where they now exist in name only).

The strength of the CNT lay in its uncompromising opposition to the state and political intrigue; in its decentralised structure and in its opposition to the universal practice of paid and permanent officials; in its concern with the objectives of workers' control of the means of production as the necessary step towards libertarian communism, while at the same time courageously putting forward the immediate demands of the toiling masses for better working conditions and a recognition of their elementary freedoms. Concessions wrung out of governments from strength as an opposition have the positive result, from the anarchist point of view, of weakening the authority of government and cannot be confused with political reformism.

To understand how it was possible for the Spanish anarchists to throw overboard all their principles, one has to understand the particular atmosphere in which Spanish anarchism flourished. It was a movement based on action:

Most Spanish militants live for the revolution and believe that it can be achieved, no matter when or how, by being engaged permanently and completely in "action." This influences their outlook to such an extent that purely ideological questions no longer interest them or, at the most, are believed to be matters for the future. Generally speaking this is the type of militant who chooses the FAI, because for him it is the only organisation for action, created exclusively by action and for revolutionary action. This type of militant eventually becomes, in fact, and in spite of his goodwill and his disinterested willingness to make sacrifices, the dead weight of the FAI, since he deprives it of other higher activities and provokes most of the differences, futile or otherwise, which absorb precious time that could be used for better things.[1]

The same observer adds that there is a tendency within the ranks of the CNT to accuse the FAI of itself being responsible for provoking this "militant's mentality" among the members of the libertarian movement, and in support of this view, he refers to a number of men who for many years dedicated their lives to action, during which some even gave their lives:

> Blinded by the "practical" and temporary results of their activities, they created a kind of "doctrine of action." . . . And the fact remains that many of these elements, carried away by the impetus of their actions, were imbued with a personal conception of the revolution, and even went so far as to put forward the idea of "the conquest of power" in order to proclaim freedom from a position of command.

---

[1] Ildefonso Gonzales, in a series of articles on *Il Movimento Libertario Spagnuolo* (The Spanish Libertarian Movement) published in the anarchist monthly *Volontà* (Naples) 9, nos. 6–9, (June–September 1952). The writer is a militant of the CNT in exile. These articles are an important contribution to an understanding of the different sections of, and influences in, the Spanish libertarian movement. No attempt is made to gloss over the weaknesses of the movement, and the study includes a number of interesting documents, particularly on the FAI.

At the other extreme were those to whom we have already referred as the "politicians of the CNT." We used this word in its pure sense, in that these men sought, not only after July 1936 but during the years preceding, to orientate the CNT away from the influence of the FAI (they have frequently referred to the "dictatorship" of the FAI) and into open political action, through political alliances, participation in general and municipal elections, and even collaboration in governments. How such activity is compatible with the federalist structure (with control from below) of the organisation is beyond our understanding.

It might seem, therefore, that of these two influences in the CNT it was the reformist "leaders" who succeeded in making their point of view prevail in July 1936, thus determining the course to be followed by the Confederation during those eventful years. But this seems to us a too superficial and inexact summing-up of the situation. We have already stated our opinion that it was an error on the part of the leaders of the CNT to concentrate their written and spoken propaganda from the beginning on the menace of "fascism." But we have also come to the conclusion that the CNT-FAI leaders' concern over the "fascist menace" was a very genuine feeling which to a large extent paralysed objective thinking on their part, just as three years later many revolutionaries throughout the world were prepared, against their better judgment, to support the "war against Nazism," believing that it would solve the problem of totalitarianism and lead to the social revolution.

Again and again in the writings of Spanish revolutionaries describing those early days of the struggle against the Franco uprising, one reads of that spirit of comradeship which swept aside all party and class barriers among the men and women who had played their part in defeating the putsch. And this gave rise to the false hope, based on the idea that everyone hated the rebels as much as the workers of the CNT, that the people would remain united until Franco's forces were finally defeated. It does not require much imagination, even with the passage of time, to live those moments of exaltation and to understand the over-optimistic political evaluation by the CNT of their anti-Franco allies of July

1936.[2] But at the same time, for seasoned revolutionaries, it is inconceivable that such a state of excitement and optimism could last long, particularly when it was clear within a week of the uprising that the government had not joined the tide of revolutionary enthusiasm or shared the people's determination to advance the struggle against Franco and the old economic order to its limits.

Nevertheless, we put forward these views as an *explanation* of the origin of the idea of collaboration in the leadership of the CNT, not only with the other workers' organisation—the UGT—but also with the political parties. Once committed to the idea of "unity" and "collaboration" other factors came into play which rapidly undermined the independence of the CNT, creating among many militants a craving for power (both as individuals as well as for the organisation), and a legalistic attitude which came to believe that the workers' victories in the economic field could be made secure by governmental decrees. This growth of the bureaucratic and legalistic mind was accompanied by a slackening of the organisational methods by which decisions were normally taken by the CNT. In other words, a leadership was created—not only by the politicians and influential members of the CNT but also by the many members who held important administrative posts and military commands—which functioned through committees and government departments, rarely consulting or giving an account of its actions to the rank and file of the organisation (i.e., the syndicates). In early 1938, the final step was taken with the creation of the executive committee of the Libertarian Movement in Catalonia. We shall refer to it in more detail in the concluding chapter of this study.

It is true that the leaders could boast that the CNT-FAI alone among the organisations held many plenums during this period at which the policies of the Confederation were discussed. But in reality these plenums were no more representative of the views of the rank and file than a House of Commons debate represents the considered

---

2   To a more limited extent one can find a parallel in the resistance movements during World War II. The optimism was short-lived with the return of the politicians after the "liberation."

views of the electorate. Time and again plenums, with momentous agendas, were called at two or three days' notice, so that it was quite impossible, within the time allowed, for the local syndicates and federations to have an opportunity to discuss the questions on which their delegates were expected to speak on their behalf. More often than not, the statement issued after such plenums would only consist of a few slogans and vague expressions of enthusiasm by the delegates, so that the rank and file's first knowledge of the decisions reached would be when they were faced with the fait accompli.

Even today, for instance, the historiographer of the CNT cannot establish whether the national plenum of Regional Committees held in September 1936 ever discussed the question of the National Defence Council (which it may be recalled was the CNT-FAI "alternative" to the Caballero government).

> The suddenness of its [the plenum's] summoning and the guarded statement on the agreements reached do not permit one to know [whether the National Defence Council was discussed].[3]

In spite of the impossibility of referring to the internal documents of the CNT-FAI, there is sufficient evidence to show that the plenums acted as the rubber stamp for the decisions taken by the leadership of the CNT-FAI, not without certain misgivings, as the regional plenum of syndicates convoked on October 22, 1936, for October 26 shows. In those four days, the syndicates had to examine the draft pact with the UGT, express their attitude to municipal councils, and deal with the resignation of the regional secretary and the appointment of his successor.

At the plenum, and following the secretary's report:

> discussion was prolonged and reasoned, many delegations taking part and expressing their various points of view, without

---

3   José Peirats, *La CNT en la Revolución Española*, vol. 1, (Toulouse: Ediciones CNT, 1951), 289.

any serious differences emerging, since all the organisation recognises that in present circumstances a strict conformity to the confederal norms cannot be demanded. Nevertheless, the majority of the delegations expressed their logical desire that whenever possible the rank and file should be consulted, requesting the committee not to exercise their prerogative save in exceptional circumstances.[4]

When we say that power corrupts those who wield it, we do not mean that such people necessarily fall victim to the temptations of bribery and material gain as is, for instance, the case in American political life. What we do firmly believe is that no one can resist the effect that power has in modifying thought and human personality. As Gaston Leval noted, "some anarchist delegates who had become ministers or officials in different categories, took their tasks seriously; the poison of power immediately took effect."[5] And only a few strong personalities can, once they have basked in it, dispense with the limelight that accompanies power.

The frailty of mankind in this respect has always been clearly understood by anarchists, and because of this they have always advocated a decentralised society in opposition to the centralisation in present-day society, which permits power to be concentrated in a few hands. In their own movement the general form of organisation has been the affinity, or functional, group; each group maintaining contact with the others through some coordinating or correspondence secretariat, but each retaining its autonomy and freedom of action. In the revolutionary syndicalist movement the same principles apply, with the syndicate as the unit of organisation. These views were in theory shared by the Spanish CNT-FAI, but in practice not always observed, and for reasons which are peculiar to the Spanish movement. We have already referred to

---

4   Peirats, *La CNT en la Revolución Española*, vol. 1, 293.
5   Gaston Leval, *Né Franco né Stalin: Le collettivita anarchiche spanuole nella lotta contra Franco e la reazione staliniana*. (Milan: Milano Istituto editoriale italiano, 1952), 81.

the "militant's mentality." One has also to bear in mind that for long periods in their history the CNT-FAI were declared illegal and therefore unable always to act organically. And the fact of the CNT being a mass organisation carried with it, to our minds, the dangers inherent in all mass movements of the creation of groups of influential militants within its ranks whose preoccupation is to safeguard the "purity" of the movement from reformist elements.

The result of all these factors was that there have always been outstanding personalities representing different tendencies, though very often the internal crises in the CNT have not been so much ideological as a clash between these personalities. It is noteworthy, for instance, that the post-war crisis in the CNT in exile, ostensibly between the "collaborationist" and "purist" tendencies, has in fact been a struggle between personalities aiming at control of the organisation.

It is also significant that many Spanish anarchists seem unable to discuss ideas without descending to personalities. A careful reading of their press, particularly in the early period of the crisis confirms, we think, such a statement. But this happens also to be the technique of every self-respecting politician in the game of power politics!

The situation created by the revolutionary workers' successes in July 1936 made possible a further building up of leaders in the CNT-FAI. Overnight the whole propaganda machinery in their hands was increased beyond belief. Besides having their own radio station and issuing daily information bulletins in a number of languages, there were some eight daily newspapers and innumerable weeklies and monthlies, covering every aspect of social activity.[6] Vast meetings were held throughout Spain addressed by "the best

---

6 José Peirats, *La CNT en la Revolución Española*, vol. 2 (Toulouse: Ediciones CNT, 1952) gives an incomplete list of more than fifty CNT-FAI periodicals published during that period, besides the daily newspapers. See also the interesting article by Juan Ferrer, "El ciclo emancipador de 'Solidaridad Obrera,'" *Solidaridad Obrero* (Paris), February 12, 1954. According to him the average circulation of *Solidaridad Obrera* before July 1936 was 7,000 copies. By 1937, it had risen to 180,000 copies daily.

orators of the movement, such as Federica Montseny, García Oliver, Gaston Leval, Higinio Noja Felipe, etc."[7] And this concentration of political power in a few hands was further aggravated by the fact that many active militants whose voices might have served as a counterbalance to those of the "influential militants" were engaged in the all-absorbing task of the collectives or with the fighting columns manning the fronts. Indeed, it is a reflection of the revolutionary integrity of the movement as a whole that so many of the men capable of running the propaganda machine and of filling administrative posts shunned these positions of power, and that in the first weeks of the struggle it was not possible to find enough men to carry on this work.

To solve the problem the Bureau of Information and Propaganda of the CNT-FAI in Barcelona decided on the creation of a School for Militants (Escuela de Militantes). In a radio talk explaining the purpose of this school it was revealed that it was "under the auspices of, and supported and maintained by, the Regional Committee of the CNT and by the FAI of Catalonia." Its purpose was "to create an organism with the exclusive aim of cultivating militants and adapting and equipping them for the work and the ideas of the organisation in its various aspects." To belong to the school it was necessary to have "personal views and a general culture, especially in social questions." But, failing these, a "desire to achieve the objectives aimed at by the school." Also, all students at the school "should have the economic backing of the syndicate to which they belong." In the course of the talk it was said that "there is no doubt that one of the major successes of our organisation has been that of creating this *original kind of institution,* since the students, while obtaining useful and interesting knowledge in all the branches of human thought, acquire, at the same time, methodically, the maximum training in their specialised subject." (emphasis added)

The historiographer of the CNT in exile makes no comment on this far from "original" institution perfected long ago by the rulers

---

7 Peirats, *La CNT en la Revolución Española,* vol. 2.

in Moscow and used by the British Labour Party and trade unions as a method for training the future party leaders and trade union bosses. To our mind such revolutionary incubators are fraught with more dangers than advantages, particularly when, as in the case under discussion, they are organised by the Propaganda Bureau with the specific purpose of turning out public speakers and journalists, who, clearly, if they are to speak or write for the Propaganda Bureau, will be expected to express the "party line" and not their personal views, the more so if they are paid propagandists.[8] Thus the official line gains a serious advantage over minority viewpoints by its monopoly over the main channels of expression.

Space permitting, we should have wished to examine in detail the whole technique of propaganda; and propaganda in Spain was conducted by all parties and organisations on such a vast scale that a study of the methods used would provide valuable lessons for the future.[9] We will, however, have to content ourselves at present

---

8   Any propaganda financed by the Propaganda Bureau had to support the official line or be starved of money. One case in point was the excellent periodical *Espagne Anti-Fasciste*, published in France, which had a large circulation among French workers and intellectuals. As soon as it dared to criticise the policy of the leadership of the CNT-FAI, funds were suspended and the journal, though it did not cease publication altogether, was considerably reduced in format and ceased to have the wide appeal of its predecessor. In a letter from Barcelona (February 1937) the Italian anarchist Camillo Berneri wrote: "Issue no. 8 of *Guerra di Classe* (a weekly edited by Berneri) will appear when it can. The committee has dealt with it in the same way as with *l'Espagne Anti-Fasciste*"; *Pensieri e Battaglie* (Paris: Comitato Camillo Berneri 1938), 261–62.

9   See footnote 6 regarding the strength of the CNT-FAI press. Their press was essentially propagandist, and as a result news items regarding the armed struggle exaggerated the victories and minimised the defeats. But they did not use their press to attack personalities in the political parties of the Popular Front or to gain party advantage for themselves (except in so far as they sought to build up their own personalities in the Popular Army and in the political and social fields). Indeed, one feels that much more could have been done through the press to gain sympathy for the anarchist cause. Perhaps the obsession for anti-fascist unity that dominated the leadership, as well as the "political" line adopted by the CNT-FAI, made it impossible for a more direct anarchist approach. The political parties, on the other hand, had no such scruples on the use of their press for party ends. And none used their press more effectively (or dishonestly) than the Communists. Jesús Hernández, the Spanish Communist Party leader,

with stating our view that the oratorical demagogues (as opposed to lecturers and speakers at group meetings and such gatherings) represent the greatest of all dangers to the integrity of a revolutionary movement. The microphone is the curse of modern times. And in some parts of Spain where they tilled the soil with roman ploughs, there was, and still is, no shortage of chromium plated microphones!

A characteristic of political demagogy is that one day one says one thing and the next one expects the people to swallow the contrary. We have already been provided with a classical example of this technique in the document of September 3, 1936, against collaboration, which was to be so soon followed by paeans in praise of government when the CNT joined Caballero. And there are many more. García Oliver, who ranked among the highest in what Federica Montseny has eloquently called the "anarchist dynasty," provides us with all the material we require for a study of the corrupting influence of power. He it was who said at a huge public meeting in Barcelona on August 10, 1936:

> The Madrid government thinks that one proceeds with the formation of an army to combat fascism without this army

---

has the following to say in his book *Yo fui ministro de Stalin* (Mexico: Editorial America, 1953), 134–35: "[Most of the political and syndical forces] lacked the propaganda sense for being seen, heard, and felt everywhere and at all times. We Communists, on the other hand, put into action the saying that 'not even God hears him who does not speak up,' and were more successful than any of the others in exploiting the agitational weapon and knew how to arouse the strongest emotions in the masses in order to lead them in our particular direction. If we decided, say, to show that Caballero, Prieto, Azaña, or Durruti were responsible for our defeats, half a million men, dozens of periodicals, millions of leaflets, hundreds of orators would all attest to the dangerousness of these citizens so systematically with such ardour and consistency that in a fortnight everybody in the whole of Spain would have the idea, the suspicion, and the conviction of the truth of the assertion firmly fixed in their minds. Someone once declared that a lie when told by one person is simply a lie; when repeated by thousands of people it is transformed into a doubtful truth; but when proclaimed by millions, it acquires the status of an established truth. This is a technique which Stalin and his cohorts exploited to perfection."

having a revolutionary spirit. The army can have only the character that emerges from the voice of the people and must be 100 per cent proletarian. To demonstrate this I must refer to the corps of Assault Guards, Carabineers, and Civil Guards who joined with the working-class masses in the struggle against fascism, forming with them a popular army which has been proved in practice to be superior to the classical concept of armed corps organised behind the backs of the people.

On December 4, 1936, at a meeting in Valencia, the same speaker, by then minister of justice, declared:

Are we interested in winning the war? Then whatever may be the ideologies or the credos of the workers or the organisations to which they belong, to win they must use the methods used by the enemy, and especially, discipline and union. With discipline and efficient military organisation, we shall win without a doubt. Discipline for those who struggle at the front and at the workbench, discipline in everything is the basis for triumph.

Six months at the Ministry of Justice converted this courageous and popular exponent of direct action into an apologist for government and work camps for political prisoners. At a public meeting addressed by him in Valencia on May 30, 1937, shortly after the fall of the Caballero government and the dismissal of the CNT ministers, he gave an account of his activities in the government.[10] It was a two and a half hour bolstering of García Oliver, the value of legislation, and the great potentialities of government. In his opening remarks he said that the title of his speech could well have been,

---

10 Juan García Oliver, *Mi Gestion al Frente del Ministerio de Justida* (Valencia: Ediciones CNT, 1937). Extracts are quoted in José Peirats, *La CNT en la Revolución Española*, vol. 2, but he unfortunately omits those remarks which from a psychopathological point of view are the most interesting.

"'From the Factory in Barcelona to the Ministry of Justice.' That is, from a worker of the Textile Syndicate of Barcelona to the structur-alising of a new Spain."[11] Later, he repeated the fact of his origin as a worker, adding: "But should anyone have any doubts about it or not know it, the minister of justice, though a worker, was García Oliver." And a few sentences later: "I was the minister of justice, García Oliver," modestly adding, "but do not believe that I did everything." What is particularly significant in García Oliver's speech is that not only does he display no embarrassment in expounding the decree laws drafted by him, which included long prison sentences for those found guilty under them, or his proposals for the *reform* of the penal system, but he also demonstrates quite clearly the deep influence exerted on him by governmentalism and his belief that the nature of governments is transformed when it includes representation of the CNT—an argument which can only lead to the position where one would advocate, in common with the Socialists and reformists, that once Parliament consisted of anarchists, we will have anarchism. "I have reasons to believe," declared Oliver:

> by interpreting the ordering of economy, that there are things which must be collectivised because they can be collectivised; that there are things which must be municipalised because they cannot be collectivised from the point of view of eco-nomic efficiency or return; that there are things which must be nationalised, because in the economic circumstances of the moment, transitory or permanent, they can be neither collectivised nor municipalised. I have reasons to believe that there are things which must still be left to the free exploitation of the small proprietors and small industrialists. All existing problems can be solved with a good government of people who work, who do not travel too much, who spend less time

---

11 By an interesting coincidence, Juan Peiró actually called *his* speech "From the Glass Factory of Mataró to the Ministry of Industry." One cannot help gaining the impression that Oliver and Peiró each considered his change of occupation—from worker to minister—as a notable achievement and a rise in status and not a very great sacrifice so far as his anarchist principles were concerned

on politics and more solving the problems and organising the work to be done.

Of the four CNT-FAI ministers in the central government, only Federica Montseny has publicly "recanted" though, as one of the "orators" of the movement, one cannot be sure to what extent this is motivated by reasons other than those of principles. In a letter to Juan López, written shortly after the "liberation" of France, she expressed the view that the question of political collaboration or abstention was neither the only nor the most important that had to be discussed:

> The problem is to make the CNT and the libertarian movement an organised and conscious force, with a definite "line," with a programme of things to be carried out immediately, and with a clear view of the morrow and its possibilities both *in* Spain and outside. . . . Perhaps we are not in agreement on all points, but I am sure we will agree on a fundamental question: in the necessity of preparing ourselves for the return to Spain with a quite different moral equipment to the one that existed in 1936. Experience must be of some use to us as well as the lessons to be drawn from events. And the CNT must be really solid, massive, organised under a firm direction with discipline and realistic objectives, without thereby losing sight of our final objectives (*notre idéal*), if we are not to lose out to the others [the political parties].[12]

Juan López, who rightly, we think, draws attention to the "authoritarian spirit" of this letter, has himself remained a supporter of collaboration. He welcomed the entry of a representative of the CNT in the Spanish government in exile (headed by Giral); supports collaboration with all the political parties opposed to Franco, with the exception of the Communists, and the necessity

---

12 Quoted in Juan López, *Los Principios Libertarios ante la Política Española (Material de Discusión)*, Brighton, February 15, 1946.

for a "realist" policy by the CNT, including participation in the government of the country. In his favour, it should be pointed out that Juan López does not call himself an anarchist; he is a syndicalist who believes in politics and "revolutionary" governments.

As we have already said, we do not know how he squares his criticism of the "dictatorship" of the FAI in the CNT, preventing real democracy and control by the syndicates, with his support of the "evolution" of the CNT to governmentalism. He is surely not suggesting that government can be controlled by the governed. By advocating the creation of what is in effect an executive council of the CNT which will be responsible to the government and not to the organisation, López, we feel, shares that "authoritarian spirit" with Federica Montseny, the late Juan Peiró (another unrepentant political collaborationist), and García Oliver (now in the political wilderness advocating an anarchist party). And these are not the only ravages wreaked by power in the ranks of the revolutionary movement. It has had its effect on many a tuppenny-ha'penny councillor, factory manager, and ersatz editor.

To what extent they will determine the future policy of the CNT we do not profess to know. Perhaps the social experiment and achievements of the Spanish workers and peasants during 1936–1939 have taught them the value of doing things for themselves without governments and "influential leaders." In which case the politicians and demagogues are going to have a hard struggle to mould the CNT-FAI to their will in the years that lie ahead.

CHAPTER IX
THE AGRICULTURAL COLLECTIVES

A critical study of the achievements of the revolutionary workers in the social and economic fields is a more rewarding task than that of following the political developments and intrigues among the political leaders and between the parties and organisations. It is more rewarding because we are face to face with the strivings of a people to convert what might easily have become a purely political struggle into a social revolution, an overturning of the whole economic and social structure of a country which had for so long been dominated by wealthy landowners and industrialists, the Church, and foreign capital. It is more interesting than any other social experiment of its kind, because it was a spontaneous, improvised movement of the people, in which the politicians played no part, save that of attempting later to destroy, control, or contain it, for such a movement threatened the whole machinery of state, of government, of capitalism, and the exploitation of man by man.

This has generally been ignored by sociologists; it has been grossly distorted by Communists in their propaganda; and soft-pedalled—for obvious reasons—by Spanish politicians. But it is to be especially regretted that so far no serious attempt has been made by the Spanish anarcho-syndicalist and anarchist movements to collect together the vast amount of material that exists on the subject of the industrial and agricultural collectives in Spain and to draw from these experiments lessons which tomorrow will be of utmost importance not only in Spain but for revolutionary movements throughout the world.

The collected material at present available in the Spanish language is contained, to our knowledge, in three volumes. There are two small books, published in Barcelona in 1937, which give firsthand accounts of collectives visited by the authors, and there are the last hundred pages of the first volume of José Peirats's history of the CNT in the Spanish Revolution, which comprise descriptions of the constitution and working of a number of collective enterprises.[1] But, in pointing out that to deal with the subject would require an entire volume, Peirats makes no attempt to relate the various experiments or to give us a general picture as to their extent or even to differentiate between the various approaches to collectivisation adopted by different regions and industries. The only study of the Spanish collectives which makes any attempt at doing this is the one by Gaston Leval.[2]

The author spent many years in Spain, and has always been particularly interested in the problems of the reorganisation of that country's economy under workers' control. During the Revolution he was able to study at firsthand a large number of collectives in Catalonia, the Levante, Aragon, and Castille. This has permitted him to draw conclusions which are valuable, for they give one an insight into the practical problems that have to be faced by all socialists and anarchists who advocate the reorganisation of our economic system along more equitable lines.

But what Peirats has not attempted to do in one hundred pages and Gaston Leval only partially in more than three hundred, we cannot hope to do in one short chapter! All we can do, therefore, is to attempt to give the reader an idea of what the Spanish collectivist movement represented, its extent and importance, and to

---

1   Augustín Souchy, *Entre los campesinos de Aragon* (Barcelona: Ediciones Tierra y Libertad, 1937); Augustín Souchy and Paul Folgare, *Colectivizaciones: La obra constructive de la Revolución Española* (Barcelona: Ediciones Tierra y Libertad, 1937); José Peirats, *La CNT en la Revolución Española*, vol. 1 (Toulouse: Ediciones CNT, 1951), 297–386.

2   Gaston Leval, *Né Franco né Stalin: Le collettivita anarchiche spanuole nella lotta contra Franco e la reazione staliniana* (Milan: Milano Istituto editoriale italiano, 1952).

deal with some of its problems. Finally, we must give some idea of the opposition met with from the political elements and describe the methods used by the Spanish government and the Communist Party to destroy these practical achievements of the people.

By so doing we shall, we think, be drawing attention to the great creative potentialities of the common people, the peasants, and the workers of Spain (potentialities shared, we believe, with the working people of all the world once they are in a position to organise their own lives) and at the same time once more underline the bitter truth revealed by political developments, that there is no common ground for unity between the revolutionary working masses and the political parties which aspire to government and power.

As all writers on Spain point out, the major economic problem is that of the land. Of Spain's twenty-five million inhabitants in 1936, 68 per cent lived in the rural areas, while 70 per cent of its total industry was concentrated in the small province of Catalonia. The solution to Spain's problems is not to convert her into an industrial country, since, apart from other considerations, she lacks the raw materials necessary for large-scale industry. The major obstacle has been that the bulk of the land has always been held by a small number of landowners, who were uninterested in developing their estates, in some cases even that they should be cultivated at all. Sixty-seven per cent of the land was in the hands of 2 per cent of the total number of landowners, 19.69 per cent owned 21 per cent, while 76.54 per cent owned 13.16 per cent. Of the latter, half owned an acre or less per head, which in most areas of Spain is insufficient to feed a peasant and his family. In the three provinces of Extremadura, Andalusia, and La Mancha alone, seven thousand proprietors, the greater part of them absentees, possess more than fifteen million acres. But the problem of the land would not be solved simply by parcelling it out among the landless peasants. The soil is poor, and there are large areas with hardly any rainfall, so that only by irrigation, the extensive use of fertilizers, and modern machinery could the peasants feed themselves and have a surplus to satisfy their other needs. Since they have no means to carry out such improvements, distribution per se of the land among individual peasants is doomed to failure. As Gerald Brenan points out:

> The only reasonable solution through wide tracts of Spain is a collective one. . . . In many districts the peasants are themselves averse to it, but the anarchist ideology in Andalusia has made it a favourite solution there and this is a factor which any sensible government would take advantage of. For the advantages of communal ownership of the land are enormous. Under present conditions one has agricultural labourers dying of hunger on estates where large tracts of corn-growing land lie fallow because it does not pay to cultivate them.[3]

The overrunning of most of Andalusia by Franco's forces early in the struggle made it impossible for collective experiments to be tried out there, but we have examples in other parts of Spain where the large estates were taken over by the peasants and worked collectively, and during the time the experiment was able to continue showed that amazing results could be obtained by these methods. Perhaps the most extensive agricultural collectivisations took place in that part of Aragon not under Franco's rule where more than 400 collectives were formed, comprising half a million people. But in the Levante too there were by 1938 more than 500 collectives. Even in Castille, a socialist stronghold in 1936, the Regional Federation of Peasants, which was affiliated to the CNT, had nearly one hundred thousand members and 230 collectives by 1937. Gaston Leval has estimated that about three million peasants, men, women, and children, succeeded in putting into practice "this system of living with immediate results, without the lowering of production which these groupings of new regimes usually produce." On the Aragonese collectivisations he writes:

---

3   Gerald Brenan, *The Spanish Labyrinth* (London: Cambridge University Press, 1943); see the chapter titled "The Agrarian Question."

The mechanism of the formation of the Aragonese collectives has been generally the same. After having overcome the local authorities when they were fascist or after having replaced them by anti-fascist or revolutionary committees when they were not, an assembly was summoned of all the inhabitants of the locality to decide on their line of action.

One of the first steps was to gather in the crop, not only in the fields of the small landowners who still remained, but, what was even more important, also on the estates of the large landowners, all of whom were conservatives and rural "caciques" or chiefs. Groups were organised to reap and thresh the wheat which belonged to these large landowners. Collective work began spontaneously. Then as this wheat could not be given to anyone in particular without being unfair to all it was put under the control of a local committee, for the use of all the inhabitants, either for consumption or for the purpose of exchange for manufactured goods, such as clothes, boots, etc., *for those who were most in need.*

It was necessary, afterwards, to work the lands of the large landowners. They were generally the most extensive and fertile in the region. The question was again raised before the village assembly. It was then that the "collectivity" if not already definitely constituted—often this had been done at the first meeting—was definitely established.

A delegate for agriculture and stock breeding was nominated (or one for each of these activities when breeding was extensively carried on), one delegate each for local distribution, exchanges, public works, hygiene and education and revolutionary defence. Sometimes there were more; on other occasions less.

Workers' groups were then formed. These groups generally were divided into the number of zones into which the municipal territory had been divided, so as more easily to include all kinds of work. Each group of workers names its delegate. The delegates meet every two days or every week with the councillor of agriculture and stock breeding, so as to coordinate all the different activities.

In this new organisation, small property has almost completely disappeared. In Aragon 75 per cent of small proprietors have voluntarily adhered to the new order of things. *Those who refused have been respected.* It is untrue to say that those who took part in the collectives were forced to do so. One cannot stress this point too strongly in face of the calumnies which have been directed against the collectives on this point. It is so far from the truth that the agrarian collectivity has brought into force, everywhere, a special current account for small proprietors and has printed consumers tickets specially for them, so as to ensure for them the industrial products they require, in the same way as they do for the "collectivists."

In this transformation of property, one must put special stress on the practical sense and psychological finesse of the organisers who in almost all the villages have conceded or given to each family a bit of ground on which each peasant cultivates, for his own use, the vegetables which he prefers in the way he prefers. Their individual initiative can thereby be developed and satisfied.

Collective work has made it possible to achieve in agriculture as well as in industry, a rationalisation which was impossible under the regime of small land ownership and even under that of big landed properties . . .

On the other hand, better quality seeds are used. This was rendered possible by being able to buy up large stocks, which the small peasant could not afford to do in the past. Potato seeds come from Ireland and selected wheat seeds only are used. Chemical fertilizers have also been used. As modern machinery properly used—tractors and modern ploughs were obtained by exchange or bought directly from abroad—permits the soil to be more deeply worked, these seeds have produced a yield per acre far superior to that which would have been obtained under the conditions which existed during previous years. These new methods have also made it possible to increase the acreage sown. In Aragon my research on the spot permits me to affirm that generally speaking *the increase in wheat crop has reached an average of 30 per cent.* An increase in yield, though in a smaller proportion, has been obtained for other cereals, potatoes, sugar beet, lucerne, etc.

In these agricultural regions the economic condition of the peasants has generally improved. It has only suffered a setback in those localities which had specialised in production for export, and which were consequently unable to place their products and obtain foodstuffs in exchange. This happened in certain regions in Levante whose produce consisted almost entirely of oranges. But this state of affairs lasted only a few months.

This latter fact is of utmost importance. It is the first time in modern society that the anarchist principle "to each according to his needs" has been practised. It has been applied in two ways; without money in many villages in Aragon and by a local money in others, and in the greater part of collectives established in other regions. The *family wage* is paid with this money and it varies according to the number of members in each family. A household in which the man and his wife both work because they have no children receives, for the sake of argument, say, five pesetas a day. Another household in which only the man works, as his wife has to care for two, three or four children, receives six, seven or eight pesetas respectively. It is the "needs" and not only the "production" taken in the strictly economic sense which controls the wage scale or that of the distribution of products where wages do not exist.

This principle of justice is continually extended. It does away with charity and begging and the special budgets for the indigent. There are no more destitutes. Those who work do so for others in the same way as others will work to help them and their children later on.

But this mutual aid extends beyond the village. Before the fascist invaders destroyed the Aragon collectives, the cantonal federations did all in their power to counteract the injustices of nature by obtaining for the less favoured villages the machinery, mules, seed, etc. . . . which were to help them increase the yield of their land. These implements were obtained through the intermediary of the Federation which undertook the delivery of the produce of twenty, thirty, forty or even fifty localities and asked in their name, from the industrial and stock-breeding centres, for the products which they required."[4]

The leadership of the UGT opposed collectivisation and advocated instead nationalisation of the means of production. But what is important to note is the widespread influence the experiments in collectivisation had on the peasants of the UGT, and, in fact, one reads of many collectives organised jointly by the CNT and UGT. In Castille, Leval points out, the collectivist movement of the CNT received considerable support from the Federation of Land Workers (UGT):

At bottom the workers of the UGT often had similar aspirations to those of the CNT. They wanted the expropriation of the large landed estates and the affirmation of social justice. In practice there was in many areas official agreement between the two peasant organisations, which always redounded to the benefit of the collectives.[5]

Interesting also to note is the help given by one region to another in organising agricultural collectives. The success of collectivisation in Castille was not only due to the efforts of the local libertarian militants and socialists. In July 1937, no less than one thousand members of collectives in the Levante had come to live

---

4   Gaston Leval, *Social Reconstruction in Spain* (London: Freedom Press, 1938).
5   Ibid.

in Castille for the purpose of helping and advising their comrades with the experience gained from their own experiments in collectivisation. And how wise were these peasants who applied the rule to all delegates that "in a well-organised collective no one must cease to be a peasant"—in other words, that delegates must continue to work in the fields with the rest.

The agricultural collectives were not rigid structures, faithful models taken from some faded blueprint. In the first place they were the spontaneous manifestations of simple people, who were ground down by indescribable poverty but who retained a spirit of revolt and a sense of justice which stood them in good stead when the time was ripe to take matters into their own hands. One of the secrets of the success of the social revolution on the land was the desire of the peasants, on the whole, to work co-operatively rather than to own and work a piece of land individually. "One has to recognise," writes Gerald Brenan in *The Spanish Labyrinth*, "that the Spanish working-classes show a spontaneous talent for co-operation that exceeds anything that can be found today in other European countries." And they also showed a willingness to learn of and to apply new methods to the cultivation of the land. There was no longer the fear that mechanisation would mean unemployment. And one could cite many cases to show how with the passage of time and the experience gained from the first experiments of communal working, the collectives adapted themselves so as to ensure more efficient production and a more effective realisation of their fundamental ideas of social justice and mutual aid.

In the descriptions of the collective enterprises one is continually struck by the concern shown by their members that those unwilling to participate should be persuaded to join eventually *by example*, by showing that their way was the better way. It is sometimes said of the Spanish peasants that their outlook was purely local. If true of the past, there seem to have been notable changes after 1936. In June 1937, for instance, a national plenum of regional federations of peasants was held in Valencia to discuss the formation of a National Federation of Peasants for the coordination and extension of the collectivist movement and also to ensure an equitable distribution of the produce of the land, not only between the collectives but for the whole country. Again, in Castille in October 1937, a merging of the one hundred thousand members of the Regional Federation of Peasants and the thirteen thousand members in the food distributive trades took place. It represented a logical step in ensuring better coordination and was accepted for the whole of Spain at the national congress of collectives held in Valencia in November 1937.

CHAPTER X

THE COLLECTIVISED INDUSTRIES

The problems confronting the revolutionary workers in industry were more complex than those facing the peasants. Too many factors were outside their control for the revolution in industry to be as thoroughgoing as that on the land.

The social upheaval that took place on July 19, 1936, did no more than change the peasant's status overnight. The large landowners had either fled or were in any case absentee landowners. From the point of view of the peasant this did not hamper him unduly in his ability to carry on, whereas the abandonment of the factories by the managers and large numbers of technicians was a serious obstacle to the resumption of efficient production in a short space of time. In the case of the peasant, the immediate problem created by the uprising was that the harvest had to be gathered on the large estates as well as on the land which had not been deserted by the owners. From the economic point of view it was a favourable beginning to the social revolution. So far as the future was concerned increased production and more modern methods of cultivation were the tasks of the peasant in the struggle against Franco. And with the exception of certain exportable goods, such as oranges, there was no real problem of markets.

How different instead was the situation in industry. Apart from the abandonment of the factories by key technicians, the problem had also to be faced that a large number of industries had become redundant because overnight important internal markets for Catalan industry had suddenly been cut off by Franco's army.

Foreign markets for Spanish manufactures were not large at any time and these too were temporarily lost. Equally important, Spain's dependence on foreign raw materials to feed her industries became a serious problem when the sources of supply were temporarily cut off and was further aggravated by the fact that when the raw materials could once more be obtained the funds were often held back by the central government from the factories needing them because they were controlled by the workers.

Most of Spain's war industry was located in territory occupied by Franco's forces, so that a further problem facing Catalonia was the necessity to create a war industry where none existed. This involved the importing of special machinery, the retooling of whole factories, and the training of workers to handle them. It also meant the creation of a chemical industry and the manufacture of many articles which had never before been produced in Spain, such as cars and lorries, which hitherto had only been assembled in Spain. Yet within the first year even this problem was successfully dealt with. These were, however, only some of the technical problems facing the revolutionary workers of Catalonia.

Politically too they were faced with opposition which used every weapon in its power to gain control over industry. This, in the end, the central government more or less succeeded in doing by the nationalisation of the war industries, which by then represented the bulk of the industrial potential. As we have already indicated, such a situation was possible because, though the workers were in complete control of the factories, the central government controlled the gold with which to purchase abroad the raw materials. without which Spanish industry was paralysed.

In the first days of the revolution, the workers simply seized those factories which had been abandoned and which were generally the largest in the region and resumed production where possible under workers' control. In some factories all the workers drew a fixed weekly wage, but in others the profits or income were shared out among the workers, an arrangement which is more equitable than that the factory owner should put them in his pocket, but which nevertheless was not compatible with the spirit of the revolution which was to do away with bosses and shareholders and not increase their number by a kind of collective capitalism. As a result, wages fluctuated in different factories and even within the same industries. The prosperous factories with large stocks of raw material and modern equipment had therefore an unfair advantage over the uneconomical factory struggling to keep going on small stocks. Such a system exists in Russia where in the kolkhozes the daily rate paid to the workers is fixed in relation to the previous year's profits. And this figure is arrived at "by exactly the same calculations that would settle the amount of the dividends to be distributed among the shareholders, if the kolkhoz were a capitalist agricultural concern" (Gide, *Return from the USSR*). But fortunately in Spain the injustice of this form of collectivisation was recognised and combated by the CNT syndicates from the beginning.

The collectivisation decree of October 24, 1936, which "did no more than legalise a situation already created by the workers," has generally been hailed by the legalists among the syndicalists as one of the achievements of the revolution.[1] The more so since the decree was the work of the councillor for economy in the Generalitat, Juan Fábregas, who was also a member of the CNT. The purpose of the decree may have been to legalise what was a fait accompli; but it was also an attempt to prevent the further development of the new revolutionary economy in Catalan industry. In October 1936, the experiment was still in its early stages. Each industry, each factory and workshop, had its own particular problems to solve as well as the general problem of industry's responsibility to the community as a whole and the part it had to play in the struggle against Franco.

The collectivisation decree, by limiting collectivisation of industry to those enterprises employing *more* than one hundred workers, excluded a very large section of the working population from participation in the experiment of workers' control. It was decreed that in all privately owned factories a workers' control

---

1   José Peirats, *La CNT en la Revolución Española*, vol. 1 (Toulouse: Ediciones CNT, 1951), 379.

committee would be created, on the one hand, to deal with the economic and social rights of the workers employed and, on the other, to ensure "strict discipline in carrying out work." They would also do all in their power to increase production by the "closest collaboration with the owner" who would be obliged each year to present to the control committee a balance sheet and minutes, which would then be passed on to the General Councils of Industry. Thus, the workers' control committee had many roles and many loyalties; and it seems that all had power except the producers!

But let us examine the situation in the collectivised industries, that is those employing more than one hundred workers or those employing less than one hundred whose owners were "declared enemies" or had fled. Actually, there was another category of industry which could come under the collectivisation decree:

> The Economic Council can also sanction the collectivisation of those other industries which, by reason of their importance to the national economy or for other reasons, it is considered desirable that they should be removed from the activities of private enterprise.

We have quoted this sentence from article 2 of the decree because it clearly reveals that the ultimate authority in the new economy was not to be the syndicates but the government of Catalonia; and that the direction and development of the economy was to rest in the hands of the politicians and economists. In this way workers' control would be reduced to but a shadow of the original objectives that the revolutionary workers had set for themselves when they took over the factories and workshops.

Management of collectivised enterprises was in the hands of a Council of Enterprises nominated by the workers themselves, who would also decide the number of representatives on this Council. But the Council would also include a "controller" from the Generalitat (Catalan government) nominated by the Economic Council "in agreement with the workers." Whereas in enterprises employing up to five hundred workers or with a capital of less than a million pesetas, the manager was to be nominated by the Council of Enterprises, in larger factories and in those engaged on national defence, the nomination of the manager must be approved by the Economic Council. Furthermore, the Council of Enterprises could be removed from office by the workers at a general meeting as well as by the General Council of Industry in cases of manifest incompetence or resistance to the instructions given by the General Council (article 20).

We must now explain the role of the General Council for Industry, which has twice appeared in this bureaucratic maze through which we are attempting to lead the reader. The General Council was composed of four representatives of the Council of Enterprises, eight representatives of the workers' organisations (CNT, UGT, etc.) and four technicians named by the Economic Council. The chairman at these Council meetings was a spokesman for the Economic Council of Catalonia. Article 25 deals with the role of the General Council, which includes formulating a general programme of work for the industry, orientating the Council of Enterprises in its tasks, and, furthermore, to undertake the regulation of total output of the industry and unify production costs as far as possible to avoid competition; to study the general needs of industry and of internal and foreign markets; to propose changes in methods of production; to negotiate banking and credit facilities, organise research laboratories, prepare statistics, etc. . . . In a word, the General Council would determine and carry out everything . . . except the actual work, which as is usual in all centralised systems was left to the workers! The powers of the General Council are revealed in article 26 of the decree, which reads:

> The decisions taken by the General Council for Industry will be at executive level, with powers of compulsion, and no Council of Enterprises or private enterprise will be able to refuse to carry them out under any pretext which cannot be justified. They will be able to appeal against these decisions only to the Councillor for Economy against whose ruling there can be no appeal.

The picture of industrial organisation in Catalonia as contained in the collectivisation decree is now complete. Apart from the greater degree of control by the workers over their working conditions than exists in nationalised industries, all the initiative and control has been transferred from the individual factories and workshops to the government offices in Barcelona. The fact of workers' representatives taking a prominent part in the Council of Enterprises, in the General Council of Industry, and even in the government does not make the structure of control any more democratic or less authoritarian. So long as the "representatives" have executive powers, then they cease to be representatives in the true sense of the word. And what is more, when the economics of industry and the control of production and distribution are in the hands of the executive, then effective workers' control is as impossible and illusory as the concept of governments being controlled by the governed, which so many Spanish syndicalists fondly cherished against all the evidence to the contrary.

Government interference from Barcelona and from Madrid succeeded in preventing the experiment of collectivisation of industry from developing to its limits. Nevertheless, there is enough evidence to show that given a free hand, that is by controlling the finances as well as occupying the factories, the Spanish workers, who showed a spirit of initiative and inventiveness and a deep sense of social responsibility, could have produced quite unexpected results. As it was, their achievements in the social services—in which they were not so dependent on government finances or raw materials and were much freer than industry from government blackmail—have been acknowledged by all observers of the Spanish scene in its earliest phases.

It speaks highly of their organising capacities and intelligence that the Catalan workers were able to take over the railways and resume services with a minimum of delay; that all transport services in Barcelona and its suburbs were reorganised under workers' control and functioned more efficiently than before; that public services under workers' control, such as telephones, gas, and light, were functioning normally within forty-eight hours of the defeat of General Goded's attempted rising;[2] that the bakers' collective of Barcelona saw to it that so long as they had the flour (and Barcelona's needs were an average of three thousand sacks a day) the population would have the bread. And to this list could be added such examples as the health services created by the syndicates which functioned throughout Spain; the schools started by the syndicalists in town and village in an effort to blot out the age-long scourge of illiteracy (47 per cent of the population); the radical steps taken to solve the problems of the aged and the sick.[3] The Spanish people were giving concrete proof that not only were they capable of taking responsibilities but that they also had a vision of society which was more humane, more equitable, more civilised than anything that politicians and governments anywhere could conceive or devise.

2   "August 5, 1936 . . . In many respects, however, life [in Barcelona] was much less disturbed than I expected it to be after newspaper reports abroad. Tramways and buses were running, water and light functioning"; Franz Borkenau, *The Spanish Cockpit* (London: Faber and Faber, 1937).

3   Gaston Leval, *Social Reconstruction in Spain* (London: Freedom Press, 1938).

CHAPTER XI

THE COMMUNISTS: SPEARHEAD OF THE COUNTER-REVOLUTION

By giving pride of place to the Communists as the spearhead of the counter-revolution in Spain, we do not in any way wish to minimise the responsibility shared with them by the Socialists and other anti-Franco parties. Nor does their action in any way detract from the often counter-revolutionary policies of the CNT-FAI leadership. We propose to deal with the role of the Communists in order to dispose of the myth, that dies hard, of the important part played by the Communist Party in the struggle against Franco, which has been spread far and wide by millions of books and pamphlets published during those eventful years and since, both by the Communists themselves and by the fellow-travelling writers of the time. These were completely duped by the stories of Communist "efficiency," of the "disinterested" aid given to Spain by Russia, and, last but not least, by the Popular Front tactics of the Communist Party. Perhaps it will also explain how a party insignificant in influence and numbers was able to play the dominating role that the Communist Party did play in Spain, not for unity and victory over Franco but as the architects of disunity, counter-revolution, and defeat.

Membership figures of the Communist Party in Spain before the February 1936 elections are consistent among non-Communist observers at three thousand, but even pro-Communist sources admit to only ten times this number. The fact remains that during the fifteen years of their existence as a party they had not succeeded in building up a solid working-class following except in Seville and

Asturias. Until 1934, faithfully following the Comintern line, their policy was one of left extremism and of opposition to all compromise with the bourgeois state. But at the time of the signing of the pact between France and Russia the Comintern dropped its left extremism tactics in favour of support for Popular Fronts and infiltration in the once despised bourgeois parties. The programme of the Popular Front in Spain was of such a mild nature that even the Socialist proposal that the land should be nationalised was dropped because it was not acceptable to the republicans. But this did not disturb the Communists with whose ability to switch policies without even the slightest blush of shame we are all too familiar. Moscow was, at that time, anxious to prove to the Western powers that it had ceased to be revolutionary and was a desirable ally. This twist of Russian foreign policy explains the swing to the right by the Communist Party in Spain, as well as in other countries, and the reluctance with which Russia took any part in the Spanish armed struggle. It was not the first occasion that the Russian leaders were prepared to sacrifice revolutionary situations, including those in which their own supporters were involved, when such struggles conflicted with Russia's foreign policy.

In the elections of February 1936, which resulted in a victory for the Popular Front, the Communists were allocated sixteen parliamentary seats as against one in the previous parliament, an increase out of all proportion to their increase in numerical strength. During the months before the Franco rising, the Communists had been seeking ways and means for increasing their numbers, for clearly while their membership remained at three thousand (or even thirty thousand) any hope of imposing their dictatorship was doomed to failure. In spite of their lip service to unity of the working classes as the basis for workers' emancipation, their role in these struggles has always been that of *dividing* the workers.[1] The reader

---

1   "At Seville the more militant sections of the workers, the dock hands and the cafe waiters belonged to them [the Communists]. The situation here was one of perpetual war with the CNT with small sections of the UGT looking on. . . . Even allowing for the fact that the atmosphere of Seville . . . was not propitious to the formation of a disciplined proletarian movement, *it must be agreed that*

may recall a reference from Gerald Brenan's *Spanish Labyrinth*, quoted earlier, in which he pointed out that in those areas where the anarchists were strongest the socialist movement was most reactionary, whereas where the anarchists were in a minority they succeeded by their militancy in driving the Socialists to the left. It was natural, therefore, that the Communists, once they had dropped their revolutionary intransigence in favour of bourgeois democracy and popular frontism, should seek to infiltrate the socialist movement in those areas where the anarchists were strongest. And in fact their first success was in Catalonia. There, the weak Socialists under the leadership of one of the most sinister figures of Spanish Socialism, Joan Comorera y Soler,

> were more to the right than any other section of the Spanish Socialists. In Barcelona, where the labour movement was anarchist, they saw their chief task in fighting anarchism.[2]

Only four days after the military uprising, the Communists merged with the Catalan Socialists to form the PSUC (Catalan Unified Socialist Party). It was the first example of a socialist party merging with the Communists and represented a move most favourable to the Communists who had no more than two hundred members in the whole of Catalonia at that time. The next step was to win the support of the other opponents of the anarchists, such as the shopkeepers, certain sections of the intelligentsia, the white-collared workers, and bourgeois republicans. Little wonder then that the membership figures of the PSUC rose by leaps and bounds during those first months. But it was entirely without revolutionary content.

The next step by the Communists was to exploit the split in the ranks of the Socialist-dominated trade union UGT. Their task was

---

the Communist penetration had destroyed all possibility of working-class solidarity. The consequences of this were felt when in July General Queipo de Llano was able to capture the city—one of the key points of the Civil War—with a handful of men." (emphasis added); Gerald Brenan, *The Spanish Labyrinth* (London: Cambridge University Press, 1943), 306–7.

2   Franz Borkenau, *The Communist International* (London: Faber and Faber, 1938).

made all the easier by the merging of the Socialist Youth Movement (two hundred thousand members, according to Brenan) with the numerically weaker Communist Youth to form the JSU (Unified Socialist Youth).

But clearly, before the Communists could impose their reactionary policies and tactics on the revolutionary workers, Russian support had to be forthcoming. Russia's adherence to the non-intervention pact coupled with the Spanish Communists' counter-revolutionary activities (in opposing expropriation of the landed estates and the factories by the workers and the creation of workers' militias; in helping the government to restore its authority, and supporting the formation of a regular police force and gendarmerie) did not further Communist influence among the workers.

Russian intervention in Spain, when it did take place, was dictated not by revolutionary motives or Stalin's love for the Spanish people but by the need for a strengthening of Russia's position in international politics. According to General Krivitsky—who claimed to be the "sole survivor abroad of the group of Soviet officials who had a direct hand in organising Soviet intervention in Spain"[3]—ever since Hitler's rise to power in 1933 "Stalin's foreign policy had been an anxious one." Only when he was sure that Franco would not have "a quick and easy" victory did he decide to intervene in Spain.

His idea was—and this was common knowledge among us who served him—to include Spain in the sphere of the Kremlin's influence. Such a domination would secure his ties with Paris and London, and thus strengthen, on the other hand, his bargaining position with Berlin. Once he was master of the Spanish Government—of vital strategic importance to France and Great Britain—he would find what he was seeking. He would be a force to be reckoned with, an ally to be coveted.

This may seem a somewhat far-fetched explanation viewed in a present-day context, but not so if one recalls that up to 1933 "there

---

3   W.G. Krivitsky, *I Was Stalin's Agent* (London: Hamish Hamilton, 1939).

was not a single country outside Russia where the Communists counted as a political force."[4] And again, according to Krivitsky, Stalin "launched his intervention under the slogan: 'Stay out of artillery fire!'" Fewer than two thousand Russians were in Spain at any time, and they were military experts and technicians, political agitators, and members of the OGPU, the notorious Russian secret police. So far as the fighting was concerned, the Russians organised the International Brigades, composed of men of all nationalities except Russian.

Not only did Russia see to it that no Russian soldier would be involved but also made quite sure that intervention was paid for in advance to the tune of five hundred tons of gold from the Bank of Spain, which were transferred to Russia as the result of a secret arrangement between the then prime minister, Largo Caballero, and the Russian representative in Spain. At the same time, Stalin sent one Arthur Stashevsky to manipulate the political and financial reins and General Berzin to organise and direct the army. The Russians had no doubts that whoever controlled the economics of a country controlled it politically, and Stashevsky immediately set about "exerting all his efforts to gather into Soviet hands the control of the finances of the republic."[5]

The hostility of the Communists to the industrial and agricultural collectives was undoubtedly politically motivated, linked with the aims of the Russian-controlled Negrín government to centralise all the economic life of the country so as to bring the workers' organisations under its control. It had nothing to do with the alleged reasons advanced by the Communists, that land was being collectivised by force and that industry was not being operated in the interests of the armed struggle.

The Russians also saw to it that not only were the International Brigades controlled by them but succeeded after only a few months'

---

4 Borkenau, *The Communist International*; this volume contains a chapter on Spain which was probably written at the end of 1937 and does not therefore present a complete picture of the Communist Party's role in Spain.

5 Krivitsky, *I Was Stalin's Agent*.

intervention in Spanish affairs to ensure that 90 per cent of all important posts in the Spanish War Department were in their hands and most of the political commissars with the republican army were Communist Party stalwarts.

The heroic struggle of the Spanish people in July 1936 had acted as a powerful magnet in drawing hundreds of militant anti-fascist exiles from Italy and Germany, as well as anti-Communist revolutionaries from all parts of the world, to join in the resistance against Franco.[6] With Russian intervention, Stalin transferred not only military and economic experts to Spain, but also the secret police. The Communist plan was to liquidate individual opponents (especially ex-Communists who "knew too much") and to destroy the revolutionary movement in Spain which had proved such a formidable barrier to any attempts by the Spanish Communist Party at political hegemony. "As for Catalonia," declared *Pravda* of December 16, 1936, "the purging of the Trotskyists and the anarcho-syndicalists has begun; it will be conducted with the same energy with which it was conducted in the USSR." And to this end, organised terror was instituted by the Communists. They, who protested loudest against the "uncontrolled elements," set up their own private prisons and torture chambers, which they called "preventoriums." No one, not even with the authority of the minister of justice, was permitted to visit these prisons. John McGovern, an Independent Labour Party MP at the time, went to Spain in November 1937 with a delegation which included Professor Felicien Challaye of the Central Committee for Human Rights, to visit members of the POUM who, at the instigation of the Communists, were held in prison without trial as "Franco's agents." In a pamphlet published on his return McGovern described his visits to the various prisons but pointed out that though supplied by the director of prisons and the minister of justice with a permit to visit the Calle Vallmajor Prison (one of the Communist "preventoriums") admission was refused, the official declaring that "he did not take any orders from the Director of

---

6   They did not form part of the carefully screened CP-organised International Brigades which only came to Spain towards the end of 1936.

Prisons or the Minister of Justice as they were not his bosses. We enquired who was his boss, and he gave us an address to the Cheka headquarters." At headquarters permission was again refused, and not even the personal intervention of the minister of justice, Senor Irujo, affected the issue. And McGovern concluded:

> The mask was off. We had torn aside the veil and shown where the real power lay. The Ministers were willing, but powerless. The Cheka was unwilling, and it had the power. We realised that if we pressed further, we ourselves would be in danger.[7]

The CNT had exposed these secret prisons months before. On March 15, 1937, sixteen members of the CNT had been murdered by Communists in Villanueva de Alcardete. To the Confederation's demands that the perpetrators of this crime should be punished, *Mundo Obrero,* the Communist mouthpiece, replied by justifying the murders. Subsequent judicial investigation had established the fact that an all-Communist gang, including the mayors of Villanueva and Villamajor, had been operating as a "defence committee" murdering political enemies, looting, levying tributes, and raping a number of women. Five Communists were sentenced to death. In April of the same year the CNT revealed, with proofs, the existence of a private prison in Murcia, in spite of the efforts of the police to suppress the details by seizing the entire edition of the organisation's newspaper *Cartagena Nueva,* which carried a first-hand account by a worker who had been taken for questioning.[8] Among those involved were police officers and Spanish members of the OGPU.

---

7   John McGovern, MP, *Terror in Spain* (London: Independent Labour Party, 1938); Emma Goldman, "Political Persecution in Republican Spain," *Spain and the World,* December 10, 1937, describes visits she made to a number of Spanish prisons in September 1937 and refers to the many prisons where permission to visit was refused.

8   Reprinted in José Peirats, *La CNT en la Revolución Española,* vol. 2 (Toulouse: Ediciones CNT, 1952).

It is impossible in the space available to detail the hundreds of cases of Communist terror that took place following Stalin's intervention in Spain's destinies.[9] So successfully had Communist propaganda and fellow-travelling journalists succeeded in convincing liberal and progressive opinion in the democracies that they, aided by Stalin, the only friend the Spanish people could look to for help, were the spearhead of the armed struggle against Franco, that the voices of the revolutionary groups appealing to the workers of the world to save the lives of Stalin's victims in Spain went unheeded. And when, in May 1937, the Communist-provoked fratricidal struggle took place in the streets of Barcelona, in which hundreds of workers lost their lives, to be followed in June by large-scale armed attacks on the agricultural collectives in Aragon, the Communists were hailed as the saviours of law and order against the uncontrollable anarchist terrorists who were attempting to seize power in Barcelona and were forcing the peasants to collectivise their lands at the points of anarchist bayonets! It was not only Hitler who realised that the bigger the lie the more chances there were of it being believed.

---

9   Hugo Dewar, *Assassins at Large* (London: Jonathan Cape, 1951), an account of the executions outside Russia ordered by the OGPU, includes a chapter that deals with these activities in Spain; Jesús Hernández, *Yo fui ministro de Stalin* (Mexico: Editorial America, 1953), the first section of this book by the ex-Communist minister in Negrín's government deals with the role of Stalin's agents in the Spanish Civil War, including a long account of the persecution of the members of the POUM at Moscow's behest and the "inside" story of the assassination of their leader Andrés Nin.

CHAPTER XII

THE "MAY DAYS" IN BARCELONA

During the life of his government, from September 1936 to May 1937, in which he was also minister of defence, the Socialist leader Largo Caballero had faithfully served the counter-revolution. He had, as Peirats puts it, saved the principle of government and had given it prestige. But in the process he had become deeply involved with the Communists and their Russian masters. It appears that Caballero had no illusions about the loyalty of the Communists, but had illusions as to his own capacities to control and direct the policies of the government, and to being the "Spanish Lenin" who, by his personality alone, could maintain the balance between the revolutionary and reactionary forces represented in his cabinet. He wanted neither the militias nor a regular army; neither the old order nor the revolutionary order; neither private property nor the expropriation of property. To the Communists he promised conscription and the building of strong defences; to the anarchists a revolutionary war—and under his personal direction. He carried out none of these promises, and his period of government was marked by military disasters, the strengthening of the institutions of state and of the power of the counter-revolution.

The "Spanish Lenin" had served his purpose as far as the Communists were concerned. His obstinacy and vanity had prevented him from becoming a willing tool of Communist policy, but by March 1937, almost completely isolated, even from the UGT on which his power and authority (as leader of that organisation) depended, it was time to replace him with a man more amenable to

Russian-inspired directives. The Communists and their reactionary allies also felt that they were now strong enough, supported by the armed forces reconstituted in the rearguard by the Caballero government, to eliminate once for all the powerful influences exerted by the revolutionary organisations. Their first objective was the POUM (the anti-Stalinist Marxist party) in Catalonia, to be followed by a concerted attack on the CNT-FAI.

From the beginning of 1937, they showed their hand by isolated armed outrages and provocations (La Faterella, Molins de Llobregat, Puigcerdá). At the same time, the government of Catalonia issued fifty-eight decrees (January 12, 1937) drafted by the councillor of finance, Josep Tarradellas, which were aimed at strangling the social revolution by increasing government control over collectivised enterprises and by imposing a new tax on them based on output. And, in March, a decree by the councillor of public order dissolved the workers' Patrullas de Control (security patrols) and ordered that members of government-controlled armed corps in the rearguard should belong to no party or organisation. At the same time the plan to "disarm the rearguard" was put into effect. Any person who carried arms without official authorisation would be disarmed and sent for trial. There can be no doubt as to the intention behind these moves.

On this occasion, however, the reaction of the rank-and-file militants was such that their "representatives" in the Catalan government were obliged to resign, and yet another government crisis was provoked. The statements issued by the Regional Committee of the CNT, and by the anarchist groups of Barcelona, were outspoken, and, though still remaining within the framework of collaboration between the organisations and parties, showed greater determination and revolutionary spirit than many previous ones. On the personal intervention of President Companys, a provisional government "of an internal character" was formed on April 26, 1937, with CNT, UGT, and Esquerra representation. But it could not halt the real crisis in which the Catalan government, with Communist inspiration, was to pit its strength against that of the Barcelona revolutionaries. Symptomatic of the atmosphere that prevailed in

1937 in Catalonia was the refusal of the Communists to join in any celebrations of May Day, coupled with the activity of the police in the streets of Barcelona obviously calculated to create disturbances. *Solidaridad Obrera* in its issue for May 2 answered these provocations in unequivocal terms:

The workers in arms are the sole guarantee for the revolution. To attempt to disarm the workers is to put oneself on the other side of the barricade. However much of a councillor and commissar one may be, one cannot dictate orders to the workers who are struggling against fascism with more sacrifices and heroism than all the politicians of the rearguard, whose cheek and impotence no one ignores. Workers: let no one allow himself to be disarmed![1]

At three o'clock the following day (May 3) the government launched its first organised attack, which provoked the armed battle in the streets of Barcelona that was to last several days at a cost of at least five hundred workers' lives. More than a thousand were wounded, and the prisons were once again filled with revolutionary militants.

We do not propose to deal in detail with the "May Days" (as the bloody struggle in Barcelona, and Catalonia in general, is usually referred to). The literature on the *facts* is extensive, and the interested reader is referred to the published eye-witness accounts as well as to the official versions by the parties and organisations involved.[2] In the present study we will limit ourselves to an examination of the political aspects of the struggle.

---

1 *Solidaridad Obrera* was the daily newspaper of the CNT in Barcelona.

2 Augustín Souchy, *The Tragic Week in May* (Barcelona: Oficina Informacion Exterior CNT y FAI, 1937) is the official CNT-FAI version published in several languages. It contains a day by day account of the struggle in Barcelona as well as of events in the provinces, followed by comments on the results and, as an appendix, the CNT Manifesto on the May Days in Barcelona. The whole of the account of the struggle in Barcelona was published as a four-page supplement to *Spain and the World* 1, no. 14, June 11, 1937. See also George Orwell, *Homage to Catalonia* (London: Secker and Warburg, 1938); Fenner Brockway, *The Truth*

The government action which provoked the May Days was the surprise attack by police in three lorries under the command of Rodríguez Salas, commissar general of public order, on the Telephone Building of Barcelona which dominated the city's busiest square, Plaza de Cataluña. Salas was bearer of an order issued by the councillor of internal security, Artemio Ayguadé (member of Companys' party, the Esquerra), authorising him to take over the building. According to the Peirats this order was issued apparently without previous consultation with the other members of the recently formed provisional government: at least, the four CNT members declared that they were unaware of the order.[3]

Taken by surprise, the workers in control of the exchange were unable to prevent the police from occupying the first floor; but this was the extent of their advance. The news, not surprisingly, spread like wildfire, and within two hours the defence committees of the CNT-FAI went into action, gathering at their local centres, arming themselves, and building barricades in readiness for any possible extension of the incident. Meanwhile, Valerio Mas, regional secretary of the CNT, contacted the premier (Tarradellas) and the minister of the interior (Ayguadé), and both assured him that they had no knowledge of the incident, though it was subsequently proved that Ayguadé had in fact given the order. In the course of the negotiations the government promised to withdraw the police. There was no shooting that night, but the following morning when the police occupied the Palace of Justice, it was clear that the events of the previous day were not an isolated incident but the beginning of a concentrated effort by the government to occupy the strategic points of the city, and once in armed control to proceed with the liquidation of the revolution once for all. But the workers of the CNT-FAI showed the same courage and initiative as in the struggle against the military rising in July 1936. With the POUM they

---

about Barcelona (London: Independent Labour Power, 1937); Frank Jellinek, *The Civil War in Spain* (London: Victor Gollancz, 1938) for a pro-Communist account with all the usual misrepresentations.

3   José Peirats, *La CNT en la Revolución Española*, vol. 2 (Toulouse: Ediciones CNT, 1952), 191.

successfully resisted the combined government- and Communist-controlled PSUC onslaught.

The reason put forward by Rodríguez Salas for the attack on the Barcelona Telephone Building was that the CNT workers in control there were "tapping" telephone calls between the ministers in Barcelona and Valencia. This justification was also advanced by Joan Comorera (public works minister in the Barcelona government and general secretary of the PSUC of Catalonia) at a public meeting in Barcelona:

> The Councillor of Internal Security, complying with his duty, decided to put a stop to an abnormal situation in the Telephone Building. The Telephone Building, as far as we know, is not the property of the CNT. It is as much the property of the CNT as of the UGT because as many men working there belong to the CNT as belong to the UGT. But it is not the property of anyone, and in any case it will be the property of the community when the Government of the Republic nationalises the Telephone. But there were serious things going on there, which the Government had to put a stop to. The fact was that all the interior controls of the Telephone Building were at the service, not of the community, but of the organisation, and neither President Azaña, nor President Companys, nor anyone else could speak without the indiscreet ear of the controller knowing it. Naturally, this had to be stopped, as it was on that particular day, just as it might have been the day after, or a month after, or a month before. So complying with orders received, our comrade Rodríguez Salas went to occupy the Telephone Building and the next moment there came the same reply as before— general mobilisation and the beginning of the building of barricades. If the councillor for Internal Security had done something outside his duty, were there not four councillors of the CNT who could demand redress and his dismissal? But they did not want to comply with normal procedure, but instead they replied to this act of the Government with a

formidable mobilisation of all groups which took possession of all the strategic places in the city.[4]

We have subjected the reader to this verbal indigestion not only in order to confirm, with Communist sources, the facts: that the attack on the Telephone Building provoked the struggle in Barcelona,[5] but because it also reveals the complete dishonesty of the Communist Party:

(1) Comorera does not, in fact, state that Azaña could not speak to Companys over the phone but that their conversations were being tapped. It was not therefore a question that the phones were not available to them.

(2) In fact, the CNT workers *were* in a large majority in the exchange. The *Daily Worker,* which cannot be accused of ever having overestimated the strength of the anarchists, wrote at the time (May 11): "Salas sent the armed republican police to disarm the employees there, *most of them members of CNT unions.*" (emphasis added) But there was never any question of *property* coming into it, since the exchange was collectivised and under joint CNT-UGT control. And the Communists as arch-legalitarians knew that this situation was sanctioned by the collectivisation decree of October 1936, and meant inter alia that the government all along had its controller on the Council of Enterprises.

(3) The CNT did, in fact, demand the dismissal of Salas and Ayguadé. This was refused. In Peirats's view, "The intransigence of the other parties, and in particular the opportunistic

---

4   Jesús Hernández and Joan Comorera, *Spain Organises for Victory: The Policy of the Communist Party of Spain Explained,* foreword J.R. Campbell (London: Communist Party of Great Britain, 1937); both speeches were delivered after the May Days in Barcelona and during the crisis of the central government. Hernández's speech was one long attack on Caballero's responsibility for all the economic and military disasters.

5   It is necessary to establish even this fact when one reads false statements, such as that of Álvarez del Vayo's, who refers to the POUM as the instigators of the uprising; *Freedom's Battle* (London: William Heinemann, 1940).

attitude of the president of the Generalitat, who resolutely opposed those sanctions, provoked the general strike and the outbreak of fighting that followed."

In the quoted passage by Comorera, one other fact cannot be overlooked: namely, the completely reactionary attitude of a party which actually complains of the revolutionary workers' vigilance in keeping a close check on the conversations that took place between the politicians. It is, of course, a quite different matter when the "indiscreet ear" is that of the Russian secret police!

There is still some confusion as to the origins of the provocation that resulted in the May Days. Behind the barricades opposing the CNT-FAI and POUM were members of the PSUC and Estat Catalá, that is, respectively Communist-controlled socialists and members of the "Catalan State" party, an extreme separatist movement. In a *Manifesto of the National Committee of the CNT Regarding the May Days in Barcelona* considerable evidence is advanced to show that leading members of the Estat Catalá had been conspiring in France to achieve the "independence of Catalonia":

> The Separatists, bourgeois in the last analysis, could not reconcile themselves to the fascist uprising that resulted in proletarian victory and threatened them with the loss of all their wealth. And in their search for some substitute solution, they entered into negotiations with Italy, in order to provoke internal strife that would furnish the opportunity for foreign intervention and facilitate the recognition of Catalonia as an independent State, thereby undermining the anti-fascist front at the same time. All those who wanted Catalonia to return to the *status quo* prevailing on July 18th, accepted these proposals.[6]

Two further interesting details in this Manifesto are the references to Ayguadé and Comorera:

---

6   Souchy, *The Tragic Week in May*, 44–48.

We must recall that Ayguadé was the Councillor of Internal Security: that he is a member of the Estat Catalá and that he fell under suspicion of being implicated in the conspiracy.

On the 20th of April, Comorera, leader of the Communist Party of Catalonia, was in Paris. Among the people he visited was the secretary of Ventura Gassol (member of the Estat Catalá) and a certain Castañer. Who is this Castañer? We are told, "Agent of the Generality."[7] Investigators have found out that he is in contact with a certain Vintro, secretary of Octavia Salta, journalist in the service of the Spanish fascists. . . . He also maintains close relations with members of the Estat Catalá, especially with Dencas and Casanovas. The former visits Castañer in his house, and the latter is visited, in turn, by Castañer.

Apart from the reference to Comorera, the CNT manifesto does not deal at all with the role of the Communists in fomenting the struggle. Peirats supports the theory that "reasons of a political nature decided the National Committee of the CNT to pass over the important and leading role played by Stalin's secret police in the May Days, that is, the real motives for that provocation." He suggests that perhaps the Committee lacked irrefutable proofs or that such proofs did not come into their hands.

---

7 These two paragraphs up to this word were deleted by the Spanish government censor when the Manifesto was first published in *Solidaridad Obrera*, June 13, 1937, but were included without deletions in the English edition of Souchy's *The Tragic Week in May*. In the French edition of the same pamphlet, *La Tragique Semaine de Mai* à *Barcelone*, the Manifesto is entirely omitted.

CHAPTER XIII
THE REVOLUTIONARY SIGNIFICANCE OF THE "MAY DAYS"

Whether or not the "May Days" were part of a carefully prepared plan does not yet seem to have been established with documentary evidence. In his book, *I Was Stalin's Agent*, General Krivitsky maintains that he was aware of the approaching May Days. Reports he saw in Moscow at the time

> made it clear that the OGPU was plotting to crush the "uncontrollable" elements in Barcelona and seize control for Stalin. . . . The fact is that in Catalonia the great majority of the workers were fiercely anti-Stalinist. Stalin knew that a showdown was inevitable, but he also knew that the opposition forces were badly divided and could be crushed by swift, bold action. The OGPU fanned the flames and provoked syndicalists, anarchists and socialists against one another.

Krivitsky also states that Negrín had already been selected by Moscow as Caballero's successor some months earlier, and that one further purpose the May Days were to serve was to provoke a crisis in the Caballero government and force the "Spanish Lenin" to resign. All this may be true, but no palpable evidence is brought forward, for instance, by Peirats who supports this view but limits himself to lengthy quotations from Krivitsky.[1] If, then, the attack

---

1   José Peirats, *La CNT en la Revolución Española*, vol. 2 (Toulouse: Ediciones CNT, 1952), 128.

on the telephone exchange was to be the signal for the Communists and their allies to attempt the armed liquidation of the revolutionary movement in Barcelona, it seems to have hopelessly misfired. Rodríguez Salas and his men arrived there at 3:00 p.m. on May 3. The attack was halted, and in Peirats's words: "the cry of alarm by the besieged workers was answered by the workers in the suburbs, and their energetic intervention initiated the bloody struggle at strong points and at the barricades."

Souchy in his detailed account of the struggle at the time points out that negotiations were opened between the CNT and the government, and lasted until six o'clock on the morning of May 4, adding: "Towards morning the workers began building barricades in the outer districts of the city. There was no fighting during this first night but the general tension increased."[2] Only when the Palace of Justice was occupied by the police did the fighting begin, and even then negotiations were proceeding between the CNT Regional Committee and the government.

The government refused to accede to the CNT demands that the police be withdrawn and that Salas and the minister, Ayguadé, be dismissed, nor would it negotiate until the streets were cleared of the armed workers. This was obviously a critical moment for Companys and the politicians. By acceding to the revolutionary workers they would be admitting that when it came to the point their power was based on a myth and that the armed workers were as strong and the government as weak as on July 19. It would mean that all these months of intrigue, of political sleight of hand, of manoeuvring could be undone in one day. There was only one course open to the government: no compromise with the revolutionary workers.

The "showdown" was avoided and government success ensured by the co-operation of the leaders of the workers' organisations, whose role throughout the struggle was a conciliatory one. Once the government refused to negotiate, they appealed to the workers

---

2   Augustín Souchy, *The Tragic Week in May* (Barcelona: Oficina Informacion Exterior CNT y FAI, 1937).

to lay down their arms, making use of the all too familiar jargon of the politicians—what will the boys at the front think, or, such action only helps Franco, etc. Meanwhile, the government resigned and a provisional one composed of one member from each party and organisation previously represented in it was formed (in this way it was possible to drop Salas and Ayguadé without any loss of face). By that time a delegation had arrived from Valencia composed of the secretary of the National Committee of the CNT, Mariano Vázquez, and the "anarchist" minister of justice, García Oliver. They were later joined by the "anarchist" minister of health, Federica Montseny. Also from Valencia came members of the executive committee of the UGT. Their efforts were directed at pacification at all costs—at least so far as the CNT leaders were concerned. And this attitude was certainly not based on a situation of inferiority at the barricades. According to Souchy, reports came in on the second day from all parts of Barcelona and from the provinces of Catalonia to the effect that

> the overwhelming majority of the population were with the CNT, and most towns and villages were in the hands of our organisations. It would have been easy to attack the centre of the city, had the responsible committee so decided. They only had to appeal to the defence committees of the outlying districts. But the Regional Committee of the CNT was opposed to it. Every proposal of attack was unanimously rejected, including the FAI.

The attitude of the CNT-FAI leaders was that the enemies of the revolutionary workers had wanted this struggle as an excuse to liquidate them, and that they should therefore refuse to play the enemy's game. On the other hand, there were a large number of militants who took the view that the CNT-FAI had been playing the government's game too long, at the expense of the social revolution and the struggle against France, and that what was now happening in Barcelona was a "showdown." Souchy—who adopted the "leaders'" position—admits in his account that perhaps at some other time this assault upon the Telephone Building might not have had such consequences. But the accumulation of political conflicts during the past few months had made the atmosphere tense. *It was impossible to stem the indignation of the masses.* (emphasis added)

Peirats also refers to the fact that the workers of the CNT could not bring themselves to carry out the often repeated appeals by the leaders for an "armistice," for "serenity," for a "ceasefire."

Discontent among them was increasing. An important section of opinion began to express its opposition to the attitude of the committees. At the head of this extremist current were "The Friends of Durruti" (Los Amigos de Durruti). This grouping was based on elements who were hostile to militarisation, many of whom had left the units of the newly formed Popular Army when the voluntary militias were dissolved.

Their organ, *El Amigo del Pueblo* (The Friend of the People), conducted a campaign against the CNT ministers and committees and advocated a continuation of the revolutionary struggle started on July 19, 1936. The confederal committees immediately repudiated the "Friends of Durruti." "In spite of this, they did not disappear," comments Peirats somewhat cryptically. It is to be especially regretted therefore, that to this "important section of opinion" the historiographer of the CNT devotes but eighteen lines. According to a Trotskyist writer, "The Regional Committee of the CNT gave to the entire press—Stalinist and bourgeois included—a denunciation of the Friends of Durruti as agents-provocateurs."[3]

---

3   Felix Morrow, *Revolution and Counter-Revolution in Spain* (New York: Pathfinder Press, 1938). Souchy, *The Tragic Week in May,* mentions that on May 5 a "newly-founded group called 'Friends of Durruti' functioning on the fringes of the CNT-FAI published a proclamation declaring that 'A Revolutionary Junta has been constituted in Barcelona. All those responsible for the *putsch,* manoeuvring under the protection of the government, shall be executed. The POUM shall be a member of the Revolutionary Junta because they stood by the workers.'

Just as the defence of Barcelona in July 1936 was a spontaneous movement of the workers, so in May 1937 the decision to be on
the qui vive against possible attacks once more came from the rank
and file. The leaders in July, as we have already shown, concerned
themselves with containing the movement. They were afraid that
the impetus which so decisively routed Franco's troops would carry
forward the social revolution to a point where it would be outside
their control. This attitude of the CNT leadership was not lost on
the politicians. What greater condemnation of the CNT leadership
than the reply given by Companys to a foreign journalist who had
predicted, in April 1937, that the assassination of Antonio Martín,
the anarchist mayor of Puigcerdá, and three of his comrades would
lead to a revolt: "[Companys] laughed scornfully and said the anarchists would capitulate as they always had before."[4]

He was right—if he was referring to the leaders who that very
month had permitted the crisis in the Generalitat to be solved
by—to quote Souchy—"proving [themselves] very compliant. They
renounced their former demands, modified the desires of the proletariat by pointing out the necessities of the war against fascism,
and urged them to concentrate their forces for the period after the
defeat of the fascists."

It is not surprising, therefore, that following the failure of
Vázquez and Oliver to persuade the workers to abandon the barricades (Oliver's radio appeal has been rightly described as an
"oratorical masterpiece which drew tears but not obedience"),
Federica Montseny was sent on behalf of the Valencia government
to try out *her* oratorical powers on the "uncontrollable" workers
of Barcelona. She came at a time when the central government
had withdrawn troops from the fronts in readiness to be sent to
Barcelona. But before leaving Valencia she obtained the government's agreement that "these forces were not to be sent until such

---

The Regional Committee decided not to concur with this proclamation. The
Libertarian Youth likewise rejected it. On the next day, Thursday, May 6, their
official statement was printed in the entire press of Barcelona." Souchy does
not give the text of the statement.

4   Lister Oak in *The New Statesman* & *Nation*, May 15, 1937.

time as the minister of health should judge it opportune to do so."[5] It is quite possible that Federica Montseny had no intention of calling the troops to Barcelona to put down the street fighting, but this does not in any way minimise the significance of her statement so far as the public was concerned or as another example of the feeling of self-importance and power created among these so-called anarchist ministers.

So far as one can judge the effect of the intervention of the influential members of the CNT-FAI was to create confusion in the ranks of the workers and oblige those of the CNT to make all the compromises. Thus, on Thursday, May 6, to show their "willingness to restore peace," the workers of the CNT agreed to leave the Telephone Building. The authorities promised to withdraw the Assault Guards at the same time. Instead they occupied the whole building, *bringing in members of the UGT to take over the jobs of the CNT workers.* Souchy writes:

> The members of the CNT saw that they had been betrayed and immediately informed the Regional Committee [which] intervened with the government. They demanded that the police should be withdrawn. . . . Half-an-hour later the Generalitat replied: the fait accompli cannot be recalled.

And Souchy continues:

> This broken agreement aroused great indignation among the workers of the CNT. *Had the workers in the outlying districts been informed immediately of this development, they would surely have insisted upon taking further measures and returned to the attack.* But when the matter was discussed later, the more moderate point of view prevailed." (emphasis added)

Once more information was being withheld from the workers and decisions taken at a higher level. And, in the words of the

---

5   Quoted in Peirats, *La CNT en la Revolución Española*, vol. 2.

Generalitat, "the fait accompli cannot be recalled." Again the workers had been betrayed.

Their compromise did not end the fighting. All it did was to make their task more difficult, for now with the telephone exchange out of their hands, their means of communication were limited to the shortwave radio station located in the CNT-FAI headquarters, from which only orders to return to work and capitulation could be expected.

When by Friday, May 7, the fighting had ceased but for occasional unimportant skirmishes, the government felt strong enough to disregard any of the demands put forward by the workers. Several thousand troops had arrived from Valencia, and with them the control of the fighting units and the forces of public order in Catalonia passed to the central government. Hostages taken by the government during the fighting were not released, in spite of solemn promises to do so.[6] Indeed, after the fighting had ceased many further arrests were made. A strict press censorship was imposed, and the various decree laws that had provoked the crisis in April were put into effect. The bourgeoisie had gained a signal victory; the social revolution had suffered a decisive defeat.

6   According to *Solidaridad Obrera*, May 11, 1937: "In the cells of the police head-quarters there are some three hundred of our comrades who must be set free immediately. They have been held for six days, and nobody has so far interrogated them."

CHAPTER XIV

THE CNT AND THE CABALLERO GOVERNMENT CRISIS

The revolutionary crisis in Catalonia had barely been "resolved" when a political crisis in the Valencia government once more distracted attention from essentials to a struggle between personalities.

At a cabinet meeting held on May 15 to examine the situation in Catalonia, the two Communist ministers, Jesús Hernández and Vicente Uribe, demanded reprisals against those responsible for the May Days. Caballero agreed but could not accept the Communists' view that the responsibility lay with the CNT-FAI and POUM. Whereupon the two Communists rose and withdrew. Caballero replied by declaring that the "Council of Ministers continues." His determination was short-lived, for the Communists' gesture was a signal for Prieto, Negrín, Álvarez del Vayo, Giral, and Irujo to rise in turn and leave. Only Anastasio de Gracia and Ángel Galarza, loyal socialist friends of Caballero, and his four staunch "anarchist" ministers remained seated.

Following conversations with the president, Caballero was again entrusted with the task of forming a government. Both the CNT and the UGT proposed a government based on the working-class organisations with representation of all the parties, led by Caballero. The Communists on the other hand proposed a government "led by a Socialist, in which all parties of the Popular Front are included, as well as the working-class organisations."

Caballero's solution was to offer three portfolios to the UGT and two to the Socialists. They were all key ministries, comprising the direction and control of the war, as well as of the country's economy. To the Communists, Left Republicans, and Republican Union, he allocated two seats each, and to his staunch friends of the CNT a further two ministries: health and justice! Both the Communists and the CNT refused to accept these arrangements. The Communists were mainly concerned that the ministry of war should not be held by the premier. Caballero could not accept this proposal, and since it was agreed by the Republicans and Socialists that a new government without the representation of the Communist Party could not be considered a Popular Front government, it was clear that Caballero would be unable to form a new cabinet which would be acceptable to the Communists. The CNT objection on the other hand was stated in a conciliatory, "more in sorrow than in anger" letter from the secretary, Mariano Vázquez, in which he pointed out that the CNT could not accept a position of inferiority with the UGT or of parity with the Communists; nor could they accept the idea that the economy of the country should be concentrated in the hands of one party.

The crisis was resolved with the president calling on Dr. Juan Negrín, a right-wing Socialist and Moscow's man, to form a government from which the UGT and the CNT were excluded. Indalecio Prieto, arch-enemy of Caballero, was to handle national defence while Negrín, besides being premier, was also in control of the economy. A Communist, Vicente Uribe, became minister of agriculture.

The CNT reaction was a curious one. In a communiqué of May 18, they declared that the Negrín government, which was formed without their participation, could not count on their collaboration.

> For the present, all we wish to state to the workers belonging to the CNT is that now more than ever before must they pay attention to the watchwords emanating from the responsible committees. Only with homogeneity in our actions shall we succeed in defeating the counter-revolution and in avoiding the "embrace of Vergara." Comrades! pay attention to the watchwords of the responsible committees! Let no one play

the game of the provocateurs! Serenity! Firmness and Unity! Long live the alliance of the workers' organisations!

One cannot avoid noting the marked difference in the attitude adopted by the leaders of the CNT to the situation during the May Days and that created by the government crisis. In the former case, they were prepared to make every compromise—indeed they ordered the ceasefire among the CNT-FAI workers without even obtaining government acceptance of any of their demands—in the name of unity and the maintenance of the "anti-fascist front" against Franco. In the government crisis they stubbornly refused to participate or to collaborate with a government which was not led by Largo Caballero. Such an attitude would not appear to us in violent contrast with that adopted during the May Days, if it indicated that the CNT-FAI leadership had learned the lessons of the Barcelona barricades and was attempting to return to its traditional revolutionary position. But this was far from being the case. In a statement to the press a few days after the formation of the Negrín government, Mariano Vázquez, national secretary of the CNT declared:

Participation of the CNT in the government is indispensable if it is intended to work with honour to end the war quickly. The workers' organisations must be represented in the government. One cannot dispense with the most vital section of the people, which works hardest in the rearguard and has most men at the fronts. To dispense with CNT collaboration in the government means driving it back to its former oppositionist role. All our enemies have dashed themselves to pieces (*estrellado*) against the glorious insignia of the CNT. Who dares to attempt to hold it back will be crushed, but the CNT will continue its forward march. Therefore, it must be reckoned with and given the place in the government that is its due.

Ignoring the threats contained in this statement, one sees above all that the idea of being in opposition has become abhorrent to these "anarchists," and their whole propaganda from now on will not be more revolutionary, but, on the contrary, it will be a daily complaint that the CNT has been *excluded* from the government and an unending lament for the good old days of Largo Caballero, when the government was a *revolutionary government*! We were under the impression that the myth of revolutionary governments had long ago been disposed of by anarchists, and that it was an illusion cherished only by Marxists. It is clear that even some of the leaders of the CNT-FAI, in spite of their attitudes and utterances, did not in fact believe at the time that there was much to choose between governments. Rather was it that they did not know how to extricate themselves, without loss of prestige, from the web of political bargaining in which they had been trapped by the more experienced politicians. They had travelled so far in their mental transformation and in their sense of personal importance and political astuteness, that they considered a return to the revolutionary position of the CNT-FAI against all governments was a retrograde step; one for which they would be condemned by history.

What, in fact, did the CNT do during those months in "opposition"?

(1) They appealed to public opinion to right the wrong of their "exclusion" from the government.

(2) They renewed their efforts to reach agreement with the UGT for an alliance.

(3) To this end they spared no efforts in attempting to rehabilitate Largo Caballero, so decisively outmanoeuvred by the right-wing Socialists (Prieto and Negrín) in the struggle for power. And Caballero naturally reciprocated since he was ousted from power and politically isolated!

This period of "opposition" was launched by a series of four vast meetings, broadcast throughout Spain, at which each of the ex-ministers gave an account of his activities in the government.[1]

---

1   An indication of the unquestioned power and prestige still enjoyed by the CNT-FAI in spite of the "May Days" defeat.

We have already referred to the speech made by García Oliver on that occasion. Even more revealing, however, was the speech delivered by Federica Montseny, a prominent member of the CNT-FAI and to this day an influential personality in the MLE (Spanish Libertarian Movement) in exile. Having played a leading role in ending the street fighting during the May Days in Barcelona, these reflections on her actions are of particular interest.

> I remained a week in Catalonia, a week of continuous work seeking the solution to all the problems, and guided by the comrades of my organisation. We were successful in our efforts. *The matter was satisfactorily solved.* It was a lesson and an experience for everybody—or rather, it should have been. And when I returned to Valencia, satisfied and convinced that we could put a feather in our caps both nationally and internationally in so far as *the workers' organisations and the government had demonstrated that they had absolute control over the masses, and that the government never had such prestige as then, in having managed to solve a problem of tremendous importance without shedding blood*—I was saying when I returned to Valencia joyfully convinced that I was returning victorious along a path covered with laurels, we found that the crisis was planned for the very day of our arrival. (emphasis added)

But this is not all. Later, the speaker dealt with the participation of the CNT in the government:

> I, as an anarchist who rejected the state, conceded it a little credit and confidence, in order to achieve a revolution from above. . . . *And those who should have been grateful to us because we abandoned the street and violence and accepted responsibility within a government, bounded by a legislation made by others did not rest until they obtained that we, the revolutionaries of the street, should return to the street.* And now this is the problem. The CNT is back in the street. Those people do not realise the terrible responsibility they bear for having made us return to the

street without the responsibility of government; an organisation and a powerful movement which have lost none of their vigour or effectiveness, but which, on the contrary, have been strengthened by acquiring a discipline and a coordination which they previously did not possess.[2] (emphasis added)

Federica Montseny's conclusions were that the participation of the workers' organisations in the government was "the most fundamental revolution made in the political and economic fields." The entry of the CNT "with a sense of responsibility, with a useful activity, with a task already realised without arguments, opens up a new future in the world for all working-class organisations." The speaker was trying to show that since the workers made the revolution, both in destroying the foundations of the existing order and in building the new society, they therefore had a right to be included as a class in the task of government. Just like García Oliver before her, Federica Montseny puts forward outworn reformist ideas as if they were revolutionary discoveries.

In a newspaper article on this subject,[3] Juan López, the CNT's ex–minister of commerce, maintained that the collaboration of the CNT had not resulted in any internal disintegration of the Confederation. If anything, the contrary had been the result.

Our influence among the workers is decisive. The sense of confederal discipline has developed immensely, and the

---

2   The following passage from Peter Kropotkin, *The Great French Revolution 1789–1793* (New York: Cosimo Classics, 2009 [1927]) is worth reading alongside Montseny's complaint that the CNT is back in the "street": "One can guess the revolutionary results which were to be expected from these representatives who always kept their eyes fixed on the law—the royal and feudal law; fortunately, the 'anarchists' had something to say in the matter. But these 'anarchists' know that their place was not in the Convention, among the representatives—their place was *in the street*; they understood that if they ever set foot inside the Convention it must not be to debate with the 'members of the right' or the 'Frogs of the Marsh'; it must be to exact something, either from the top of the galleries where the public sat, or through an invasion of the Convention, with the people at their back."

3   *Fragua Social* (Valencia), September 6, 1936.

moral and organic unity of the CNT is not surpassed by any organisation or party.

To measure the health of an organisation in terms of "discipline" and "organic unity" is, in our opinion, dangerous, misleading, and unconvincing. *All* politicians and trade union leaders dream of discipline for the masses. The CNT leaders proved to be no exception to the rule. In case it may be said that we have misinterpreted Juan López, we will quote from a further article published by him a month later.

> Everyone must be disposed towards an inflexible view of the internal discipline of our movement. There must be for the libertarian movement in this period of war and of rapid transition, a real single command. That is to say, a single voice and a single front. Local problems, regional crises, absolutely everything must be resolved by the direct intervention of the supreme organs of our movement. Contradictory positions must be discarded, and, since we are united by a single ideal, we must defend one interest.[4]

Juan López was not alone in proposing and desiring centralised control in the CNT. Some months earlier, on March 28, 1937, the National Committee called a conference of all the confederal and anarchist press, which was held in the Casa CNT-FAI in Barcelona. Peirats writes:

> Its principal objective was the subordination of all the organs of expression of anarcho-syndicalism to the directives of the National Committees. Certain dissonances had to be suppressed, such as the freedom to criticise by certain periodicals which had raised themselves to the position of being repositories of principles and snipers at the weaknesses of the Committees and the confederal ministers. The result of this

---

4   *Fragua Social* (Valencia), October 7, 1937.

conference was the most effective answer to the ill-founded illusions of those who believed in a chimerical confederal discipline.[5]

Though the conference agreed with most of the projects put forward, the proposal that the libertarian press should virtually become the mouthpiece of the committees was only accepted by a majority vote, "a hollow victory if one takes into account that at the end of the conference the minority reiterated its decision to disregard the vote."[6]

The CNT as a movement did not suffer by the policy of collaboration and centralisation in the same way as have so many other working-class organisations in similar circumstances, simply because to a very large degree the leaders were unable to impose their decisions on the rank-and-file militants. The swiftness with which they mobilised their forces in Barcelona during the May Days, and the difficulty which the "influential militants" had in persuading them to abandon the barricades is surely proof of this. But there can be no escaping the fact that the defeat forced on them during the May Days was followed by a noticeable demoralisation among the revolutionary workers. The organised armed attacks on the collectives in Aragon, costly and useless military campaigns carried out for political considerations only, serious shortages of food and raw materials, the growing number of refugees as Franco occupied more towns and villages could not but have a serious effect on morale.

It is true that during this period the CNT was not in the government, and there are those apologists of collaboration who put forward the view that the attacks on the workers' positions following the May Days could not have taken place had there been

---

5   José Peirats, *La CNT en la Revolución Española*, vol. 2 (Toulouse: Ediciones CNT, 1952).

6   Even more drastic steps to control the press were taken less than a year later at the CNT's national economic plenum (Pleno Nacional Economico Ampliado) held in Valencia. The measures proposed are discussed in a later chapter.

CNT ministers in the Negrín government.[7] But we believe that to put forward such an argument is to close one's eyes to the realities. Above all, it is to ignore the all-important fact that the Caballero government had at least one victory to its credit: *that of re-establishing the authority of government*, which during the first two months of the struggle did not exist. In this task Caballero was greatly assisted by the influential members of the CNT-FAI in his cabinet and by the growing bureaucracy in all departments of public life, in which members of the CNT-FAI played an important role.

And just as the provocation during the May Days was carried out in spite of the presence of the four CNT ministers in the government, so would similar acts against the revolutionary workers have been committed whether the CNT was in the central (Valencia) government or not. As Federica Montseny so succinctly put it on one occasion: "In politics we [the CNT-FAI] were absolutely ingenuous."

---

7   This view is put forward in violent terms by Horacio Prieto, formerly national secretary of the CNT, in the article "La Politica Libertaria," *Material de Disussion* (Brighton), February 15, 1946.

CHAPTER XV
THE FAI AND THE POLITICAL STRUGGLE

Insofar as the present study is an attempt to draw some of the lessons of the Spanish Revolution, we do not propose to deal with the last eighteen months in the same detail as we have the first year of the struggle, for obvious reasons.

By July 1937, the state and the institutions of government had once more reasserted themselves; the armed struggle against Franco, once controlled by the government and professional militarists and fought as a war of fronts, could no longer be turned into victory (the whole northern front had collapsed, and in the south, Malaga had been lost); and the workers' organisations were being torn by the struggle between personalities and by a growing centralisation. The much vaunted word "Unity" had become synonymous with blind acceptance by the workers of instructions from the "supreme organisms," whether of the state or of their own organisations.

The UGT was split by the political struggle going on for its control between the Communists and the right and left wings of the Socialist Party. The CNT was floundering in the mire of compromise. The committees and the syndicalist bureaucracy in the economic councils, in the military commands, in the security forces, in the municipalities and every other state institution were completely isolated from the aspirations of the revolutionary masses, and, in the name of unity and the victory over Franco, were throwing overboard principles and the revolutionary conquests of the workers one by one. As we have already stated, the "May Days" in

Barcelona could have been the signal for calling a halt; instead, the actions of the leadership were a confirmation that the revolution had been defeated.

As if to seal this defeat came the plenum of the FAI held in Valencia at the beginning of July 1937, at which it was proposed to reorganise the Federation in a way that would make it possible greatly to increase its membership and its "influence." But it was clear from previous statements—assuming their actions were not sufficient evidence—that this reorganisation of the FAI was not an attempt to safeguard the revolution but to stake some claim in what might be left of the revolution after the "exigencies of the war" and the politicians had done their best to emasculate it. In a circular issued by the Peninsular Committee of the FAI in October 1936, participation by anarchists in "organisms of an official nature" is justified on the grounds that the situation demands it. The Committee goes on to deal with the future role of the CNT, which in the economic reconstruction of the country will be obliged to collaborate with all sections of the "anti-fascist bloc," for it cannot be undertaken by any one sector of the community but demands a "single organism in which are concentrated the common interests" of industry and agriculture. This view is justified on the grounds that

> if we introduce discord in the economic field and break up the efforts which are being made to bring this [reconstruction] about, we shall create a chaotic situation. For these reasons and in foreseeing future developments, we must anticipate the disappearance, in certain circumstances, of the syndicate as we know it at present; and in others the fusion of our organisation of struggle with similar ones belonging to other tendencies.

Now the idea behind the FAI plan becomes clear. In a few sentences this is what they say: since the syndicates will be interested exclusively in economic questions and will be able to have only a professional influence on the activities to which they have been assigned, it will be necessary for an external force to exist which will direct this economic robot towards those ends "to which humanity aspires." This external force is the Specific Organisation (Organisación Especifica). And we need hardly add that for this task the FAI considered itself the ideal choice! This is the first step in the conversion of the FAI to the role of a political party. The second step is to tighten up its form of organisation. The FAI founded in 1927 at a conference held in Valencia had the "affinity group" as the basis of its organisation. The groups were federated in local, comarcal, and regional federations. The union of all the federations, including the Portuguese Federation, constituted the Iberian Anarchist Federation (FAI), and expressed itself through the Peninsular Committee.

At the plenum of Regional Committees held in Valencia in July 1937, it was declared that

> the affinity group has been, for more than fifty years, the most effective organism for propaganda, for contacts and anarchist activity. With the new organisation that is required of the FAI the organic role of the affinity group has been eliminated. It is the intention of the plenum that the affinity groups must be respected, but that by reason of the decisions taken by the FAI they will not be able to participate organically in the FAI as affinity groups.

The new bases of organisation of the FAI were to be the geographical groups, by districts and suburbs. These were to be joined in local, comarcal, provincial, and regional federations. The regionals made up the FAI. Applications for membership would be examined by a commission attached to every district and suburban group and local federation. So far as the reorganised FAI was concerned, admission with full rights was granted to (a) militants who already belonged to the FAI; (b) all those who belonged to syndical, cultural, and other organisations linked to anarchism before January 1, 1936. Others, who did not comply with these conditions but whose references were satisfactory would be granted conditional membership, not being allowed to hold any post in the organisation for the first six months.

These were the conditions for joining the new FAI, but what of the declarations of principles? Bearing in mind that the intention was to increase the membership "in the shortest possible time," it is not surprising that the document contains no statement of principles, unless the following paragraph is to be taken as such:

> As anarchists, we are the enemies of dictatorships, whether of races or of parties; we are enemies of *the totalitarian form of government* and believe that the future direction of our people will be the result of the joint action of all sections of the community which agree on the creation of a society without class privileges; in which the organisms of work, administration, and communal living are the principal factor for providing Spain, through federal norms, with the outlets which will satisfy its different regions. (emphasis added)

From an organisation which declares its opposition to the "totalitarian form" of government but not to government itself, one cannot expect any reference to opposition to the state. More so when one reads elsewhere in this document:

> The FAI, without disregarding—indeed conceding the greatest importance to—the war; without renouncing its final objectives, proposes to further the Revolution *in all the popular organisms in which its activities may be effective* in determining in a progressive direction the outcome of the present revolution.

And later:

> We advocate the total disappearance of the bourgeois hangovers which still subsist and we are making every effort to encourage all organisations which will contribute to this end. Nevertheless, we believe that, in contrast with our attitude of

opposition in the past, *it is the duty of all anarchists to take part in those public institutions which can serve to secure and further the new state of affairs.*" (emphasis added)

Members of the FAI who hold public office

are required to give an account to the committees of their mission and activities, maintaining close contact with them for the purpose of following at all times their *inspiraciones*[1] in every specific case. Any member of the FAI designated for a public office, whatever its nature, can be disauthorised or removed from office as soon as such action is deemed necessary by the competent bodies of the organisation.

The foregoing is a clear statement of the intentions of the FAI to play the role of a political party in the affairs of government. For to be able to nominate members to hold "public office" the FAI would have to be recognised by the government as one of the parties forming the "anti-fascist bloc." They were fully aware of the implications of their actions from an anarchist point of view, but were undeterred, and meetings were held in the principal cities of Spain to launch this monster in the name of anarchism.

In a statement to the International Anarchist Movement,[2] the FAI asked for understanding of their actions and respect for decisions taken only after "free and passionate discussion." (No mention, however, is made of the fact that those members of the FAI serving at the fronts, and there were many, had no say in these deliberations.)[3]

---

1   The meaning of "inspiracion" is "inspiration," or in the less euphemistic language of the professional politicians: "orders, directives."

2   "Federacion Anarquista Iberica al Movimiento Internacional," *Information Bulletin of the CNT-FAI* no. 367 (Spanish Edition, Barcelona), September 20, 1937.

3   A. Ildefonso in his series of articles on the "Movimento Libertario Spagnuolo," *Volontà* (Naples) 6, no.7, June 30, 1952: "It is true to say that in that period the best militants of the libertarian organisations were to be found among the combatants, and that on their return they found themselves faced with the

For instance, the new structure of the FAI, in which a form of public activity is accepted, as well as special aspects of political activity, such as the participation of the FAI in all the organisms created by the revolution and in all places where our presence is necessary to accelerate activity and to influence the masses and the combatants, has been the subject of many violent discussions, without such action being in itself a fundamental modification of our tactics and our principles but simply and solely a circumstantial adaptation to the necessities of the war and the new problems created by the revolution.

Nevertheless, opposition to the reorganisation of the FAI in Spain was considerable, particularly in Catalonia, where at a regional plenum of groups, a number of delegates withdrew. Two months later, in an article published in *Solidaridad Obrera* (October 12, 1937), Gilabert, secretary of the local federation of anarchist groups in Barcelona again referred to the "large minority" *(minoria considerable)* in opposition, adding that "the differences reached the point where some groups threatened to provoke a split." A committee was nominated to find a solution, which was that the large opposition should be free to continue as affinity groups, "but that their resolutions of an organic nature will be taken into account only in relation to the numbers they represent." This proposal, however, had to be put to a Peninsular Congress for ratification.

The plan to boost the membership of the FAI by broadening its basis seems not to have met with the success hoped for. Before July 1936, the members of the FAI were estimated at 30,000. And, according to Santillán, by the end of 1937 the figure stood at 154,000.[4] But what had been gained in quantity had been lost in

---

fait accompli. In reality they could not see the significance of these tactical transformations in their true light, overwhelmed and somewhat 'impressed' as they were by 'the tremendous responsibilities of the hour,' and totally absorbed by the fever that gripped everyone over certain concrete achievements of that revolution which they had dreamed of for so many years."

4   Diego Abad de Santillán, *Por qué perdimos la guerra* (Buenos Aires: Imán, 1940).

revolutionary content; the urge to create the mass movement had been achieved at the expense of individual values and anarchist principles.

PART 2

INTRODUCTION

During the last eighteen months of the struggle, the revolutionary and anti-fascist movements were living a lie. With the control of economic life and of the military struggle in the hands of Stalinist agents supported by all the political enemies of the revolution, and with the willing or unwilling connivance of many who called themselves revolutionaries, there could be no other outcome than a victory for Franco and his allies. The military offensives launched by the Negrín government were either ghastly failures or costly adventures in which military successes were quickly turned into retreats. Political and not military considerations dominated all these offensives, so that even the advocates of a single command, military organisation, and an iron discipline—"similar to that of the enemy"—were to be bitterly disappointed with the results.

Only when the archives of the CNT-FAI are available to the student of the revolution will the true feelings of the militants and leaders at the time be really known, for their press, plastered with victory slogans, militarist propaganda, the glorification of war, and threats for those who shirked their "duty" for the "patria," was no longer the voice of the organisation as a whole but the mouthpiece of the government and the "revolutionary" chauvinists. Yet, even without the evidence, one cannot believe that these leaders of the CNT-FAI were so naive as still to hope for a military defeat of Franco, but that many of them shared the views of some members of the government, that every effort should be made to prolong the war at any cost until the outbreak of hostilities between Germany and Britain, which everyone knew to be inevitable sooner or later. Just as some hoped for victory as a result of the international conflagration, so many Spanish revolutionaries gave their support to World War II, because they believed that a victory of the "democracies" (including Russia!) would result in Spain's automatic liberation from the Franco-fascist tyranny. In these hopes one sees the curious combination of political opportunism and naivety. The former is common to all mass organisations, but it is the combination of the two that is a special characteristic of the Spanish revolutionary leadership—and of which Federica Montseny appeared to be aware when she said: "in politics we were quite ingenuous." We have seen how from the first days of the struggle in Spain they were outwitted and outmanoeuvred by the politicians on every issue. Equally significant is that their contact with politicians had no ideological influence on the politicians, whereas a number of leading members of the CNT were in the end won over to the very principles of government and centralised authority, not "circumstantially" but permanently (Horacio Prieto, García Oliver, Juan Peiró, Juan López, to mention only a few of the most *destacados militantes* that come to mind).

With the defeat of the revolution in May 1937 by the central authority the leaders of the CNT-FAI no longer represented a force to be reckoned with by the government, which proceeded to take over the militias, abolish the workers' patrols in the rearguard, and smash the collectives, thus pulling the teeth of the revolution; and it was left to the leaders of the CNT to break its heart.

The last eighteen months of the struggle are marked not only by military disasters in which tens of thousands of lives were sacrificed but also by a determined effort to transform the CNT beyond recognition *from within*. It is this development with which we propose to deal in the pages that follow. It is, we think, of great importance to the libertarian revolutionary, for while some Spanish militants conveniently explain every step taken as being determined by "circumstances" it seems to us that the rapid growth of an authoritarian leadership in the CNT, as well as the inability of the rank-and-file members and militants to prevent it, in fact stem directly from the compromising of basic principles from the beginning of the struggle in July 1936.

CHAPTER XVI

FROM THE MILITIAS TO MILITARIZATION

> We are not interested in medals or in generals' sashes. We
> want neither committees nor ministries. When we have won,
> we will return to the factories and workshops from which we
> emerged, keeping away from the safe deposits, for the aboli-
> tion of which we have long struggled. It is in the factory, in
> the fields and the mines that the true army for the defence of
> Spain will be created.
> —Buenaventura Durruti (reported in *Solidaridad Obrera*,
> September 12, 1936)

> The government has posthumously granted the rank of
> lieutenant colonel to the illustrious libertarian leader
> Buenaventura Durruti, on the anniversary of his death.
> —Headlines in *Solidaridad Obrera*, April 30, 1938

In spite of its tradition of violence the CNT-FAI had also an anti-
militarist and anti-war tradition. It was summed up at the Saragossa
Congress (May 1936) in a *Proposal on the politico-military situation*
as follows:

> Sixthly: to undertake an agitational campaign of the spoken
> and written word against war and against all that which tends
> to encourage war. The setting up of anti-militarist commit-
> tees which will establish direct relations with the IWMA

in order to be informed on international matters, and will encourage a hatred of war and resistance to conscription among young people by means of leaflets and pamphlets.

Seventhly: in the event of the government of Spain declaring mobilisation on a war footing the general revolutionary strike will be declared.

It should be noted that this statement was published only two months before the military rebellion, and with the knowledge that such a rising was being organised. Indeed, in the preamble to the proposal in question, we read:

Bearing in mind that Spain is passing through a situation which is clearly revolutionary, and that if the CNT does not endeavour to come out in defence of liberties which are being whittled away by all the politicians (*gobernantes*) of the right and the left, its activity will be at the mercy of the ebb and flow of politics. It is therefore necessary to agree on common action to combat in depth all repressive laws and those which are against the freedom of association and expression.

Aware of the breakdown of the present democratic regime, and believing that no solution to the present political and social situation will be found through Parliament, and that with the breakdown of the former it could provoke a rightist reaction or alternatively a dictatorship—no matter of what kind—it must be the CNT which, by reaffirming its apolitical principles, openly declares itself on the ineffectualness and failure of parliamentarianism.

Within a month of the rising—August 1936—these declared principles and tactics were to be put to the test, for the Madrid government issued a decree ordering the mobilisation of the Reserves of 1933, 1934, and 1935. This was answered by young Catalans who held a mass meeting at the Teatro Olimpia in Barcelona to declare their "refusal to return to the barracks." The CNT in an equivocal manifesto supported their cause. It was equivocal, because it was not an attack on mobilisation and the principle of conscription but a defence of young people who declare *Abajo el ejercito! Vivan las milicias populares!* (Down with the Army! Long Live the Popular Militias!). The manifesto ends, however, on a strong positive note directed to the governments of Catalonia and of Madrid:

> We cannot defend the existence of nor understand the need for a regular army, uniformed and conscripted. This army must be replaced by the popular militias, by the People in Arms, the only guarantee that freedom will be defended with enthusiasm and that no new conspiracies will be hatched in the shadows.

Meanwhile a plenum of local and district groups of the FAI stated its position in these terms:

> The plenum . . . accepts the fait accompli of the popular militias as an inevitable necessity of the civil war. The plenum expresses its opposition to the militarization of the militias, while recognising, nevertheless, the need for the organisation of action, which is indispensable in any war.

The real significance and sincerity of the foregoing can best be judged, we think, by being read in conjunction with the statement issued by the Committee of Militias on August 5, which declared that

> The central committee of Anti-fascist Militias of Catalonia has decided that soldiers of the 1934, 1935, and 1936 classes should report immediately to the barracks and that there they put themselves at the service of the Committees of Militias which have been constituted under the jurisdiction of the central committee.

Now, this central committee, it will be recalled, was in fact, if not in name, the "revolutionary government" of Catalonia and was composed of representatives from all the political parties and workers' organisations. Santillán and Aurelio Fernández represented the FAI, while Durruti, García Oliver, and Asens were the CNT's representatives.

In the central committee's first proclamation of resolutions, *the carrying out of which was obligatory for everyone (cuyo cumplimiento es obligatorio para todo los ciudadanos)*, article 7 makes it quite clear—in case the passage we have italicised did not—that the committee intends to give the orders and be obeyed:

> The committee trusts that, in view of the need to build up a revolutionary order to deal with the fascist nuclei, its orders will be obeyed without the need to have recourse to disciplinary measures.

Thus is it clear that from the beginning the revolutionary leaders saw the struggle as one in which they would be not the guides or coordinators of the popular enthusiasm but its controllers; that the alternative to the bankrupt central government and the Generalitat was not new forms of organisation but the Jacobin government in the guise of El Comité Central de Milicias Antifascistas; that the answer to a military uprising was not the "people in arms" but a "popular" army of volunteers and conscripts attempting to emulate the militarists at their own profession: war!

In the circumstances it is not surprising that the position of the revolutionary leaders changed from week to week. By the end of August 1936, a new attitude can be detected. Prominently displayed in *Solidaridad Obrera* (August 29) is a "Proclamation issued in all the areas occupied by the Durruti Column" and signed by the "centuries' delegate, José Esplugo," which

> in the names of the anti-fascist committees, and *interpreting the decree of the Madrid government calling up the reservists of 1934 and 1936, notifies them of the ineluctable duty of joining the ranks,*[1] either in the various districts or with the columns.

---

1   The original texts reads: "*hace saber la obligacion ineludible de incorporarse a filas.*" Our translation is based on the most favourable interpretation of the words "*obligacion ineludible*"! (emphasis added)

For some leaders, like García Oliver, for instance, the militia stage had been left behind by early August 1936, less than a month after the military uprising. At a large meeting which he addressed in Barcelona he declared that "the People's Army which has grown out of the militias must be organised and based on new concepts." And he outlined the steps actually being taken to achieve these ends:

> We are going to organise a revolutionary military school in which we will train a technical command which will not be a copy of the old officialdom, but simply technicians who will follow, furthermore, the directions (*indicaciones*) of the officer-instructors who have demonstrated their loyalty to the people and to the proletariat.

Seven months later, Minister of Justice García Oliver, in an address to the students of the Military School warned them in these words:

> Officers of the Popular Army, you must observe an iron discipline and impose it on your men who, once they are under your command, must cease to be your comrades and be simply cogs in the military machine of our army.

So much for the Popular Army "based on new concepts."

The formation of the Caballero government early in September 1936 and the growing power of the Communists was the signal for an all-out attempt to build a government-controlled military machine. Whether such a step would ensure victory against Franco was doubtful, but that it was an effective blow to the revolution there could be no doubt. The *mando unico* (single command) was a myth to the very end, the generals being pawns in the hands of the political parties.

Political considerations dominated the choice of military commanders, and campaigns costly in lives and materials were launched merely for party political ends.

We do not believe that the leaders of the CNT had any illusions about the sincerity of the politicians but, having discarded the revolutionary solution in favour of a governmental one from the very beginning, they were committed to the political game in which they felt they could play an effective role only so long as they were able to occupy key posts in the machine of state. In the first months the militants of the CNT offered some resistance to the reactionary, governmental policies advocated by the leaders and though eventually through their virtual monopoly of the press and other channels of propaganda and the rapid advance by Franco's forces, which threatened Madrid, and other material difficulties, the various measures were accepted as "inevitable in the circumstances," etc. . . . . the CNT leaders found themselves always one step behind the political parties so far as sharing out the key jobs was concerned. Having developed a bureaucratic and legalistic mind, the political game became a kind of obsession for these men.

The reactions of the confederal militiamen to militarization is described as follows by Peirats:

The confederal and anarchist columns were the most reluctant in accepting the new situation *(modalidad)*, which they interpreted as a decisive step in the direction of orthodox militarism, towards the legalisation of war, and to barrack discipline. When the higher committees *(comités superiores)* of the CNT-FAI opted in favour of the general militarization of the militias, a matter which the CNT ministers were pressing for from government level, serious confusion resulted on all the fronts where members of the Confederation were engaged. Noisy meetings took place between the combatants and the committee's delegations which were sent to the front lines to carry out their, admittedly difficult, mission. Many intransigent militiamen who had joined the armed struggle purely as volunteers rescinded their undertaking and left for the rearguard. Later they returned to rejoin. The Durruti column, following militarization, became the 26th Division. The revolutionary and comradely climate miraculously persisted between the new officers and the troops until the end of the war.[2]

Even the Columna de Hierro, to whose revolutionary intransigence in the early days of the struggle we have already referred, disbanded at a public meeting in which it declared that it was doing so "with the aim of not isolating itself from the struggle which is being waged against fascism." Perhaps these brave men had cause later to regret their decision.

Once committed to the idea of militarization, the CNT-FAI leaders threw themselves wholeheartedly into the task of demonstrating to everybody that their rank and filers were the most disciplined, the most courageous members of the armed forces. The confederal press published innumerable photographs of its military leaders (in their officers' uniforms), interviewed them, wrote glowing tributes on their elevation to the exalted ranks of colonel or major. And as the military situation worsened so the tone of the confederal press became *more* aggressive and militaristic. *Solidaridad Obrera* published daily lists of names of men who had been condemned by the military tribunals in Barcelona and shot for "fascist activities," "defeatism," or "desertion." One reads of a man sentenced to death for helping conscripts to escape over the frontier. And a news item from Valencia published in *Solidaridad Obrera* (April 21, 1938) with the heading "Sentencia Cumplida" (Sentence Carried Out) reads:

---

2   José Peirats, *La CNT en la Revolución Española*, vol. 2 (Toulouse: Ediciones CNT, 1952); presumably the good relations between "the new officers and troops" which Peirats refers to applied simply to the former Durruti Column. One cannot imagine that in Colonel Cipriano Mera's division, for instance, such a *compañerismo* could exist on Mera's own statement that the situation would be "from now on, an iron discipline, which will be worth what is offered freely. From today I will only deal with captains and sergeants!" One feels that the uniform went to Mera's head. He was by trade a building worker and a leading member of the CNT in Madrid. So far as we know he is now in the collaborationist camp of the CNT in exile.

Sentence was approved in the case made out at court martial against Lt. (Administration) Mariano Sanz Navarro for the crime of abandoning his post. He appeared before the Permanent Tribunal of the Court of Justice of the 22nd Army Corps on the 17th inst. and execution of sentence took place in the village of Villafamat to where he was transferred and sentence carried out to set a greater example. The soldiers of the garrison were present and filed past the body cheering the Republic.

This campaign of discipline and obedience through fear and terror—we have for reasons of space only briefly dealt with the question, though the confederal press of the time contains abundant material—did not prevent large-scale desertions from the fronts (though not often to Franco's lines) and a falling output in the factories.

There is documented evidence of the falling off of output in the war industry as a result of the nationalisation of all factories engaged on war production, thereby indicating that with all its shortcomings workers' control in the factories resulted in greater productivity than when the government took over in the name of greater efficiency (though in reality for the purpose of controlling those potential armouries of the people in arms). There is no reason to doubt that for the same reasons the morale of the militiamen was highest when government control and regimentation of the armed forces was non-existent.

But from the anarchist point of view there are two vital objections to militarization:

(1) that it would result in the deformation of the armed struggle which began with a socio-revolutionary character to a national war the outcome of which would matter only to the ruling class;

(2) that militarization implies centralisation of power, the mobilisation and conscription of a whole people, and is the negation of individual freedom. We shall discuss these questions in greater detail in our final chapter.

CHAPTER XVII

THE EXTENDED NATIONAL ECONOMIC PLENUM OF JANUARY 1938

The *Pleno nacional economico ampliado* of the CNT held in Valencia in January 1938 was the first comprehensive gathering of the Confederation since the Saragossa Congress of May 1936. It was attended by more than 800 delegates representing some 1,700,000 members. The minutes are not available, and it is necessary to refer to the fragmentary reports published in the press as well as a pamphlet published by the National Committee of the CNT in which are printed the resolutions adopted by the plenum. In that plenum, in the words of Peirats:

> One of the anomalies that is noted is the advance expression of opinion by the National Committee on all the items on the agenda. This conflicts with traditional procedure. Though all the opinions previously discussed by the National Committee with the delegates present at the plenum were put forward, the procedure would have been denounced in other circumstances as irregular and captious. Inadmissible too, in other circumstances, would have been the deliberative intervention of the National Committee in all discussions and in particular in defending its *Dictamenes* (Opinions).[1]

---

1   José Peirats, *La CNT en la Revolución Española*, vol. 3 (Toulouse: Ediciones CNT, 1953).

According to the general secretary of the CNT the purpose of the plenum was the examination of certain fundamental questions; to demonstrate the maturity achieved by the organisation during eighteen months of constructive experiments in the economic field; to solve these problems with *"precisión, claridad y positivismo,"* as well as to create the general impression that the workers were capable of solving the problems created by the situation, by imposing on themselves whatever sacrifices were necessary and by overcoming any existing shortcomings. And finally, to study the economic situation as a whole "outside political and war considerations" and seek the solution which was most rational and relevant.

It is not surprising in view of the growing centralisation of the organisation that many of the resolutions at this plenum sought to increase the power of the administration, both in the control and management of industry as well as of the internal life of the organisation. Thus, the controversial point four on the agenda (which was one of only three resolutions which were decided by vote—the remainder being adopted unanimously) proposed the creation of work inspectors for those factories "which are in the hands of the workers." The need for these inspectors is explained in a memorandum by the National Committee in these terms:

> We know that the overwhelming majority of workers and militants have carried out their duties and have sought by every means to increase production. Nevertheless, one is aware that there are totally irresponsible and ignorant minorities in the rearguard who have not produced the kind of results that were to be expected.

The inspectors were to be nominated by the National Federation of Industry, and their duties and powers are summarised under three headings:

> 1. These delegates will put forward the expected norms which will effectively orientate the different industrial units with a view to improving their economy and administration. They

will not be allowed to function on their own account; it will be up to those in charge (*encargados*) to carry out and see that others discharge the decisions of the councils, to whom they are responsible.

2. For greater efficiency and operation, and in cases where it should be thought necessary, the councils will propose that they should be empowered to apply effective sanctions on those organisms or individuals who have deserved them by reason of their failure to carry out their duties.

3. The organisation will agree to the extension of the coercive powers accorded to the organisms which have to use this right and make the order defining these powers. These dispositions concern only those industries which are in the hands of the workers.

To appreciate the real power of the inspectors one has to take note of the eleventh point on the agenda which deals with "The establishment of norms of work." The proposals on the subject include for a syndical control committee being established in each factory

which will take part in the management council and be vigilant so far as the satisfactory execution of work is concerned. It will collaborate and always try to help in perfecting methods of work and increasing production. The syndical control committee will report to the junta sindical (syndical board) on all details concerning the undertaking. It will propose to the technical administrative council the nomination of distributors and responsible officers for the enterprise. It will make easier the exposure of troublemakers, reporting cases of incompetence which come to their notice. It will endeavour to improve as far as practicable the material conditions of work. It will propose promotions in the professional classification of those who have deserved it and have not been noticed by the distributor. It will concern itself with hygiene, propaganda, the strengthening of the moral bonds among workers in socialised industry. It will periodically check the accounts and will also communicate its criticisms and praise to the Technical-Administrative Council as well as to the junta sindical, and will place itself at the disposal of the work delegate for whatever he may require.

Furthermore, the Consejo Nacional de Economia

Will prepare a producer's rulebook, containing a list of the rights and duties of all engaged in the economic contract of confederal production, summarising the main agreements reached by the extended economic plenum.

But this is not all. Every worker will have a work card as well as his syndical card and producer's rule book! The potentially dangerous purpose to which the work card could be put was revealed in the section dealing with the unsatisfactory worker. It is so important that we are transcribing it in full:

The manager who acts as the responsible official in the employment section, in production, and in the *comité* for syndical control, can propose the dismissal of a worker, and, in agreement with the general manager, speedy decisions will be taken.

In the case of unjustified absence from work; in cases of persistent lateness; in cases where a worker fails to reach the production targets required; in the cases of those who tend to be "trouble-makers," in that they create dissension between the workers and the managers (*los responsables del trabajo*) or the trade union representatives.

Once dismissal has been sanctioned the worker can appeal to the junta sindical, which, advised by the technical and administrative council, has the final word.

[When a worker has been dismissed according to the rules as outlined above] the industry is obliged to find him work elsewhere, providing him with the relevant work certificate.

If at a new place of work he were to relapse into his bad habits and were again dismissed by the recognised procedure, he would not be offered further work in that area and would be directed by the industry to another locality where he would be given work if it were thought necessary.

If even after this change another lapse were to occur, through obstinancy, then his past record would be entered on his work card and union card, leaving it to the discretion of his union to decide on what sanctions to apply in the form of temporary suspension from work, sanctions which are to be used only as a last resort.

As the engagement of staff for any enterprise will be checked by the bureau of the technical administrative council of the syndicate, all workers and employees will have a dossier in which will be entered details of their professional and social achievements. The technical administrative council will receive staff through the different sections of the syndicate, who will vouch for their respectability and professional capacities.

This is what the CNT in January 1938 describes as the "*organizacion responsable*"! We have no hesitation in describing the *carnet de trabajo* (work card) as a badge of slavery which even the reactionary and accommodating trade unions of America or Britain would resist to the last man, but which was adopted by the CNT with 516 votes in favour, 120 against, and 82 abstentions.

Of the measures to tighten up the "unity of the organisation," item 8 on the agenda is the most significant. It calls for a drastic reduction in the number of publications issued, ostensibly because of the paper shortage, the unnecessary duplication of coverage, and the reduced number of "competent comrades" to edit them. This word "competent" assumes a somewhat sinister meaning when we also read that a further reason for reducing the press is the need to give a homogeneous orientation to the publications. "One must call a halt to public disagreements in the movement." To this end it was laid down that in Barcelona, Valencia, and Madrid, morning and evening daily papers "must appear" (*deben parecer*) while in other towns, which are listed, morning papers "can be published" (*puede editarse*). This *ukase* is followed by the solemn warning that

> all dailies which do not keep to this plan will have to disappear, being considered uneconomical and unnecessary.

What the newspapers and periodicals shall print in their columns is also stated categorically. Thus, all the dailies are "under obligation" (*quedan obligados*) by decision of the national plenum to devote a page or half a page a day to the peasants. Bulletins published monthly by each National Federation of Industry will deal with activities of industry and "will not in any form deal with political and military developments, recognising these matters to be the exclusive province of the dailies." Similarly, the National Federation of Peasants will publish a monthly magazine which

> will have to limit its contents to the study and technical orientation [of agricultural questions] dropping completely any references to aspects of political and syndical orientation, since it is the exclusive task of the dailies to deal with the political aspects and of the bulletins to deal with syndical problems.

The move to control *political opinion* is patently clear. It would be interesting to know what changes took place in the editorial staffs of the CNT dailies and the political significance of these changes. And, last but not least, by whose orders these changes were made. Such information is not readily available, but it represents some of the vital material needed for an accurate assessment of where the real power of the organisation lay during those troubled years.

The direction taken by the CNT in its January 1938 plenum is so blatant and reactionary that nothing more surprises us. Not even the creation of an executive committee of the MLE (Spanish Libertarian Movement) in Catalonia early in April of the same year:

This executive committee will function by the following internal machinery. All decisions will be taken unanimously or by majority vote, and in the event of voting being equal, one will proceed to the reappointment of the whole committee.

All local and comarcal organisms of the three movements [CNT, FAI, FIJL] will approve and carry out the decisions of this committee.

The executive committee of the Libertarian Movement will be advised by a military commission, who will have studied the various problems in advance.

In agreement with the *comités* of the Movement, the executive committee will have the power to appoint those who will sit on the military and political advisory committees.

The executive powers of this executive committee include the immediate expulsion of those individuals, groups, syndicates, locals, comarcals, or committees which do not respect the general resolutions of the Movement and who harm it by their actions.

They will also penalise members who give support to those who have been expelled from the three organisations for the reasons above mentioned.

The executive and punitive powers of this committee will apply to the front-line forces as well as to the rearguard.

Nothing now was left—not even the illusion that the CNT was a revolutionary organisation controlled by its members. Now it was an easy matter to find common ground with the UGT leaders for signing yet another of those pacts of unity which abounded in a Spain which nevertheless continued to be more and more divided as the months went by.

CHAPTER XVIII
THE UGT-CNT PACT

The "evolution" of the CNT as evidenced by the Valencia plenum of January 1938 undoubtedly facilitated the negotiations for reaching agreement on a "Pact of Unity" with the socialist-controlled unions of the UGT. The revolutionary intransigence of 1936 had long since been replaced in the minds of the leaders of the CNT by a concern for what they considered the organisation's "rightful share" of the prizes of government at all levels, not only in the existing "exceptional circumstances" created by the armed struggle but for the future in the event of a miraculous victory over Franco.

The only effective unity is that forged by the working people themselves at their places of work and in their communities; a unity born out of common problems and needs, and mutual respect. This had occurred in many factories and collectives in Spain from the very beginning but was impossible in those cases where, for instance, the UGT was under the political sway of the Communists or the right-wing Socialists. And all that could be attempted by the CNT was to respect the rights of those who disagreed with their views on the social and economic reorganisation of the country and, at the same time, defend their own equal rights from outside interference.

The leaders of the CNT and UGT, who were anxious to arrive at some agreement as to their respective share of political power in the future destinies of Spain, were prepared to eliminate the differences which separated the two organisations by a piece of paper bearing their signatures and described as a Pact of Unity! The sense of their own importance displayed by leaders, their belief that real, human problems can be bypassed with a kind of bargaining at a high level are surely the most obscure aspects of power politics.

In the draft proposals put forward by the CNT and UGT, respectively, for the Pact of Unity one is immediately aware that the UGT made no concessions to the revolutionary objectives of the CNT with the exception of paying lip service to the importance of workers' control, which it considered "one of the greatest and most valuable of the workers' conquests" and demanded that the government should *legalise* workers' control "which defends the rights and duties of the workers so far as production and distribution are concerned." The CNT, on the other hand, in what appears to be a desperate attempt to find common ground with the reformist UGT outlines the function of a national joint committee as that of "ensuring the effective participation of the proletariat in the Spanish state and of undertaking to defend, *now and always*, a really democratic regime, opposing all totalitarian ideas and ambitions." On the question of "national defence" the CNT proposed among other things that the Confederation and the UGT should "assist in every way in the creation of an efficient regular army to win this war and to guard our liberties in the future." The CNT advocated workers' control but also the formation of a National Economic Council, composed of representatives of the syndicates and the government, whose function will be to

> direct production, distribution, credit, trade, and matters of compensation, acting through national councils of industry—which shall be constituted in the same way as the Economic Council.[1]

The Spanish Anarchist Federation, commenting on these documents, said of the UGT proposals that they were "from the beginning to the end a recapitulation of the government's point of

---

1   The text of these proposals and the comments by the FAI were published in *Spain and the World* 2, no. 3, March 4, 1938.

view," and that the UGT leaders were not interested in effective unity and "are only playing to the gallery." Of the CNT proposals the FAI commented:

> [They are] a product of the dual necessity of demonstrating our will to co-operation and of maintaining our principles. In it we have made every concession consistent with the latter and with the defence of our revolutionary conquests.
>
> The CNT has again demanded co-operation and representation in the anti-fascist government, particularly in the departments of war and economics. . . . On the other hand, the CNT has accepted the nationalisation of the war industries, railways, banks, telegraphs, etc. and has made many concessions, only reserving the principle of syndical representation on the governing councils of these organisations.[2]

The *Programme of Unity of Action between the UGT and the CNT* which was the outcome of the proposals put forward earlier by the two organisations is a document which clearly recognises the ultimate power and authority of the government and the state and seeks to insinuate the workers' organisations wherever possible into the institutions and machinery of government and state. Even on the question of the collectives the government would have the last word:

> 1. The UGT and the CNT recognise that lawful form should be given to collectives and therefore think that legislation on the question is necessary to settle which of them are to be continued, the conditions of their constitution and working, and to what point the state should have a say in them.
> 2. Such collectives as are amenable to the legislation in question and are of recognised economic usefulness will be helped by the state.

---

2   *Spain and the World* 2, no. 33, April 8, 1938; see also José Peirats, *La CNT en la Revolución Española*, vol. 3 (Toulouse: Ediciones CNT, 1953), chapter 28.

3. Legislation regarding collectives should be planned and put
before the government by the National Council of Economy.[3]

Who, one is tempted to ask, will decide which collectives are of
"economic usefulness" and to whom? And by giving the legislators
the powers to determine which of them shall continue, they remove
the very basis of the collectives: *that of being the spontaneous creation
of the people who work in them.*

In the CNT-UGT programme it will be left to the government
"to control production and regulate internal consumption, which
are the basis for our export policy." As for wages:

> The UGT and CNT advocate the establishment of a
> minimum salary based on the cost of living; and *taking into
> account both professional standing and individual production.* In
> this connection they will uphold the principle of "to him
> that produces better and more, more shall be given, without
> distinction of age or sex, so long as the circumstances arising
> from the needs of national reconstruction last." (emphasis
> added)[4]

Such methods of increasing production make necessary a new
bureaucracy of production experts, rate-fixers, timekeepers, and
other parasites, quite apart from the fact that in the process the

---

3   José Peirats, *La CNT en la Revolución Española*, vol. 3.
4   This very un-anarchistic sentiment cannot be wholly attributed to the influence
of the UGT in drafting the document. It reflects a growing mentality of the
union boss who echoes the complaints of the middle classes about "slackers"
among the workers and the need to penalise them. Much more shocking than
the sentence quoted from the UGT-CNT document is the campaign conducted
by *CNT,* organ of the CNT in Madrid, in favour of issuing producers' cards
with the purpose of eliminating "work slackers." These cards, according to the
Spanish Labour Bulletin (New York), June 7, 1938, "showing that the bearer
has done his or her share of work to help win the war, would entitle them to
their ration card without which no food can be procured." The popular slogan,
declared the Madrid organ of the CNT, should be: "He who doesn't work shall
not eat."

workers are divided and disunited by grievances. Piecework is the very antithesis of *mutual aid*, on which the collectivisations of the Spanish Revolution were based and which, for instance, distinguished them from the Russian collectives.

Indeed, yet another example of this attempt to destroy the spirit of mutual aid is contained in the proposals regarding agricultural collectives. The UGT-CNT proposals were that the land should be nationalised,

> the benefits of which should preferably be made over to the rural collectives and co-operatives, especially those set up by the CNT and UGT. . . . *The state should adopt a policy of helping* existing collectives, particularly those of the UGT and CNT and the legally constituted voluntary syndicates of country workers." (emphasis added)

The government would have the task of assisting the peasants in the acquisition of machinery, seeds, etc., and the granting of credits through the National Bank of Agricultural Credit. Thus, control would at all times be in the hands of the central authority, and this could only be achieved at the expense of local initiative.

In passing, it should be noted that the proposals concerning agriculture are in direct contradiction with the spirit of the decisions taken by the peasants' syndicates at their plenum in Valencia in June 1937, in which it was agreed to coordinate their activities on a national scale *not through the intervention of the state but by the workers' own organisms*. And that spirit of mutual aid was clearly indicated in article 26(e) of their constitution, which reads:

> Though initially collective and individual enterprises will consider themselves at liberty to deduct their needs from what they produce, it is nevertheless understood that both enterprises declare as their objective an equitable distribution of the production of the agricultural industry in such a way

as to ensure an equal right to all consumers throughout the country, in the widest sense of the word.

The references to workers' control in the CNT-UGT pact are in fact no more than a declaration that the workers' organisations will participate in joint consultation boards in industry, while the allocation of raw materials and production and distribution will be under the direction of the government. And it is too obvious to deserve elaboration that without economic control there can be no such thing as workers' control.

Of the CNT-UGT pact, the eminent Socialist leader, Luis Araquistáin, said at the time: "Bakunin and Marx would embrace over that document of the CNT"—to which the Barcelona anarchist weekly *Tierra y Libertad* made the following spirited reply, without nevertheless making any specific reference to the pact itself, though one could read into their critical remarks disapproval of the whole document:

A love for phrases frequently leads to building on the quicksands of grave historical errors. The phrase, "embrace between Marx and Bakunin," symbolizes a unity of divergent ideas such as neither the present reality nor the expectations of the future can guarantee. It is a phrase, therefore, which, when unqualified, may cause much confusion.

The "embrace" in striving for social reconstruction among all of us? Yes. The "embrace" for those who want a revolution which will emancipate the proletariat? Yes, also. The "embrace" of fighters against a common enemy, now and later? Yes. Those who follow the ideals of Bakunin and those who follow Marx are united today and should be united tomorrow to save the Spanish people and their revolution.

But those who continue as anarchists and Marxists have not obliterated—nor can they—with an "embrace" the fundamental differences that separate them. Even though the revolutionary tactic, the direct action of the proletariat itself, unites us, the fundamental dividing line remains. For as long as we, the anarchists, think that the state cannot be the organ of the revolution, that it should not be tolerated as a political entity which assumes responsibility for emancipating the people; so long as the Marxists, on the other hand, continue to think that the state has to be made the instrument, either transitory or otherwise, for constructing a free society—complete union will be impossible.

Marxists and anarchists may reach an agreement and fulfil it so long as in so doing they do not violate any essential principles. But between dictatorship and freedom, between state centralisation and direct association of the people, there is a great distance that cannot be spanned unless it is recognised by all that freedom is the only basis for real socialism.

For the revolutionist whose convictions derive from the lessons of history, there is no sentiment of race or patriotism which can obliterate the fundamental contradictions between the two theories; nor is there possible a synthesis between two historical currents that clash and repel each other. There is unity for specific struggles. There is an "embrace" for a common revolutionary upheaval. But authority and freedom, the state and anarchism, dictatorship and the free federation of the peoples, remain irreconcilably antagonistic until such a time as we all will understand that no real union is possible except by the free choice of the people.

In short, the "embrace of Bakunin and Marx" would be real only if the socialists, who according to Marx want eventually to achieve anarchism, will give up the classic paradox of resorting to a dictatorship of the state for suppressing the state.

The terms of the UGT-CNT pact were never implemented, even though both organisations were offered, and accepted, seats in a reshuffled Negrín government following the dismissal of the minister of national defence, Indalecio Prieto, and, according to the arguments put forward by the pro-governmentalist syndicalists, should have been in a position to make demands on the government.[5] But these were mere illusions, which some of them to this day seem unable to shake off.

---

5   Prieto, a right-wing Socialist, who was the declared enemy of Caballero, as well as of the anarchists, was dismissed by his erstwhile Socialist friend Negrín on the grounds of his "pessimism" as to the outcome of the war. Prieto, in a speech delivered to the Party some months later, declared that the real reason was his refusal to be dictated to by the Communists; Indalecio Prieto, *Como y porque salí del Ministerio de Defensa Nacional* (Paris: Imprimerie Nouvelle, 1939).

CHAPTER XIX
THE CULT OF THE ORGANISATION AND OF PERSONALITIES

The title of this chapter may appear, at first sight, paradoxical, for one would assume that the cult of the organisation as all-powerful and all-wise implies the complete subjection of the individual personality to its commands. But the all-powerful organisation, whether it be the Catholic Church, the Communist Party, or the industrial empire, is inarticulate without the "inspired guidance" of the leader, be he a pope, a Lenin, or a Ford. The larger the organisation, the greater is the need for general submission to its will and the suppression of the individual conscience, which is entrusted to the safekeeping of those who, for various reasons, assume the role of mouthpieces and infallible guides.

In theory, the CNT by its decentralised structure might appear to have safeguarded itself against these dangers. In reality this was not the case, and to our mind this was because the individual member of the CNT, while holding strongly his personal views, was always very conscious of belonging to a group, or syndicate, which in turn was part of a local federation, which in turn was part of a regional federation, which itself was part of a national federation. The organisation existed independently of the individuals who belonged to it. It was immutable, based on principles that were inviolable. The mistakes were human ones, but the organisation was surrounded by an almost religious aura, a feeling that whatever happened the CNT would always be there. When we read a manifesto by the National Committee which ends "Viva la *inmortal* CNT," we cannot dismiss the adjective as pure demagogy but must equate it with a religious faith. And the fact is that the CNT, illegal for a large part of its history, has time after time re-emerged when again permitted to function legally stronger than ever, at least numerically and in the lip service paid to its immutable principles. But internally, on a *human* level, the struggle between the reformist and revolutionary factions also grew stronger and always seemed to be linked to outstanding personalities. The Peiró-Pestaña polemic in 1929 illustrates both the clash of personalities as well as the mystical approach to the CNT. Peiró, many of whose actions and utterances were in direct contradiction with the principles of the CNT, nevertheless never denied

> the indispensability of the permanent and essential nature of basic principles. Confederal congresses can modify all the principles of the CNT which they consider should be modified. What no congress can do, and even less, what no man, however much "vision of reality" or "practical spirit" he may possess, can do is to deny the principles which are the essential basis, the foundation and raison d'être, of the CNT: anti-parliamentarianism and direct action. . . . For if it were possible to do so, then the CNT would have no reason for existing. And I, now, simply defend that which gives the CNT its raison d'être.[1]

Less than a year later, in 1930, Peiró's name is to be found among the signatories to a Manifesto on *Inteligencia Republicana*, which was an attempt to create a Popular Front to put into effect a kind of democratic political and social programme. A month after its publication the following statement by Peiró was published in *Acción Social Obrera*:

> Always a believer in frankness, unable to withhold from public knowledge what I do in private, I added my signature

---

1   José Peirats, *La CNT en la Revolución Española*, vol. 1 (Toulouse: Ediciones CNT, 1951), 32.

to a political manifesto. . . . It is clear that in signing the manifesto I was in conflict with my ideas, and I state that my action, right or wrong, was carried out in the full knowledge of this contradiction. I formally give notice that it was then and is now an entirely personal action. No one could say that I tried to influence others to follow in my steps. It is a matter of gestures in which the individual has to act spontaneously.

Nevertheless, I have only yesterday received statements warning me that my personal action is not only contemptible and a flagrant error, but that it also carries within itself certain dangers, against *that which is over and above me. And because I could not and do not wish to harm that which is dear to me, I realised that there were two ways only open to me: either to withdraw my signature from that manifesto or to be submerged in my own ostracism* . . .

Therefore, I declare that *in order to avoid any kind of dangers against those things that for me must be sacred,* from this moment I cease all activity in the realm of ideas and in the organisation's press and will take my place as one more among the many who in silence follow the vanguards who guide our fortunes." (emphasis added)[2]

Eight years later Peiró explains how it was possible that he who, for tactical reasons, was opposed to the entry of the CNT into the government should, nevertheless, have himself become a minister: "Thought is independent of discipline. Thought belongs to the individual, everything else he owes to the collectivity, to the organisation to which he belongs."

One would be tempted to comment at length on these, to us, important documents which help to explain how it was possible in 1936 for the leaders—or if one prefers Peiró's expression "the vanguards who guide"—to pursue policies in direct contradiction with the principles so long advocated in congresses and in the press.

---

2   Ibid.

Every compromise, every deviation, it was explained, was not a "rectification" of the "sacred principles" of the CNT but simply actions determined by the "circumstances," and that once these were resolved there would be a return to principles.

The member of the CNT could not *act* as an individual. *Cumplir con su deber,* an exhortation a thousand times repeated in the confederal press and from the public platform, meant sinking one's personal values and feelings for the greater interest of the organisation.

One militant, Marcos Alcón, describes how when he refused an order by the local federation of the CNT to take up a post in the municipality, he was called to a meeting at which delegates of the local federation and the Regional Committee were present. After giving his reasons for non-acceptance of the post, he was told by the regional secretary, Mariano Vázquez, that "my duty as a militant required that I should go wherever the Organisation sent me."

Alcón was one of the militants who resisted, situating the organisation in its proper perspective. He declared:

> I belong to the CNT because I believe it represents the objectives we are pursuing. When it does not fulfil the role we have assigned to it and has the presumption of obliging me to betray my personal convictions, then I will cease to belong to it.

That is, the organisation must serve man, not man the organisation. But it seems to us that the cult of the organisation is both its strength and its weakness. In an anti-authoritarian organisation the achievement of that strength contains also the seeds of its destruction, for it presupposes that the organisation will think and act as one man, and to this end it becomes necessary to build up dominating personalities whose word is not questioned and whose actions are beyond reproach. The dominating personalities were the outstanding orators and the "men of action." As Ildefonso González points out:

A number of men who, for many years devoted their lives to action, in which often they also lost their lives, belonged to the FAI and surrounded themselves with a mystical aura. Blinded by the "practical" and momentary results of their activity, they created a kind of doctrine of action.[3]

One such man was García Oliver, and his "glorious" past conferred on him in July 1936 tremendous prestige and power in the eyes of the workers. On every possible occasion the confederal press and propaganda department added glamour to his name. These personalities had to be continually kept in the public eye. The lengths to which the sycophants went is displayed in a report published in *Solidaridad Obrera* (August 29, 1936) on the occasion of Oliver's departure to the front. He is variously described as "our dear comrade," "the outstanding militant," "the courageous comrade," "our most beloved comrade," who, the article continues,

> with his warm eloquence has raised storms of rebellion in the larger gatherings of workers, who has electrified the people in the public squares with his simple words, and who has defied the bullets with his proverbial courage, is about to leave once more for the place of danger.

The propaganda department of the CNT-FAI, in their *Information Bulletin* devoted the whole front page in one issue to a profile of "A Man—García Oliver":

> Men like this comrade must occupy prominent and responsible positions from which they can communicate to their

3   A. Ildefonso Gonzáles, in a series of articles on *Il Movimento Libertario Spagnuolo* (The Spanish Libertarian Movement) published in the anarchist monthly *Volontà* (Naples) 9, nos. 6–9, (June–September 1952). The writer is a militant of the CNT in exile. These articles are an important contribution to an understanding of the different sections of, and influences in, the Spanish libertarian movement. No attempt is made to gloss over the weaknesses of the movement and the study includes a number of interesting documents, particularly on the FAI.

brothers their courage and their dynamism. And we would even say—their strategy.

His dynamism, linked with his fearlessness, is like an invincible line of bayonets (*valladar*) against fascism. What is more, we would then see the combatants recover that spirit of sacrifice which made them rise, facing the perils of an unequal struggle with bared chests.

Men, carried forward by a symbol, die smiling; thus died our militiamen and thus will die the men, soldiers today of the Popular Army, moulded (*plasmados*) by the spirit of comrade García Oliver.[4]

References are also made to his "creative genius" and comparisons made with "that other great figure, our immortal Durruti, who rises from his tomb and cries, 'Forward.'" This unbelievable mystical demagogy is not an isolated example. The confederal press of the period provides us with unlimited examples. What is equally serious is that people such as García Oliver *obviously thought of themselves in these exalted terms,* as is evidenced, for instance, by the broadcast speech he made at the time of the May Days in Barcelona:

You know me well enough to understand that in these moments I work through the impulse of my freest (*liberrima*) will, because you know me well enough to be convinced that no one, either before or now, or in the future, no one will succeed in drawing from my lips a statement which is not felt by me. Yes, having said this I must declare: all who have died today are my brothers; I kneel before them and I embrace them all equally. *Salud*! comrade workers of Catalonia.

The press, the radio, and the public platform can be both the weapons for man's emancipation as well as for his subjection. They are always dangerous when monopolised by a few people. It is significant that most of the oratorical giants of the revolutionary

---

4   Spanish-language edition of the CNT-FAI information bulletin, August 27, 1937.

movement in Spain became the reformists, the revisionists, and the politicians. In our opinion the process of disintegration was halted only by the victory of Franco.[5] Even so, the effects are still visible in the Spanish revolutionaries in exile among whom the collaborationist, interventionist ideas have divided the movement into two opposing camps, bitterly hostile towards one another.

It goes without saying that an organisation which encourages the cult of the leader cannot also cultivate a sense of responsibility among its members which is absolutely fundamental to the integrity of a libertarian organisation. As we have more than once pointed out, it was fortunate that large numbers of workers in the CNT were not hypnotised by these supermen. Nevertheless, they were unable, in the deteriorating economic and political situation, to restore the revolutionary movement to its traditional position. Too many "leading militants" were occupying positions of power—and we must stress the fact that they were important positions.[6]

It would make a revealing study if a list were compiled of the members of the CNT-FAI who during those years accepted positions of power in the reconstituted state and government, and if alongside each flame were indicated the present political affiliation or point of view of the persons concerned. We believe that such a

---

5   In 1938, for instance, David Antona, who was regional secretary of the CNT of the Centre, was appointed governor of the province of Ciudad Libre (formerly Ciudad Real), and one reads of the guerrilla fighter, Jover, chief of the 28th Division in the reorganised "Popular Army," being embraced by Premier Negrín "in front of the acclaiming soldiers" and promoted to the rank of lieutenant colonel.

6   According to José Peirats, *La CNT en la Revolución Española*, vol. 3 (Toulouse: Ediciones CNT, 1953), 319, by 1938, the libertarian movement was divided into two main tendencies: "that represented by the National Committee of the CNT was entirely fatalistic; that of the Peninsular Committee of the FAI represented a tardy reaction against that fatalism." But between these two positions was a third tendency, which "was not circumstantialist but permanent, in favour of a far-reaching rectification of tactics and principles, and represented by Horacio Prieto. This tendency would have converted the FAI into a political party with the task of representing the libertarian movement in the government and in the organisms of the state, as well as participating in electoral campaigns. This was the harvest from all the sowings of ideological compromises and weaknesses which had affected the CNT as well as the FAI from July 19 [1936]."

document would provide one of the most important lessons to be learned from the social upheaval that took place during 1936–1939. It would certainly be a warning to future revolutionary movements and a further confirmation of the validity of anarchist theory on the corrupting effect of authority and power.

CHAPTER XX
THE RANK AND FILE'S RESPONSIBILITY

One of the criticisms levelled at the original English edition of the present work by both sympathetic and hostile readers was that we had over-emphasised the faults of the leaders of the CNT-FAI and at the same time had, to use one writer's words, been "over-charitable" to the rank-and-file members of the revolutionary organisations.[1] We believe their criticisms to be valid, though we also believe that we have erred in the right direction! And for the same reasons that in Orwell's *Animal Farm*, though Boxer, the hard-working, willing horse was, from the point of view of cold historical analysis, a simple, credulous creature, he emerges from that "revolution" the most human (or whatever the equivalent is in animal terms) and

---

[1] George Woodcock, in a long and important review of *Lessons of the Spanish Revolution*, titled "The Spanish Revolution Examined," in the American journal *Resistance* 9, no. 4 (February 1954). It should be added that the review and the book itself were subjected to a vulgar attack by J. García Pradas in a series of articles published in the collaborationist journal from Toulouse *España Libre* nos. 346–353 (July–September 1954), with the significant title "Respecto a la CNT" (Respect for the CNT!). To our mind these articles carry little weight since they studiously avoid our documentation and attack our conclusions with opinions which are based on the unquestioning acceptance of the "circumstantialist" policy of the CNT and the rejection of anarchist principles as the only *means* by which anarchists can achieve, or try to achieve, their ends. They are worth reading, however, as "textbook" illustrations of many of the criticisms we have made of the authoritarian, nationalistic mentality and demagogic approach of a large number of militants of the CNT.

unforgettable character; the one who, in spite of the pigs of Animal Farm, remains the burning hope for the future.

If one pauses to ask oneself: what aspect of the struggle in Spain justifies the application of the word "revolution," one is struck by the fact that it was only at the level of the anonymous men and women, in the fields and factories and in the public services, in the villages and among the militiamen of the first days, that one had real glimpses of a thoroughgoing, revolutionary change in the social and economic structure of Spain. Politically, by which we mean at the governmental level at which the revolutionary leaders operated, all the concepts of state and government remained unchallenged. (Parliament, it is true, though it had not been dissolved, did not function. But it could be equally argued that the destitution of Parliament without the abolition of government is, if anything, a very big step towards dictatorship; certainly not a revolutionary step in the progressive sense.) The illusion was cherished, however, that the nature of government could be changed for the good. In the words of Federica Montseny, the "direct intervention" of the CNT in the central government "was considered by us as the most far reaching revolution that has been made in the political and economic fields."

We have already described these as outworn reformist ideas, including the one which believes that the presence of CNT ministers in a government gives the workers "direct representation" in the economic and political destinies of the country.

We can understand—without however sharing the view—that the revolutionary workers might consider that so long as they could get on with their social revolution at the point of production, the schemings and the job-hunting among the politicians and their own leaders were no concern of theirs. And this view was encouraged by the fact that in the early months of the struggle the directives and decrees emanating from the government, not to mention the patriotic exhortations of the committees of the CNT-FAI, were generally ignored. Even when the government had re-established its authority it is clear from their acts of resistance that the workers and peasants had not been converted to the idea that the social revolution could be achieved through government, and in spite of declarations such as that of Montseny in which she "conceded to [the state] a little credit and confidence, in order to achieve a revolution from above."

The rank and file saw—or "instinctively felt"—more clearly than the leaders, and we have no doubt in our mind that the action of the workers in raising the barricades in Barcelona in May 1937 was a last desperate attempt to save the revolution from strangulation by the Jacobins and the reactionary politicians who had insinuated themselves once more into positions of power. Barcelona in May 1937 was to the Spanish Revolution what Kronstadt, sixteen years earlier, had been to the Russian Revolution.[2]

There were at least three ways in which the revolutionary movement could express its disapproval of the counter-revolutionary actions of the government and of the various committees of the CNT-FAI:

(1) *By recalling and replacing the members of the committees.* As far as we know this was not done at any time during the struggle, but we lack documentation to indicate that at any time the workers in their syndicates or those in the armed forces were ever in a position to express in a deliberative manner either their approval or disapproval of the activities of the committees.[3]

---

2   See Voline, *The Unknown Revolution: 1917–1921* (London: Freedom Press, 1955 [Oakland: PM Press, 2019]).

3   So many of the documents on which one has to rely for information concerning the various plenums held during the period are simply the official summaries published by the confederal press from which were eliminated any controversial or acrimonious discussions. For the public the impression had to be created of unanimity in the ranks of the CNT. That everything did not flow so smoothly can be gathered, for instance, from José Peirats's account of the plenum of October 1938, for which he had not only the official accounts published in *Solidaridad Obrera* but also the unpublished notes of a member of the FAI who was present; *La CNT en la Revolución Española*, vol. 3 (Toulouse: Ediciones CNT, 1953). For the observer outside the Spanish movement the procedure for the nomination of members of the National and Regional Committees, of the newly created subcommittees, the coordination committees, and the executive

(2) *Through discussion in the confederal press.* As we have shown in earlier chapters the press was being more and more controlled by the committees, who apart from their obsession to make the public believe that the organisation was "united," in making it speak with one voice—that of the "responsible committees," it is unlikely that they would allow the press to be used for criticism of their activities. If one is to sustain the myth of the inspired leadership no one must be allowed to declare that it has feet of clay!

(3) *By direct resistance to orders and decrees.* Here there is considerable evidence of disapproval. Generally speaking, however, resistance was not coordinated (except of course in the early weeks), and the workers found themselves faced with a fait accompli to which they succumbed not because they were convinced but, in part, through a misguided loyalty to the "anti-fascist" struggle and by an awareness that the government had by then the necessary strength to crush the resistance as well as to enjoy the support of the leaders of the CNT.

To illustrate the resistance to government encroachment on the workers' revolutionary achievements, as well as of the duplicity of the CNT leaders, we will consider two incidents in detail, one which occurred after the May Days of 1937, the other before.

---

committee (in Catalonia) is obscure. (To judge from the conversations we have had with Spanish syndicalists it seems obscure to them too.) It is surely time that some authoritative light was shed on these important organisational matters. And at the same time other aspects of the same questions could be examined, such as: How directly represented were the rank-and-file members at the plenums, and what were the powers of the delegates? It would also be of interest to know how many of the delegates at the national plenum of October 1938 held government and municipal posts or how many at the Enlarged National Economic Plenum in January 1938 held managerial or supervisory jobs. Only when a clearer picture of the organisational functioning of the CNT in that period is available will it be possible to judge the responsibility of the rank and file and, equally important, to test the validity of the theoretical arguments put forward by the advocates of anarcho-syndicalism.

The first was in Catalonia, where after the defeat of the Franco uprising most of the public services, including public entertainments, were taken over by the workers. For some reason or other this service remained outside the collectivisation decree of October 1936.[4] But on February 1, 1938, an announcement was made by the department for economy of the Generalitat that the industry was being taken over by the Controlling Commission of Public Entertainments in Catalonia, composed of three nominees of the Generalitat and the undersecretary of the department. One might imagine that the three nominees, all belonging to the CNT, had been appointed by the syndicates concerned. Not at all. In this particular case we have the advantage of firsthand testimony from an active member of the industry affected by the order.[5]

It is clear from Marcos Alcón's account that all kinds of pressures were brought to bear by the Regional Committee which succeeded only in dividing the workers. Failing to convince them, even by the bait of three posts in the government department that was to take over, the next step was to publish the intervention decree and face them with the fait accompli. To this they replied with the general strike of the industry. More parleys with the Regional Committee, which, as a last resort, referred the matter to the recently formed *executive* committee (whose president was no other than García Oliver), who replied that "we had to accept." The struggle was ended, but one can safely assume that the conclusions drawn by the rank-and-file members were that the Regional and executive committees were working for the Generalitat and not for them.

The second case we submit to the reader refers to the incidents in the working-class centre of Vinalesa which resulted in a number of peasants being killed by the government forces. Briefly, the facts are these. Early in 1937, a decree was issued by the Ministry of Commerce taking over all transactions connected with the export of goods and produce (which many of the collectives had been

---

4   See chapter X.
5   Marcos Alcón, "Datos para la historia," *Cultura Proletaria* (New York), May 22, 1943.

carrying out themselves). Among other things this meant that the government would control and dispose of the foreign currency received in payment for these exports. The decree was naturally viewed with suspicion by the collectives and resisted. The government replied by sending armed guards to Vinalesa. Again they were resisted. But for the intervention "of the confederal (CNT) ministers and committees it would have had the gravest repercussions in all the region including the fronts."[6]

At the regional plenum of the peasant syndicates of the Levante, held in Valencia in March of that year, the Vinalesa incident was discussed by the delegates who also protested against the action by the government and called for the liberation of the CNT members of Torres de Cuarte.

The National Committee suggested that the incidents could possibly be attributed to individuals "planted" in the syndicates and in the country to foment unpleasant incidents. It appealed to everybody to avoid encouraging such situations, which, coupled to the mental blindness of those in authority, could result in wholesale massacres. It put forward its explanation of the incidents, which in its opinion had been of help to the enemy. It added that nobody had taken the trouble to inform the Regional and National Committees beforehand of what was about to happen nor of a mobilization which was carried out without its knowledge or authorization. The Committee had taken up the question of those who had been arrested and had been assured that they would not be subjected to any injustice. Furthermore, it had taken steps to demand other assurances to prevent similar occurrences arising. It appealed to everybody to do absolutely nothing without first consulting the Committees "that have to shoulder the responsibility for what happens."

The National Committee's statement that "nobody took the trouble to advise the Committee of the CNT beforehand" is of particular interest because *the minister of commerce at that time was a member of the CNT, Juan López*! He issued the decree, presumably

---

6   José Peirats, *La CNT en la Revolución Española*, vol. 2 (Toulouse: Ediciones CNT, 1952), 78.

without consulting the workers in the collectives, for, when the government sought to implement it, they resisted. And whichever government department was responsible for the use of armed force against the peasants of Vinalesa, the minister of commerce, as such, and a member of the government, shared in the responsibility for that action.

From the two examples we have discussed it is quite clear that the revolutionary workers had their share of responsibility for allowing the government to re-establish its cadres and its authority and for permitting the growth of a leadership within their own organisation. They paid dearly for their political ignorance and good faith. But one cannot equate their responsibility with that of revolutionaries with long years of experience of struggle and even suffering, who not only did not warn the workers of the dangers of executive power but were the very people to use it, advocate it, and bask in the lime- light of public notoriety.

CHAPTER XXI
SOME CONCLUSIONS

We embarked on this brief study of the Spanish Revolution with a feeling of humility, and now in attempting to draw our conclusions we do not propose to assume the role of the politico-military strategist whose blueprint would have ensured victory. We leave this task to whoever may have such presumptions. That we have expressed our indignation at those men who in Spain usurped their functions as representatives in order to become the directors of the destinies of their fellow-beings is, we trust, sufficient proof that in our criticisms we do not intend to put ourselves in a position similar to theirs. But what happened in Spain—and in particular the role played by those who declared that they were acting in the name of anarchism, libertarian communism, and the social revolution—is of profound importance internationally to all who call themselves anarchists and revolutionaries.

But we should first express our point of view that the lessons of the Spanish experience have no bearing on the *validity* of anarchism as a philosophy of life. Anarchists and libertarians are seeking a form of society in which all men and women will be free; free to live the kind of life in which they will find fulfilment and a sense of purpose. It does not imply either uniformity and conformity or the guarantee of eternal happiness. It is based not on a scientific formula but on our emotions, our feelings for the kind of life that we should like to lead. All that science does for us is to confirm that fundamentally the great majority of our fellow beings desire and need similar surroundings of freedom in which to develop. If science, on the other hand, indicated the contrary view, it would not destroy the *validity* of our aspirations. All it would indicate is that the difficulties in the way of attaining the anarchist society would be even greater than they are at present. And this is not an insurmountable obstacle, unless one believes in some kind of slavery of the mind to scientific infallibility.

The importance, therefore, that a critical study of the Spanish Revolution has for anarchists is not of the *objectives* of anarchism but on the *means* by which it is hoped to achieve them. It raises also the ever-recurring problem of the role of anarchists in situations, albeit revolutionary, in which it is clear that the solution cannot be an anarchist one.

It is generally agreed among the Spanish anarchists (FAI) and syndicalists (CNT) that the situation created by the militarists' uprising and the workers' reaction to it in the first days could not be successfully resolved by the CNT-FAI and their sympathisers without the collaboration of other elements.

For the sake of interpreting as accurately as possible their point of view, we must add that many militants have since declared that they had underestimated the extent of the uprising, and because of this much valuable time was lost. Had the initial successes been followed up, they argue, by organising armed columns immediately, Franco would not have had time to reorganise *his* forces, and the uprising would have been destroyed before the bulk of his war potential in Morocco could have been put into the field. It is also the general opinion that had agreement with the UGT been reached from the beginning it would have been unnecessary to make any compromises to the politicians.

Actually, as we have seen, there were many difficulties of a political nature on both sides which prevented this union of the two organisations, and, in the circumstances, for the leadership of the CNT, the problem became one of choosing between the lesser and greater evils: either the victory over Franco through a moderate Popular Front government or a victory for Franco with all that this might entail. There can be no doubt that their minds had been made up in the first days of the struggle when the revolutionary action of the workers, such as the expropriation and reorganisation of the essential public services under workers' control, was in its early stages. As a result, far from ensuring that the revolution should be as far-reaching as the workers were able to lead it, their decision to recognise the state and the authority of democratic government created confusion in the workers' ranks, and instead of seeking to destroy bourgeois institution through the creation of revolutionary organisms, they found themselves occupying posts in those very institutions which all their experience had taught them should be destroyed as the first step in any thoroughgoing revolution. As one observer rightly pointed out in the early months of the struggle, "An old rule about revolutions was once more confirmed; a revolution must either be carried through to the end, or had better not start at all."[1]

Having decided against an attempt to destroy the bourgeois state, single-handed if necessary, the CNT-FAI accepted the lesser evil; that anything was preferable to Franco, that every compromise should be made in the name of unity and for victory over Franco, justifying this position on the grounds that defeat would also mean the defeat of all the revolutionary gains made by the workers.[2]

---

1   Franz Borkenau, *The Spanish Cockpit* (London: Faber and Faber, 1937).

2   A phrase used by Durruti, the anarchist guerrilla leader who was killed in Madrid in November 1936: *Renunciamos a todo menos a la vitoria* (Let us give up everything except victory) was extensively and, in our opinion, dishonestly used by the collaborationists in the CNT-FAI as an indication that even the great Durruti was in favour of abandoning the revolutionary objectives of the anarchists in favour of a victory at all costs over Franco. We have nowhere seen in Spanish sources the text of an interview Durruti gave to a journalist, Pierre Van Paassen, and published in the *Toronto Star* in September 1936. In it Durruti clearly and uncompromisingly indicates what the role of the anarchists should be, refusing to be diverted from anarchist principles by considerations of expediency.

"For us it is a question of crushing fascism once and for all. Yes, and in spite of government.

"No government in the world fights fascism to the death. When the bourgeoisie sees power slipping from its grasp, it has recourse to fascism to maintain itself. The liberal government of Spain could have rendered the fascist elements powerless long ago. Instead it temporised and compromised and dallied. Even now at this moment, there are men in this government who want to go easy with

On the other hand, the governments of Barcelona and Madrid (the latter, it should be remembered, *only after attempts at a compromise with Franco had failed*) also realised that they could not win the war against Franco without the support of the CNT-FAI and in a desperate effort to stave off defeat were prepared to make considerable concessions to the revolutionary workers, which they would obviously withdraw once they felt that the immediate danger of Franco had passed and the shattered apparatus of government was again strong enough to impose obedience.

The questions which a revolutionary organisation in such a situation has to seek to answer are:

(1) How best can the common cause (i.e., the struggle against Franco) be prosecuted?

---

the rebels. You can never tell, you know—he laughed—the present government might yet need these rebellious forces to crush the workers' movement . . .

"We know what we want. To us it means nothing that there is a Soviet Union somewhere in the world, for the sake of whose peace and tranquility the workers of Germany and China were sacrificed to fascist barbarism by Stalin. We want the revolution here in Spain, right now, not maybe after the next European war. We are giving Hitler and Mussolini far more worry to-day with our revolution than the whole Red Army of Russia. We are setting an example to the German and Italian working-class how to deal with fascism.

"I do not expect any help for a libertarian revolution from any government in the world. Maybe the conflicting interests in the various imperialisms might have some influence in our struggle. That is quite possible. Franco is doing his best to drag Europe into the conflict. He will not hesitate to pitch Germany against us. But we expect no help, not even from our government in the last analysis."

"You will be sitting on top of a pile of ruins if you are victorious," said Van Paassen.

Durruti answered: "We have always lived in slums and holes in the wall. We will know how to accommodate ourselves for a time. For you must not forget, we can also build. It is we who built these palaces and cities here in Spain and in America and everywhere. We, the workers, can build others to take their place. And better ones. We are not in the least afraid of ruins. We are going to inherit the earth. There is not the slightest doubt about that. The bourgeoisie might blast and ruin its own world before it leaves the stage of history. We carry a new world, here in our hearts. That world is growing this minute."

Quoted in Felix Morrow, *Revolution and Counter-Revolution in Spain* (New York: Pathfinder Press, 1938).

(2) What measures must be taken to extend and consolidate the social revolution?

(3) How can the government be prevented from building up its power, which it will eventually use to further the counter-revolution?

The CNT-FAI sought to answer these questions by participation in the government and in all governmental institutions. Their arguments can, we believe, be summarised as follows:

(1) that the central government would be the rallying point for all the "anti-fascist" sectors; that it could organise a popular army with a unified command; that it controlled the finances and was therefore in a position to buy arms and raw materials needed for waging the struggle;

(2) that by having representatives of the CNT in the government it would be possible to *legalise* the revolutionary gains and influence the other ministers in the direction of further "revolutionary" legislation;

(3) that only by being in the government could the interests of the workers be safeguarded, and any attempts to undermine the revolution prevented by the CNT ministers in that government.

Anarchism and Syndicalism

In organisations with a mass following, the small anarchist minority can only retain its identity and exert a revolutionary influence by maintaining a position of intransigence. By that we do not mean that they should oppose those actions the workers may take to improve their economic situation and working conditions. On the contrary, anarchists should be the first to encourage such activity, recognising nevertheless that such activity is essentially reformist and cannot itself result in the social revolution which aims at the abolition of all classes and privileges.

Indeed, as we have seen in the trade unions, negotiations for wage increases, because of the complexities of the whole economic set-up and the serious repercussions wage increases in one industry can have on other industries and on the cost of living generally, are in fact no longer struggles between workers and employers. They are matters determined at government level, by tribunals in which eminent legal minds interpret agreements in relation to cost-of-living indices and other statistics and whose decisions are binding on workers and employers alike. We have perhaps put the extreme case, but it represents a definite trend particularly in the highly industrialised countries. The mass organisation, instead of being a weapon of struggle against economic injustice and privilege becomes a vast prison in which the individual loses his identity, a helpless cog in the capitalist machine of production and cost-of-living statistics.

But it seems to us that such dangers are present even in a mass syndicalist organisation (and in spite of the revolutionary spirit that might have guided its founders both in framing its aims and principles and in the safeguards written into its constitution to prevent the growth of an internal bureaucracy) *the moment such an organisation opens its doors to all workers.*[3] Herein, surely, lies the dilemma: for a workers' organisation to be successful in its immediate role of improving the conditions of its members, it must speak with one voice—that is, it must aim at having a mass membership. But demanding that workers who join must first subscribe to the ideological objectives of the organisation means that they must be subjected to some political test. Such tests may ensure the political homogeneity of the organisation but will also condemn it to being without a mass following. In fact, such organisations as the CNT, though their declared objectives were *comunismo libertario,* admitted all workers, irrespective of their political sympathies or

---

3   In the struggle for leadership in the CNT during the years immediately preceding the Rivera dictatorship, the anarchists charged Seguí and his syndicalist friends with showing a general tendency to reformism and of being too ready to accept mediation *by the state* in labour disputes. Yet Seguí is generally considered by Spanish anarchists as one of the outstanding personalities in the history of the Spanish revolutionary movement.

their lack of any. Many workers joined the CNT simply because it energetically championed their interests in the day-to-day struggle; others perhaps because in their particular locality the CNT was numerically stronger than the UGT. And it must be added in this connection—and also because it helps to explain in part how the committees succeeded in gaining more and more power to direct the policies of the CNT—that during the struggle against Franco, membership of the two workers' organisations more than doubled as a result of all workers being obliged to join one or the other of these organisations.

Some revolutionaries suggest that a solution to this dilemma is the creation of an ideologically pure revolutionary syndicalist organisation whose members are also members of the mass organisation. But such an organisation would be syndicalist in its structure but a revolutionary party in fact and, as has been proved in practice, is doomed to failure.

Because of the views we have expressed, anarchists are frequently referred to as "individualists," by which term is meant that they are opposed to organisation and the discipline that membership of an organisation involves. To a certain extent, anarchists are themselves responsible for this confusion. Within the anarchist movement there are those who believe that our activities should be concentrated on the creation of a revolutionary syndicalist—or more accurately, an *anarchosyndicalist* organisation—to counteract the reformism of the trade unions. Others instead believe that our energies should be used to spread anarchist ideas among our fellow workers and in every direction open to us, at the same time participating in the workers' struggle wherever we can, without losing our identity as anarchists, since our objective is to infuse these workers with revolutionary ideas. Because these anarchists do not believe that the creation of an anarcho- syndicalist organisation is an essential first step in building up a conscious and militant revolutionary movement, the tendency among those who do is to refer to them as "anti-organisers" and even "individualists."

We must assume, for space reasons, that the reader is familiar with the tenets of anarcho-syndicalism. To our mind the differences existing between anarchists and anarcho-syndicalists are not ideological, but rather differences of appreciation.

To be consistent, the anarcho-syndicalist must, we believe, hold the view that the reason why the workers are not revolutionary is that the trade unions are reformist and reactionary; and that their structure prevents control from below and openly encourages the emergence of a bureaucracy which takes over all initiative into its own hands, etc. This seems to us a mistaken view. It assumes that the worker, by definition, must be revolutionary, instead of recognising that he is as much the product (and the victim) of the *society* he lives in as we all are, more or less. And trade unions, just like other self-contained concentrations of human beings, such as prisons, armies, and hospitals, are small-scale copies of existing society with its qualities, as well as its faults.

In other words, the trade unions are what they are because the workers are what they are and not vice versa. And for this reason, those anarchists who are less interested in the revolutionary workers' organisation consider the problem of the *organisation* as secondary to that of the *individual*; that there is today no shortage of people able to absorb themselves in the day-to-day negotiations between worker and employer, but there are only too few to point out the futility of such action as an end in itself. And we have no fears that when sufficient workers have become revolutionaries they will, if they think it necessary, build up their own organisations. This is quite different from creating the revolutionary organisation first and then looking for the revolutionaries (in the reformist trade unions in which most workers are to be found) afterwards.

We have introduced this long parenthesis on the relation between anarchists and syndicalists, because it has such an important bearing on the role of the revolutionary—and in particular the anarchist—movement in Spain, both before and during the struggle against Franco.

From its foundation in 1910, the CNT was rarely free from internal struggles between the reformist or revisionist elements and the anarchists whose specific task was to maintain the anarchist spirit with which the organisation had been infused by its founders.

These struggles were in part reflections of world events (such as the war of 1914–1918, in which some were pro-Allies, others neutral, or the Russian Revolution, which resulted in defections among prominent members, including Nin and Maurín, who were to become the founders of the Spanish Communist Party—and later its victims).

They were also exacerbated by the fact that so often these struggles were also clashes between would-be leaders of the organisation. Men such as Seguí, Pestaña, Peiró played dominating parts— one might even say *personal* roles—in the development of the CNT, and though eventually the revolutionary position prevailed in the manifestos and resolutions of the organisation, in action the reformist, revisionist tendency continually manifested itself either by the actions of individuals who then presented the organisation with the fait accompli (Seguí by his pact with the UGT, carried out behind the backs of the members of the CNT; Nin by taking it upon himself to affiliate the CNT to the Third International) or by behind-the-scenes negotiations with the politicians: "I have asked to speak," said Juan Peiró at the CNT congress held after the proclamation of the Republic in 1931, "in order to affirm that from the year 1923 not a single National Committee nor a single Regional Committee has ceased to be in contact with the political elements," not—he added—in order to establish the Republic but to get rid of the dictatorship of Primo de Rivera. And during the period 1936–1939 this political activity reached its climax with actual participation of the CNT in the government with all its consequences. And there are no signs that the revisionism of the CNT ended with the defeat. The position of the MLE (the Spanish Libertarian Movement) in Spain today (1957) is not clear; in exile, it is divided into two camps, with a majority calling for a return to the revolutionary principles of the CNT and a minority in favour of a continuation, even an extension, of the collaborationist policy.

What has been the role of the anarchists in these internal struggles of the CNT? At a national anarchist conference held in Barcelona in the winter of 1918, with the specific purpose of discussing what should be the relation of the anarchists to the syndicalist organisation, it was agreed that though a mass movement of workers such as the CNT could not be described as anarchist, "it must be impregnated as much as possible with the libertarian or anarchist spirit *and be led and directed by them.*"[4] In 1922, at a congress of anarchist groups held in Madrid, it was resolved

> that all anarchists should enrol in the CNT and treat it *as their special field of action.* Up to that time many had held aloof from the syndicalist organisation, which seemed to them to represent a narrowing conception of anarchism as a philosophy for all men; it was now urgent that they should bring their full influence to bear upon it if they did not wish to see it captured by the Bolshevists, who were practising their usual infiltration tactics. (emphasis added)[5]

The policy of making the CNT "their specific field of action" could only result in the FAI losing its anarchist identity and independence, the more so when so many of the leaders of the CNT were also leading members of the FAI.[6] The outcome of this dual role was that by the end of 1936 the FAI had ceased to function as a specifically anarchist organisation, having thrown overboard all its principles if only by the participation of some of its members in the governments of Catalonia and Madrid as representatives of the CNT (Santillán, Herrera, Oliver, Montseny, etc.), and finally the fusion of the FAI, the FIJL (Libertarian Youth Federation), and the CNT into one organisation: the MLE (Movimiento Libertario Español—the Spanish Libertarian Movement).

Thirty years earlier, Malatesta, with that profound understanding of his fellow men which inspired all his writings, had clearly

---

4   Gerald Brenan, *The Spanish Labyrinth* (London: Cambridge University Press, 1943).

5   See A. Ildefonso Gonzáles, on *Il Movimento Libertario Spagnuolo* (The Spanish Libertarian Movement) published in the anarchist monthly *Volontà* (Naples) 9, nos. 6–9, (June–September 1952), particularly on the "Tendenze nella FAI." He points out among other things that "some old militants believe that the period before the constitution of the FAI was more brilliant for Spanish anarchism, from the point of view of the strictest observance of anarchist principles."

6   *Pensiero e Volontà* (Rome), April 16, 1925.

seen the effects of the fusion of the anarchist movement with the syndicalist organisation when he wrote:

> Every fusion or confusion between the anarchist movement and the trade union movement ends either in rendering the latter unable to carry out its specific task or by weakening, distorting, or extinguishing the anarchist spirit.

Anarchism and Violence

We have all along considered that it was outside the scope of this study to engage in an analysis of the military aspects of the struggle in Spain, quite apart from the fact that such a subject is not within the competence of the present writer. But it would be shirking the responsibilities we have assumed were we not to attempt to deal with certain questions of principle arising from the development of the armed struggle.

Violence, contrary to popular belief, is not part of the anarchist philosophy. It has repeatedly been pointed out by anarchist thinkers that the revolution can neither be won nor the anarchist society established and maintained by armed violence. Recourse to violence, then, is an indication of weakness not of strength, and the revolution with the greatest possibilities of a successful outcome will undoubtedly be the one in which there is no violence, or in which violence is reduced to a minimum, for such a revolution would indicate the near unanimity of the population in the objectives of the revolution.

Unless anarchists declare that the only revolution or insurrection that will meet with their support is the one that will usher in the libertarian society, they must face the situation created by those uprisings, the objectives of which represent only a step towards the desired society, and declare what their position in such struggles will be. Generally speaking, their position has always been clear; that every manifestation of the people for their emancipation should be supported by anarchists as anarchists. That is to say, ready at all times to make concessions to the common cause but without, in so doing, losing their identity. We believe that such a position requires that anarchists should fearlessly expose what they believe to be the mistakes of a revolution and, at the same time, by retaining their freedom of action be prepared to withdraw their co-operation once they believe that the objectives of the struggle have been sacrificed to expediency.

The use of violence has been justified both as a principle and as a means to an end; hardly ever, however, by anarchists. At the most, anarchists have justified its use as a revolutionary necessity or *tactic*. The misunderstanding is in part the result of confusion in terms for which the anarchists themselves are responsible. We refer, of course, to those who call themselves pacifist anarchists, or non-violent anarchists, and who thereby imply that those not included in these categories must be violent anarchists! The fallacy, to our minds, is that of making non-violence a principle, when in fact it is no more than a tactic. Furthermore, the "non-violent" advocates fail to make a distinction between violence which is used as a means for imposing the will of a group or class and that violence which is purely defensive.

In Spain the attempt to seize power by force was made by Franco and his military and Phalangist friends. To this end they had a carefully prepared plan to occupy all the important cities of Spain. What should the people have done on the July 19? In the opinion of that eminent advocate of non-violent methods Bart de Ligt, the best way to "fight" Franco would have been for the Spanish people to allow him to occupy the whole country "temporarily" and then to have "let loose a great movement of non-violent resistance (boycott, non-co-operation, and so on) against him." He continues:

> But our tactics also include, and far more than modern military tactics do, an effective international collaboration. We are no party to the deceitful idea of non-intervention; wherever humanity is threatened or attacked, all men and women of good-will must intervene in defence. In this case also, from the very beginning, a parallel movement of non-co-operation

from the outside should have been organised to support that inside, in an endeavour to prevent Franco and his friends from getting the materials for war, or at least to keep these down to the minimum.

That the advocates of non-violence cannot be dogmatic is shown by what follows:

And even in the situation as it is at present, all sincere war resisters should have intervened systematically on behalf of the Spanish people and especially on behalf of the libertarian revolution, by fighting Franco with the methods indicated above . . . whatever the methods used by the Spanish people to defend itself, it is in a legitimate state of defence, and this is truer still of those revolutionaries who—during the Civil War—are striving to bring about the social revolution.

"Once again the international working-class movement has neglected one of the noblest of its historic tasks by falling in with the deceitful measures of Imperialist Governments, either self-styled democracies or actually Fascist countries, and abandoning those who fought in Spain with unequalled heroism for the emancipation of the working-class and for social justice. If it had intervened in time, the masses of Spain would still have been able to dispose of the military clique in 1936 and to concentrate on social reconstruction. If it had done so, *violence would have been kept down to a minimum and the possibility of a real revolution would have been so great as to change the face of the world.*" (emphasis added)

Earlier in his analysis of Spain, Bart de Ligt pointed out that

Considering the ideological traditions and the social, political and moral conditions under which this civil war broke out in July 1936, *the Spanish anti-militarists could do nothing else than resort to arms before the military invaders.* But by so doing they found themselves obliged to use the same weapons as their enemies. They had to engage in a devastating war which, even in the event of victory, must bring about conditions both objective and subjective as unfavourable as could be to the realisation of the social revolution. If we look at things closely we see here again a kind of dictatorship; if men wish to defend themselves against a violent invader, it is the invader who dictates to the defender what methods of combat he shall use. On the other hand, if the defender can rise immediately above violence, he is free to use his own, and really humane methods.

It goes without saying that we would rather see victory go, if only partially, to those who fight for justice, peace and freedom, even with gun in hand, than to those who can only prolong injustice, slavery and war. But we must admit that the Spanish people, in its fight against Fascism, has chosen the most costly and ineffective method it could, and that it did neglect to get rid of the military clique at the proper time, which is to say, long before the Civil War broke out.[7]

Any Spanish reader of the above must be permitted to shake his head and sigh at the naivety displayed in this presentation of the non-violent case. *If* the international proletariat had supported the Spanish workers, *if* the military clique had been sacked, and *if* a thousand and one other conditions had been fulfilled . . . who knows *what* might have happened in Spain! But let us not forget the all-important sentence in what we have quoted above. If all these *ifs* had been realised, Bart de Ligt admits that "*Violence would have been kept down to a minimum and the possibility of a real revolution would have been so great as to change the face of world.*" In other words, an admission that under certain conditions violence need not degenerate, a position which many advocates of non-violence dogmatically sweep aside as untenable.

---

7   Bart de Ligt, *The Conquest of Violence* (London: George Routledge and Sons, 1937).

It is when the use of violence is prolonged and the armed struggle ceases to be related to its objectives that we find ourselves on common ground with the self-styled non-violence anarchists, and consider that anarchists, in justice to themselves and to their fellow workers, must question the validity of the prolongation of the armed struggle. In Spain that situation arose after a few months. The delays in following up the initial successes and the failure to prevent the establishment of a bridgehead from Morocco permitted Franco to reorganise and reinforce his army and to launch his large-scale offensive from the south and threaten Madrid with encirclement. Faced with this situation, the leaders of the CNT-FAI capitulated to the Popular Front point of view for militarization. The consequences of this capitulation have been dealt with at some length in the course of this study. Could the CNT-FAI have acted otherwise? That is a question which perhaps one day the Spanish revolutionaries will be prepared to face and answer.

We will limit ourselves to the expression of an opinion in general terms. We believe that anarchists can only participate in those struggles which are the expression of a people's will to freedom and justice. But when such struggles should be organised and conducted with the same ruthlessness as that of the enemy, with armies of conscripts schooled in blind obedience to leaders; by the militarization of the rearguard and censorship of the press and of opinion; when secret prisons are connived at, and to express criticisms is considered High Treason (as in the trial of the POUM leaders) . . . before that stage has been reached, anarchists who are not afraid of unpopularity or the "judgment of history" should declare their inability to co-operate and conduct their struggles against both regimes in whatever way they consider consistent with their aspirations and their principles.

Means and Ends

The distinction between the libertarian and authoritarian revolutionary movements in their struggle to establish the free society is the means which each proposes should be used to this end. The libertarian maintains that the initiative must come from below, that the free society must be the result of the will to freedom of a large section of the population. The authoritarian, on the other hand, believes that the will to freedom can only emerge once the existing economic and political system has been replaced by a dictatorship of the proletariat which, as the awareness and sense of responsibility of the people grows, will wither away and the free society emerge.

There can be no common ground between such approaches. For the authoritarian argues that the libertarian approach is noble but "utopian" and doomed to failure from the start, while the libertarian argues, on the evidence of history, that the authoritarian *methods* will simply replace one coercive state by another, equally despotic and remote from the people, and which will no more "wither away" than its capitalist predecessor. The free society can only grow from the free association of free men (that is men whose minds are free from prejudices and who ardently believe in freedom for others as well as themselves).

In the course of preparing this study one of the conclusions we have come to is that *only a small section of the Spanish revolutionary movement was in fact libertarian,* a view we are not alone in holding. The position was put, succinctly and not without sadness, we think, by an old militant writing under the pen name of "Fabio" in the anarchist review *Tiempos Nuevos* (April 1945). He pointed out that

> Had collaboration been considered a mistake, the matter would not be serious. Errors can be corrected. By not collaborating any more, the question would be settled. What collaboration revealed has no possible solution. It is what a very few of us had suspected for some time: that there were a few, not many, hundred anarchists in Spain.

Furthermore, it would seem that the cult of action had blinded a very large number of seasoned militants to the disastrous consequences of action becoming an end in itself. They were themselves victims of the illusions which they had so often criticised in the socialists, of believing that power was only evil when in the "wrong hands" and for a "wrong cause," and not that "power tends to corrupt, and absolute power corrupts absolutely," anarchists and syndicalists included.

Thus, they were prepared to use the weapon of war, which they had as recently as May 1936 so outspokenly denounced, both in the name of the social revolution and as a means of defeating "fascism." Indeed, all the policies of the CNT-FAI after July 1936 were in direct contradiction with everything the organisation stood for as stated in its *Dictamenes aprobados por el congreso* (Opinions approved by the Congress) in Saragossa in May 1936.[8] It is worth examining some of the more outstanding of these.

In the *Dictamen sobre la situacion politica y militar*, which we have already quoted at the beginning of Chapter XVI, the organisation's position with regard to parliamentary democracy was made quite clear. Yet in spite of its recognition of the "bankruptcy" of the present social and political institutions, the CNT-FAI after July sought to re-establish it as the most effective means of dealing with the situation created by the military uprising. It believed that the armed resistance and the economy of the country could only be effectively organised from above. This position was expressed time and time again but never in a more barefaced way than in an obviously inspired front-page editorial published by *Solidaridad Obrera* (February 21, 1937) in which one reads:

> When Madrid found itself without government and was master of its own destiny, it organised its own defence. This shows that the governors were an obstacle. On all occasions when the people run their own lives, victory follows. When one takes on the responsibility of ruling and directing a people with such extraordinary ethical and moral backgrounds, those who direct the war and the revolution must

8   Which are reproduced in full in *El Congreso Confederal de Zaragoza* (Toulouse: Publicaciones CNT, 1955), 179–202.

not feel these endemic doubts and vacillations. There is no justification for it other than a lack of leadership.

When one lacks faith in the people one is governing one resigns. To govern without faith in the national future is tantamount to preparing for the defeat. In these supreme moments in the life of Spain, only those men who have absolute certainty in victory can direct its destiny. Men who combine courage with intelligence. The revolution has to be felt both in the mind and in the heart. Optimism and ability are indispensable qualities in overcoming the enormous difficulties opposed to victory. This must be realised at all costs. Our lamented Durruti used to say: "We renounce all except victory." This is our motto. To lead the people, it is indispensable that those in charge of governing the masses should embody this thought: "To be obeyed, the first thing one needs to have is authority." And the only way to obtain it is by ability. And this implies talent, a gift of leadership, faith in the destiny of the people one is governing; activity, foresight, anticipating events, and not being taken in tow by them.

The date of this extraordinary piece of double-think is important, for in February 1937 the CNT had four ministers in the government! But some readers may find it difficult to understand why, if "on every occasion when the people act on their own initiative, victory follows," the CNT should be so anxious to join the government or how a government which "has faith in the people" needs to "impose obedience."

Again, the *Dictamen sobre Alianzas Revolucionarias* (Opinions on Revolutionary Alliances), with a view to the "overthrow of the existing political and social regime," declares that

1. The UGT, on signing the Pact of Revolutionary Alliances, clearly recognises the breakdown of the system of political and parliamentary collaboration. As a logical consequence of this recognition, it will cease to offer any kind of *political*

and *parliamentary* collaboration with the regime at present in being.

2. In order that the social revolution shall be an effective reality, it is necessary to destroy completely the existing political and social regime that regulates the life of the country.

The apologists of the CNT-FAI's policies will probably argue that to defeat Franco it was necessary to change the organisation's tactics—the more so since the UGT had not accepted the Alliance.

To answer the last point first. From July until September 1936 neither of the workers' organisations were directly represented in the central government. During that period, what attempts were made to form a revolutionary alliance with the UGT? (And a revolutionary alliance does not mean a pact between the leaders which is what the CNT-UGT pact of 1938 was but, as the term implies, with the revolutionary sections of the UGT.)

The apologists' first argument on tactics ignores the significance of two paragraphs quoted above, in which reference is made to the recognition of "the breakdown of the system of political and parliamentary collaboration" and to the fact that the social revolution demands the complete destruction of "the political and social regime that regulates the life of the country." These are not declarations of tactics but statements of fact, of experience of the nature of political collaboration, embodied in a principle. The leaders of the CNT-FAI may have been right in believing that a social revolution and the defeat of Franco were not possible, but in our view *by the very same reasoning* they should have also come to the conclusion that *even less could be hoped for* from government and political collaboration.[9] The fact, of course, is that they chose to discount the

---

9   Juan López, ex-minister of commerce and a leading exponent of the anti-anarchist and governmentalist position in the CNT described the results of political collaboration at a meeting in Madrid of the newly created "National Committee of the Libertarian Movement" (of which he was general secretary) with exceptional frankness (which can be explained by the fact that the date was March 11, 1939, the place Madrid, the struggle in its last hours, and the CNT leaders

correctness of the anarchist analysis of the social problem on the grounds that the situation was so exceptional that it had not been foreseen and allowed for by anarchist theoreticians in their writings! This very characteristic Spanish presumption, which so often is a cover for ignorance, is restated in an issue of *Solidaridad Obrera* (February 2, 1938):

> We are very much aware that above all THE WAR DISPOSES, that is to say that we have to devote all our efforts to this terribly absorbing struggle *whose demands were certainly not foreseen in any doctrinal text.* (emphasis added)[10]

One of the consequences of this "circumstantialist" policy was that the slogans of the propagandists of the CNT-FAI soft-pedalled the social revolution and instead used its really powerful propaganda machine to play up "the anti-fascist" struggle and to seek to exploit crude nationalistic and patriotic sentiments. The use made by Franco first of the Moors and later of the Italians and Germans was all grist to their mill. This, and the insistence of the CNT-FAI

---

proposing to liquidate the Communists before they were liquidated themselves): "Our position vis-à-vis the Communist Party: we have more than sufficient justification to launch ourselves against them and to eliminate them, but it is equally true that we would have the same justification so far as the Socialists and Republicans are concerned. The policies of the Popular Front have been the cause of all our disasters and our present situation, viewed internationally as well." This confession was followed by López outlining the policy to adopt in the circumstances, and his words are worth repeating for they clearly reveal the *political* approach which dominated the thought and actions of so many leaders of the CNT, an approach, we would add, which threatens and is in direct contradiction with the tenets of an organisation *controlled from below*. López's words were: "In this sense we can make our criticism of the Communists, but intelligently, seeking the right moment. Our public position must be the following: 'We do not seek the extermination of the Communist Party nor of any party but, on the contrary, that they should all join the Popular Front and give their maximum efforts to the National Defence Council.' This said, however, the Communists will not have access to power."

10 In spite of the fact that the Spanish "problems" were foreseen in the writings of Errico Malatesta, Alexander Berkman, Emma Goldman, Camilo Bertoni, et alia!

leaders on militarization and the continuation of the armed strug-gle *at all costs,* seem to us further confirmation of our opinion that the Spanish revolutionary movement was more than tinged with nationalism (as well as of regionalism). The lengths to which it went is illustrated in a speech by Federica Montseny at a mass meeting in Madrid on August 31, 1936, that is, only a few weeks after the uprising when the revolutionary enthusiasm was strongest and the "military" situation still not in any way desperate. She said of Franco and his friends:

> with this enemy lacking dignity or a conscience, without a feeling of being Spaniards, because if they were Spaniards, if they were patriots, they would not have let loose on Spain the Regulars and the Moors to impose the civilisation of the fascists, not as a Christian civilisation, but as a Moorish civilisation, people we went to colonise for them now to come and colonise us, with religious principles and political ideas which they wish to impose on the minds of the Spanish people.[11]

Thus spoke a Spanish revolutionary, reputedly one of the most intelligent and gifted members of the organisation (and still treated as one of the outstanding figures by the majority-section of the CNT in France). In that one sentence are expressed nationalist, racialist, and imperialist sentiments. Did anyone protest at that meeting?

But to return to the "Opinions" of the Saragossa Congress of May 1936. On the subject of "Duties of the Individual for and to the Collectivity and the Concept of Distributive Justice" it is declared that

---

11 Reported in *Solidaridad* Obrera, September 2, 1936. Also reported by *Solidaridad Obrera* September 12, 1936, is a speech by J.P. Fábregas (prominent member of the CNT) in which he declared: "I have a blind faith in the destiny of our land, because I believe in the pure essence of the race, because I am quite certain that we symbolise right, justice, and freedom.

Libertarian communism has nothing in common with any system of coercion: a fact which implies the disappearance of the existing system of correctional justice and furthermore of the instruments of punishment (prisons, penitentiaries, etc.).

The view is expressed that "social determinism" is the principal cause of so-called crime, and that once the causes have been removed crime will cease to exist. Thus, the causes will disappear "when man's material needs will be satisfied as well as giving him the opportunity to receive a rational and humane education." And in concrete terms:

> For this reason, we hold the view that when the individual fails to carry out his duties both in the social order and in his role as a producer, it will be the task of the popular assemblies, in a spirit of conciliation, to seek the just solution to each individual case. Libertarian communism will therefore base its "correctional action" on medicine and on pedagogy, the only preventives to which modern science accords such a right. Where any person who is a victim of pathological symptoms threatens the harmony that must exist among the people, therapeutic pedagogy will be used to seek to cure the disorder and to arouse in him a moral feeling of social responsibility which an unhealthy heredity has denied him.

To what extent were these methods applied or even advocated by the revolutionary leaders in their dealings with their fellow humans or in their press? Again, we can hear the objections from the self-styled revolutionary "realists" that in the particular situation through which Spain was passing it was not possible to apply them—not even presumably in the period when the ministers of justice and public health were both members of the CNT! And that, in any case, deserters, "cowards," black-marketeers, supporters, and soldiers on Franco's side, the neutrals, the pacifists, the "slackers," the misfits, and the indifferent were not victims but "traitors who had to be taught a lesson"!

How can it be said that they are not the products of the society in which they live? In a society without violence there would be no cowards; without wars there would be no deserters; where there is no shortage of goods there is no black-market . . .

The fact of the matter is that for the revolutionaries as well as the government *all means were justified* to achieve the ends of mobilising the whole country on a war footing. And in those circumstances the assumption is that everybody should support the "cause." Those who do not are made to; those who resist or who do not react in the manner prescribed are hounded, humiliated, punished, or liquidated.

Thousands of members of the revolutionary movement held official positions in para-governmental institutions. They sat on the popular tribunals, as well as guarding and running the prisons. There is no evidence that they objected to the punishments and the hundreds of death sentences meted out by the tribunals. The CNT press provides a gloomy catalogue of death sentences pronounced and executed, without a murmur of disapproval. Any comments are in fact of approval. "May it serve as an example!" was *Solidaridad Obrera's* headline (September 16, 1936) to the announcement of the execution of a rebel leader in Minorca.

One could even say that the attitude of the CNT-FAI to legalised violence during the period 1936–1939 is such as to make their collaborationist deviation pale into insignificance. Violence for them was no longer a weapon of defence against armed attack by Franco's forces. It was the weapon of revenge (the execution of "fascist" prisoners), of intimidation (public execution of deserters), of deterrence ("The death penalty for the thief"—*Solidaridad Obrera,* September 17, 1936). We say without hesitation that an anarchist cannot justify the shooting of any person who is unarmed, *whatever his crime.* Even less justification is there in executing those who refuse to kill or who have helped "the enemy" with information, etc. We believe that the revolutionary struggle, while it lasts, can be adequately protected from fifth columnists by their detention—under the best possible conditions. "And are we to spare the lives of those men who have been responsible for the extermination of hundreds of our comrades?" we shall be asked by those Spanish workers who believed with the anarchist Gonzalo de Reparaz in the philosophy of "Terror against Terror"[12] or with Juan Peiró's "Revenge and a fierce revenge. An eye for an eye and a tooth for a tooth."[13] And there is only one answer: Yes!

There are many ways of changing society. One is by exterminating, morally or physically, all those who disagree with your way of thinking; the other is by first convincing sufficient people of the rightness of your ideas. Between these two extremes are a number of variations on the first theme, but, we submit, there can be no variations on the second. The self-styled "realists" among the libertarians believed that compromise is morally justified, since it produces results. If we are to judge the "results" by the history of the international socialist and communist movements or by the *Platformists*[14] in the international anarchist movement and the "circumstantialists" of the Spanish CNT-FAI, we can only draw one conclusion: that where the means are authoritarian, the ends, the real or dreamed of future society, is authoritarian and never results in the free society. Violence as a means breeds violence; the cult of personalities as a means breeds dictators—big and small—and servile masses; government—even with the collaboration of socialists and anarchists—breeds more government. Surely, then, freedom as a means breeds more freedom, possibly even the Free Society!

To those who say this condemns one to political sterility and the ivory tower our reply is that their "realism" and their "circumstantialism" invariably lead to disaster. We believe there is something more real, more positive, and more revolutionary in resisting war than in participating in it; that it is more civilised and more revolutionary to defend the right of a fascist to live than to support

---

12 *Solidaridad Obrera*, January 30, 1938.

13 Ibid.

14 The group of Russian anarchists in exile who in 1927 issued a project for the organisation of anarchists with the title "Plateforme d'organisation de l'organisation de l'Union générale des anarchistes (Projet)," which ostensibly was directed to Russian anarchists in exile, but the very fact that it was published in French indicated that it was also intended for the international movement.

the tribunals which have the legal powers to shoot him; that it is more realistic to talk to the people from the gutter than from government benches; that in the long run it is more rewarding to influence minds by discussion than to mould them by coercion.

Last, but not least, the question is one of human dignity, of self-respect, and of respect for one's fellows. There are certain things no person can do without ceasing to be human. As anarchists we willingly accept the limitations thus imposed on our actions, for, in the words of the old French anarchist Sébastien Faure:

> I am aware of the fact that it is not always possible to do what one should do; but I know that there are things that on no account can one ever do.

London
July–December 1952; *January–April* 1957

BIBLIOGRAPHY (1957)

Principal Sources

Books

Brenan, Gerald. *The Spanish Labyrinth: An Account of the Social and Political Background of the Civil War*. London: Cambridge University Press, 1943.

De Companys a Indalecio Prieto: Documentacion sobre las industrias de guerra en Cataluna. Buenos Aires: Ediciones del Servicio de Propoganda Espana. 1939.

De Julio a Julio: Un año de lucha. Valencia: Fragua Social, 1937. [French edition with title *Dans la tourmente: un an de guerre en Espagne*. Paris: Tribord, 1938.]

De Santillán, Diego Abad. *Por qué perdimos la guerra: Una contribucion a la historia de la tragedia Española*. Buenos Aires: Imán, 1940.

———, ed. *Timón: Sintesis de orientacion politico social*. First Series nos. 1–6. Barcelona, July–December 1938. Second Series Nos. 1–5. Buenos Aires, November 1939–March 1940.

De Santillán, Diego Abad, and Luce Fabbri. *Gli Anarchici e la Rivoluzione Spagnuola*. Geneva: Carlo Frigerio Editore, 1938.

García Oliver, Juan. *Mi gestion al frente del ministerio de justicia*. Valencia: Comisión de propaganda y prensa del Comité Nacional de CNT, 1937.

Ildefonso, González. "Il Movimento Libertario Spagnolo" *Volontà* (Naples), 9, nos. 6–9 (1952) [reprinted as a pamphlet (Naples, 1953)].

Leval, Gaston. *Né Franco né Stalin: Le collettività anarchiche spagnole nella lotta contro Franco e la reazione staliniana.* Milan: Milano Istituto editoriale italiano, 1952.

———. *Social Reconstruction in Spain.* London: Freedom Press, 1938.

López, Juan, ed. *Material de discusion para los militantes de la CNT de España.* Brighton: Milford Haven, 1945–1946.

Montseny, Federica. *Militant Anarchism and the Reality in Spain.* Glasgow: Anti-Parliamentary Communist Federation, 1937.

Peirats, José. *La CNT en la Revolución Española.* vols. 1–3. Toulouse: Ediciones CNT, 1951–1953 [in English: *The CNT in the Spanish Revolution,* vol. 1–3. Oakland: PM Press, 2011–2012].

Peiró, Juan. *Problemas y cintarazos.* Rennes: Imprimeries Réunies, 1946.

Souchy, Augustín. *The Tragic Week in May.* Barcelona: Oficina Informacion Exterior CNT y FAI, 1937 [also French and Spanish editions of the same pamphlet].

Souchy, Augustín, and Paul Folgare. *Colectivizaciones: La obra constructiva de la Revolución Española.* Barcelona: Tierra y Libertad, 1937.

Newspapers

CNT-FAI Information Bulletin. Spanish, English, and Italian editions, Barcelona, 1937–1939.

Spain and the World (London), 1936–1939 [53 issues].

Files of *Fragua Social* (CNT daily, Valencia), *Solidaridad Obrera* (CNT daily, Barcelona), *Tierra y Libertad, Mujeres Libres,* and other anarchist and syndicalist journals published in Spain, 1936–1939.

Other Sources

Berneri, Camillo. *Pensieri e Battaglie*. Paris: Comitato Camillo Berneri, 1938.

Borkenau, Franz. *The Communist International*. London: Faber and Faber, 1938.

———. *The Spanish Cockpit*. London: Faber and Faber, 1937.

Caballero, Largo *Mis recuerdos*. Mexico: Ediciones Unidas, 1954.

Casado, Colonel S. *The Last Days of Madrid: The End of the Second Spanish Republic*. London: Peter Davies, 1939.

De Ligt, Bart. *The Conquest of Violence: An Essay on War and Revolution*. London: George Routledge and Sons, 1937.

Hernández, Jesús. *Yo fui un ministro de Stalin*. Mexico: Editorial America, 1953.

Hernández, Jesús, and Joan Comorera. *Spain Organises for Victory: The Policy of the Communist Party of Spain*. London: Communist Party of Great Britain, 1937.

Jellinek, Frank. *The Civil War in Spain*. London: Victor Gollancz, 1938.

Krivitsky, Walter Germanovich. *I Was Stalin's Agent*. London: Hamish Hamilton, 1939, chapter III.

McGovern, John. *Terror in Spain*. London: Independent Labour Party, 1938.

Morrow, Felix. *Revolution and Counter-Revolution in Spain*. New York: Pathfinder Press, 1938 [a critical study from the Trotskyist angle].

Orwell, George. *Homage to Catalonia*. London: Secker and Warburg, 1938.

Peers, Allison. *Catalonia Infelix*. London: Methuen, 1937.

Prieto, Indalecio. *Como y porque sali del Ministerio de Defensa Nacional*. Paris: Imprimerie Nouvelle, 1939.

Sartin, Max. *Berneri in Spagna*. New York: Biblioteca de l'Adunata dei Refrattari, 1938.

BIBLIOGRAPHICAL POSTSCRIPT (1972)

I

In the bibliography to *The Grand Camouflage* the author Burnett Bolloten declares that in the preparation of that great work he had consulted no less than 2,500 books and pamphlets on the subject and lists those he has either quoted from or found useful. His bibliography runs to seventeen pages, yet what strikes the reader is the minute number of works published between 1945 and 1960. Spain was an unprofitable subject so far as the publishing world was concerned. For instance, Mr. Bolloten's work though completed in 1952 was not published until 1961. During those years it was offered to numerous American publishers including five university presses and was turned down by all of them. Times have certainly changed and what with the ever-growing number of PhDs in search of a subject and insatiable printing machines and publishing empires in search of reprints and authors, the Spanish Civil War has emerged from its undeserved oblivion. Whether the reader will be more enlightened at the end than he was when he started reading some of the most popular works in print is another matter.

There are a number of important works which have appeared since 1957 (when I completed the revised version of *Lessons of the Spanish Revolution*), and which could have been used to advantage in the present volume, but because I was not attempting to write a history but seeking only to draw conclusions from the revolutionary aspects of the struggle, I would have found myself mainly involved in adding footnotes which would have simply underlined the arguments but not changed them. The advantage gained would, I thought, be offset by a cluttering of the argument with a surfeit of detail, apart from the fact that there is a limit to the amount of revision and expansion a work can stand without having to be completely rewritten, and I had no intention of doing that. On the other hand, I feel I must take advantage of the publication of my work in English to refer to some of the important works that are now available to the student of the Spanish Revolution.

II

Gerald Brenan's *Spanish Labyrinth* (London: Cambridge University Press, 1943) is still the best book on the social and political background and contains a valuable bibliography; it is available in a paperback edition. Max Nettlau's *La anarquia a través de los tiempos* (Barcelona: 1935) has been published in Italian translation as *Breve Storia dell'Anarchismo* (Cesena: Edizioni l'Antistato, 1964) and contains chapters on the origins of anarchism and on collectivist and communist anarchism in Spain. Also by Nettlau is *La Première Internationale en Espagne* (1868–1888) (Dordrecht, NL: Reidel, 1969), a six hundred–page monumental source work on the subject, patiently edited by Renée Lamberet. Apart from being beyond most people's purse it has defeated all attempts I have made to read it; probably it is a work not meant to be read but to be consulted (and only by the student steeped in the subject of the origins of the First International in Spain). Much more readable, though also a work of scholarship, is Casimiro Martí's *Origines del anarquismo en Barcelona* (Barcelona: Editorial Teide, 1959), which was I think the first serious study of anarchism to emerge from Franco's Spain.

Of the more recent background material covering the first three decades of the present century, a reprint of M. Dashar's pamphlet *The Origins of the Revolutionary Movement in Spain* was issued in 1967 (London: Coptic Press, 1967), while José Peirats in *Los anarquistas en la crisis Española* (Buenos Aires: Alfa, 1964) devotes the first one hundred pages of his work to the years leading up to

July 19, 1936, as he also did in the first six chapters of volume 1 of his history of the CNT so frequently referred to in the present work.

The first two hundred pages of Gabriel Jackson's *The Spanish Republic and the Civil War* (Princeton, NJ: Princeton University Press, 1965) deal with the Republic of 1931 in considerable detail.

III

The best general work on the Civil War is Pierre Broué and Émile Témime's *La Revolution et la Guerre d'Espagne* (Paris: Éditions de Minuit, 1961). It is a work of scholarship and *engagement*, both authors being deeply involved in salvaging the truth about the war and the revolution, and it is good to see that at last it is available in English translation [*The Revolution and the Civil War in Spain* (London: Faber and Faber, 1972)]. If not sabotaged by the reviewers it should become the standard general work and help to counteract the harm done by the most popular and least *engagé* general work published in the same year: Hugh Thomas's *The Spanish Civil War* (London: Eyre & Spottiswoode, 1961). I have explained elsewhere at length why I consider the latter to be the most cynical book on the Civil War that I have read and will not repeat the arguments here.[1] A revised edition of *The Spanish Civil War* has since been published by Penguin Books (1965). In the preface to it the author writes that the new edition "slightly expands the economic and social aspects of the war. The origins of both the Communists and the Anarchists in Spain have been further explored. Otherwise, the book remains much the same as it did when it first appeared." In fact, the only significant "expansion" is the eleven-page chapter on "The Collectives," a subject which Mr. Thomas had overlooked in the original edition—apart from minor references! However, he has gone from strength to strength and is now considered an authority on the collectives by some after having contributed a much longer piece in the volume on Spain edited by Raymond Carr, *The Republic and the Civil War in Spain* (London: Macmillan 1971).

---

1   See *Anarchy* 1, no. 5 (1961).

IV

More material has been published on the collectives in the past few years notably the critical work by Frank Mintz, *L'Autogestion dans l'Espagne Révolutionnaire* (Paris: Bélibaste, 1970), which seeks to answer practical questions such as "Why did collectivization take place?" "How was collectivization carried out?" "Are there aspects of originality about the collectivization?" The merit of this work is that the author seeks to bring together material from a wide range of published sources and to summarise the results. It is, however, typical of many theses in not being easy to read, but it is a valuable contribution to the subject.

A major source work on the collectives which has just appeared is Gaston Leval's *Espagne Libertaire, 1936–1939* (Paris: Éditions du Cercle et Éditions de la Tête de feuilles, 1971). This is a slightly expanded version of *Né Franco né Stalin: Le Collettivita anarchiche spagnole nella latta contro Franco e la reazione staliniana* (Milan: Milano Istituto editoriale italiano, 1952) with which the reader is by now familiar, if only because of the many occasions I have referred to it in my own work.

A contribution from Spain is Albert Pérez-Baró's *30 meses de collectivisme a Catalunya* (Barcelona: Ediciones 62, 1970). The author is a militant of the CNT from pre-1936 years and was closely connected with the legislation on collectivisation in Catalonia. I have not managed to see a copy of this work but Frank Mintz describes it in the *CIRA Bulletin* (Lausanne) no. 22 (1971) as "indispensable for the understanding of many events which marked the economic transformation of Republican Spain." The same writer reviews another work from Spain (incidentally, both volumes are in Catalan) Josep Maria Bricall's *Política económica de la Generalitat (1936–1939) Volum primer: evolució i formes de la producció industrial* (Barcelona: Ediciones 62, 1970), which he considers "fundamental." "It contains documentation and statistics more detailed than anything so far published on Spain and Catalonia" and is richly illustrated.

On the subject of the Spanish economy, a work which I have found impressive and instructive is Ramón Tamames's *Estructura económica de España* (Madrid: Ed. S.E.P., 1960 [3rd revised and expanded ed., 1965]). This is both a source work and a critical study of some eight hundred pages covering every aspect of the Spanish economy. It does not in fact deal with the collectivisations of 1936–1939, though the few pages on agrarian reform in the Second Republic are to the point. The author quotes interesting and significant figures on land expropriation during the revolution. By May 1938, no less than 5.7 million hectares (14 million acres) had been occupied of which: 6 million acres were expropriated because their owners had abandoned them or for political reasons, 5 million acres because of its social use, and 3 million acres were taken over only provisionally (p. 46). Another interesting "statistic" is given on page 11, where he points out that the gross national product did not increase at a comparable rate with the population growth after the civil war, with the result that "in the years 1939–1950 there was a very noticeable fall in the standards of living in Spain."

V

Of the source books on the revolution Peirats's three-volume history *La CNT en la revolución Española* (Toulouse: Ediciones CNT, 1951–1953) is still the most important work available to the student, and it is encouraging to see that it is now back in print in a new edition (Paris: Ruedo Ibérico, 1971). But undoubtedly the most impressive source book to have appeared since Peirats, and in English, is Burnett Bolloten's *The Grand Camouflage*, which first appeared in 1961 with the sub-title *The Communist Conspiracy in the Spanish Civil War* and mysteriously disappeared from the publishers' lists soon after only to reappear in 1968 under another publisher's imprint with the subtitle *The Spanish Civil War and Revolution 1936–1939* and an introduction by H.R. Trevor-Roper which is of interest in describing the difficulties encountered by the author in looking for a publisher in the first place and the conspiracy of silence that followed its publication. Professor Roper suggests that perhaps it is that "the Anglo-American literary establishment is still stuck in the fashionable postures of the 1930s which Mr. Bolloten implicitly undermines?" The main clue to what he means by this is Orwell's essay on "The Prevention of Literature," written early in 1946 when Orwell's literary diatribes had been transferred from his wartime bêtes-noires, the fascists, the pacifists, and the anarchists, to the Russians and the fellow-travelling intellectuals, and I assume that the key passage in that article to which Professor Roper refers is:

> Fifteen years ago, when one defended the freedom of the intellect, one had to defend it against Conservatives, against Catholics, and to some extent—for they were not of great importance in England—against Fascists. Today one has to defend it against Communists and "fellow-travellers." One ought not to exaggerate the direct influence of the small English Communist Party, but there can be no question about the poisonous effect of the Russian *mythos* on English intellectual life. Because of it known facts are suppressed and distorted to such an extent as to make it doubtful whether a true history of our times can ever be written.

This is not the place to try to unravel Orwell's political confusionism, because anyway I agree that so far as the Spanish Civil War is concerned the "line" put over by the Communists at the time—that is, fascism versus democracy, the latter being represented by the Popular Front government, which had been victorious at the general election of February 1936—was swallowed hook, line, and sinker by the right-thinking left, not to mention eccentric conservatives such as the Duchess of Atholl, but I think that Bolloten's masterpiece was not published in the fifties simply because, firstly, there was no "interest" in the English-speaking world in the subject, and, secondly, that when it was published it was sabotaged by the academics who monopolise the reviews and who resented the intrusion of a mere journalist in a subject that they had just "discovered" as a lucrative field of exploitation, as well as the fact that Bolloten undermined the whole basis of their *élitiste* approach with the opening paragraph of this remarkable work:

Although the outbreak of the Spanish Civil War in July 1936, was followed by a far-reaching social revolution in the anti-Franco camp—more profound in some respects than the Bolshevik Revolution in its early stages—millions of discerning people outside Spain were kept in ignorance, not only of its depth and range, but even of its existence, by virtue of a policy of duplicity and dissimulation of which there is no parallel in history.

I have twice paid homage to Bolloten, and I can do no more than quote from what I wrote when I reviewed both Thomas and Bolloten in *Anarchy* no. 5 (July 1961):

It is significant that another book, *The Grand Camouflage: The Communist Conspiracy in the Spanish Civil War* by Burnett Bolloten which appeared at the same time as Mr. Thomas' has either been ignored or, where it has been reviewed with the Thomas book, has received scant treatment. This is a pity because it is a so much more important work and in spite of the fact that it does not attempt to present a complete picture of the Civil War the reader will learn more from its 350 pages about the real issues in that struggle than from the 700 pages of Thomas' comprehensive "history." . . . The reason why Mr. Bolloten's book is more interesting than the title would lead one to believe is that in order to analyse the counter-revolutionary role of the Communists he first had to give the reader a picture of the social revolution that took place and this he does in chapter after chapter with references which sometimes occupy more space than his text. For instance the chapter on "The Revolution in the Countryside" is only twenty pages long of which more than seven are source references. But in those references is material for a large volume.

And when I had to write an introduction to a Spanish translation of my own work, I said that I had decided against further expansion of the text in spite of the many books that have appeared on the Spanish Civil War since 1957,

> because in my opinion only one—Burnett Bolloten's *The Grand Camouflage* is a valuable source work as well as being one of the few which has a realistic grasp of the subject. I have not made use of Bolloten here because it would have meant examining all his sources, assessing them and producing five volumes at least! But I urge all serious, committed, students of the subject to study Bolloten *and follow up his footnotes*. I am immodest enough to suggest that Bolloten also illuminates the thesis expounded in the pages that follow.

But I also urge readers of Professor Trevor-Roper's introduction not to assume that he is in sympathy or summarises the work he is introducing, whatever he may write. Indeed, it is a vivid illustration of the crass ignorance of the academics—Professor Roper is Regius Professor of Modern History at Oxford University—when he writes:

> The Anarchist revolution of 1936 has been described before, but seldom, I think, as vividly as by Mr. Bolloten. His description of it, amply documented from direct, local sources, is one of the most fascinating parts of his book. But it is, in effect, only the introduction. *For that revolution, while it effectively dissolved the old Republic, contributed nothing to the immediate task of resisting the rebellion of Franco.* (emphasis added)

What did? And the Professor replies, as did all the fellow-travellers of the thirties: "That force proved to be the Communist Party." And on what grounds does he base his assertions?

The Spanish Communist Party was negligible in strength in 1936. Spain has never accepted Communism, or indeed fascism or any ideology that has taken firm root in Europe. The European ideas which it has embraced have been the rejected heresies of Europe—or, if orthodoxies, orthodoxies radically transformed by their passage over the Pyrenees. Not Marx but Bakunin is the prophet of Spanish radicalism. And so, in 1936, while the Anarchists were able to make a revolution, the Spanish Communists were too weak even to think of conspiracy. At most they had 40,000 members, represented by 16 deputies in the Cortes. Nevertheless, within a year, the Communist Party was the effective master of the Republican Government. *By the end of the war, General Franco was really fighting not against the Popular Front but against a Communist dictatorship.* (emphasis added)

I must resist the temptation of analysing the passages I have italicised, but I have quoted Professor Roper at length because his way of dealing with the facts and his very thought processes are typical of the academic historians, who at least in the English-speaking world have "taken over" the Spanish Civil War, though there are signs of counter-action. Noam Chomsky in his long essay on "Objectivity and Liberal Scholarship," which is included in the Pelican volume published in 1969 with the title *American Power and the New Mandarins* deals with the effect of what he calls "the counter-revolutionary subordination" in the writing of history, and he illustrates his arguments by reference to the attitudes of historians to the Spanish Civil War and, in particular, to the revolution in the street. He examines in some detail one of the works of liberal scholarship (Gabriel Jackson's prize-winning *The Spanish Republic and the Civil War*) and concludes, "It seems to me that there is more than enough evidence that a deep bias against social revolution and a commitment to the values and social order of liberal bourgeois democracy has led the author to misrepresent crucial events and to overlook major historical currents."

One suspects that the publication at long last of Broué and Témime's work in English translation owes much to Professor Chomsky's connection with the MIT (Massachusetts Institute of Technology), which bought the English rights, and it is, I think, significant that though it appears with the very respectable imprint of Faber and Faber [1961] it carries the uncompromising title *The Revolution and the Civil War in Spain,* just as Bolloten's work now appears with the subtitle *The Spanish Civil War and Revolution 1936–1939,* whereas a decade earlier it was presented as an exposure of *The Communist Conspiracy in the Spanish Civil War.* Perhaps the Thomas-Joll-Raymond Carr unholy trinity who scratch each others' literary backs at every turn is at last being rumbled. Mr. Carr's skilful review of Broué and Témime in the *Observer* makes it quite clear that he sees the red light but is also confident that the intruders can be successfully elbowed out. And with a volume selling at £6 not many people will be able to afford it. The publishers should be pressed to bring out a cheap paper edition.

A source work that the serious student should not ignore in spite of its serious shortcomings is *Tres Días de Julio* by Luis Romero (Barcelona: Ariel, 1967). In this six hundred–page work, copiously illustrated, the author who is a prize-winning Spanish novelist, attempts to summarise what was happening in all the principal towns and cities of Spain on three crucial days in July 1936, that is on July 18, 19, and 20. In a commemorative article on "Spain 1936" which I wrote for *Freedom* in 1963 I outlined the kind of "history" I would like to see. It was a day-to-day account of the activities of the two workers' organisations, CNT and UGT, beginning with the founding of the Republic in 1931; the first section would take one to the elections in February 1936, the second, "but in much greater detail," would cover the period from February to the military uprising in July, and the third section "would seek to recreate the events of say the month following the uprising, and this would show how far the work of 'demolition' of the existing order went and to what extent the revolutionaries were able to create new social and economic organisations to take its place and deal with the multiple problems not only created by the military uprising but which exist in any society with large concentrations of population."[2]

---

2   *Freedom,* July 20, 1963; reprinted in Freedom Reprints vol. 13, *Forces of Law & Order* (London, 1965).

Señor Romero spent three years on this work, and though from various references I feel sure that it is a serious contribution, the fact that the author has chosen to present his material as literature and not as history, and without a single footnote as to sources, nor even a bibliography, no serious student can use it as source material without further research, though I think the informed reader will read it with considerable interest as a dramatic work. For example, of the occasion when Companys summons the Catalan anarchists to meet him at the Generalitat, Romero writes: "The cars stop in the middle of the Square of the Republic. On the main balcony of the Generalitat a huge flag of Catalonia flutters. A corps of Mozos de Escuadra guards the gateway. The street intersections seem to be taken over by Assault Guards and citizens wearing armbands with the Catalan colours! The representatives of the CNT and of the FAI, armed to the teeth, get out of the cars; the Mozos de Escuadra remain calm. A commandant, who must surely be their chief, advances towards the group which has assembled at that very gateway: Durrruti, García Oliver, Joaquin Ascaso, Ricardo Sanz, Aurelio Fernández, Gregorio Jover, Antonio Ortiz, and 'Valencia.' 'We are the representatives of the CNT and of the FAI; Companys has called for us, and here we are. Those who are accompanying us are our bodyguards.'"

Good dramatic stuff but also factually accurate.

Obviously, what was said is of less interest for Señor Romero as a novelist but much more important for Peirats or myself, who are concerned with the revolution, though the atmosphere in which these discussions and decisions were taken are relevant, and it is in this context that I think Señor Romero's book is of interest. But since he does not quote his sources one can only use his material with reservations.

VI

There have been surprisingly few critical works published in the past fifteen years. José Peirats wrote a *Breve storia del sindicalismo libertario spagnolo* (Genova: Edizioni RL, 1962), which covers more or less the same topics as were dealt with in my *Lessons* and is considerably more critical than he allowed himself to be in his three-volume history. The Spanish original was later published with the title *Los anarquistas en la crisis política española* (Buenos Aires: Libros de Anarres, 1964). Apart from dealing in greater detail with the years of the Republic (1931–1936) it is identical with the Italian edition, though in the interim period Peirats and some of his friends split from the official Spanish movement in exile and according to one writer found themselves "cut off from any support from the rank and file." That writer, thirty-two-year-old César M. Lorenzo is, according to the publisher's blurb, "son of militants of the Spanish CNT who sought refuge in France after the fall of Catalonia," and his book *Les anarchistes espagnols et le pouvoir, 1868–1969* (Paris: Le Seuil, 1969) is a mine of detailed information, much of it documented, but it suffers from two major faults. The first is that this four hundred–page book is dominated by Horacio Prieto who is quoted by the author or included in footnotes almost on every other page,[3] and one would find no reason to object if it could be shown that Prieto, in fact, dominated the thinking of the CNT-FAI in Spain and in exile to this extent. He didn't by any means, though there is no denying that he was what the Spaniards called "an influential" member of the organisation—one could dub him the "anarchist minister-maker" for it was he who, as the national secretary of the CNT, manoeuvred the entry of the four CNT ministers into the Caballero government in November 1936. For my part I have all along looked upon him as one of the most unpleasant political intriguers that the CNT has thrown up and every reference to him in Lorenzo's book confirms the impression I had gained from what I had read by him previously. But to illustrate the pro–Horacio Prieto bias, I

---

3   Not to be confused with the socialist leader *Indalecio* Prieto. The only thing these two Prietos had in common was that they supported the right wing of their respective organisations. I have quoted Brenan as saying that the CNT got on better with the right-wing Socialists, with Prieto, than with Caballero. It is quite clear that the CNT's right-wing Prieto had a very strong *penchant* for the Socialist's "Lenin": Caballero!

have opened the volume at random (there being no index, which is regrettable in such a well-produced book, and inadmissible in a four hundred–page volume which the publisher offers as an "histoire lumineuse et déconcertante" but understandable in view of the fact that the Horacio Prieto bias to which I have referred would emerge in a most embarrassing way!) at page 283 and sure enough Horacio Prieto is mentioned by name no less than three times, as he is on page 284, though only twice on page 285, but on this page the author starts quoting from a lecture delivered by Prieto to the National Committee of the CNT on economic problems and their solution. Lorenzo describes the lecture as "very long and very technical" and that "in his introduction and in his conclusion, he declared that political and economic action were inseparable, that libertarian communism was only utopian, that the CNT itself was an institution similar to a state with its standing orders, its rules, its operation subjected to moral and ideological norms, its administrative network, and its directive organisms. He stressed the importance of the political keys to economic power (the gold reserves in particular) and the importance of legislation, indicating that libertarians could not achieve anything worthwhile in economic matters if they did not have access to its keys." I could find such arguments stimulating if M. Lorenzo did not then go on to quote Prieto verbatim where he dismisses the attempts by the workers to collectivise the land and industry as best they could in these terms:

> Collectivism such as we know it in Spain is not anarchist collectivism but the creation of a new capitalism, even more incoherent than the old capitalist system that we have just destroyed; it is a question of a new form of capitalism with all its defects. with all its immorality, which is reflected in innate egoism, in the ever-present egoism of the workers who administer a collective. It is fully proved that there does not exist among us today the observance of, or any love or respect for, the libertarian morality which we claim to defend or to propagate.

And so on, for three pages. One must not be afraid of criticism, but one suspects those who criticise the anarchists and anarcho-syndicalists for not being good anarchists, while at the same time arguing that non-authoritarian methods, will never lead to the bringing about of anarchism. Prieto, the anarchist minister-maker, believed even during the struggle in 1936–1939 that unless anarchists participated in the power game they would never make headway, and he continues to this day advocating the anarchist party. And this brings me to the second fault, or weakness, of M. Lorenzo's book, and it is that he has no other ideas himself, and so his conclusion after exposing for four hundred pages the political frailty even of anarchists when they taste the sweet fruits of power, is Prieto's, that there is no anti-authoritarian alternative to the power struggle. In which case there is no future for anarchism, other than as a personal philosophy for an elite.

This could have been a very important book if only M. Lorenzo had not shown such loyalty to his father . . . Horacio Prieto!

VII

I have not been seeing the libertarian Spanish press in exile regularly for some six years, though what I have seen would indicate that those concerned with its publication are more interested with keeping together the ageing movement in exile on illusions about the past and exaggerated hopes for the future than in drawing lessons from their unique experience. A journal which gave one hope that this pattern was about to be broken was *Presencia* (*Tribuna Libertaria*) which first appeared in Paris November–December 1965. I assume that only ten issues appeared, but they do include some original material. Of particular interest to this writer was a projected symposium on the theme "Did the Spanish libertarian movement in 1936–1939 renounce continuing the revolution to its conclusion." In introducing the series (no. 5) the editors suggest that the theme could be put more simply in the following terms: "If the July 19, 1936 were to repeat itself—as if by magic it were to occur in exactly the same form and in the same context—should the libertarian movement act as it did?"

Alas, in spite of inviting such luminaries of the Spanish libertarian movement as García Oliver, Federica Montseny, and Santillán, only Peirats and Cipriano Mera contributed.

Peirats's contribution is important, for it is even more critical than he was in the volume referred to earlier, and the key statement he makes is surely that

> there is no doubt that there was a renunciation of the revolution as soon as the military uprising in Barcelona and Catalonia had been resolved. And in spite of the fact that the revolution could not have occurred under better circumstances. . . . It is true that the hardest part of the task would have to be assumed by the most determined minorities. In particular the seasoned militants of the CNT-FAI. But the populace, which understood the gravity of the issues involved, shouldered them massively, preventing any upsetting of the situation. The renunciation took place precisely at the moment when a group of outstanding members of the CNT-FAI went to the Generalitat to listen to the flattery which president Companys showered on them. For the historian, this group of distinguished men entered as conquerors and in a short space of time left as the conquered.

Peirats underlines the charge when later he writes: "Truly speaking it was not a case of renunciation but rather of a surrender of the revolution." There could be no excuse for anarchists, who know more about the machinations of the political and state machine than anyone, to offer excuses such as that they had been caught unawares or that they were ingenuous so far as politics were concerned "in view of the ease with which some of them adapted themselves to political protocol and the situation." Indeed, Peirats observes that "in the period 1936–1939 there emerged a new class, heir to all the tasks previously held by the class that had disappeared. And it included some sections of the libertarian movement." In his conclusions Peirats also accuses the CNT-FAI luminaries of being narrow-minded revolutionaries lacking imagination, "without a real anarchist morality," and in the circumstances they did what anybody else would do and took the easy road and "opted for the least effort." But for Peirats anarchists *cannot* do what "everybody else would do in the circumstances." So when he poses the question "What could the libertarian movement do?" he soon finds himself concluding that half the question can be answered by posing another question: "What should *not* have been done?" We are back to "Means and Ends" and Peirats makes a number of stimulating observations on the subject. In the following issue of *Presencia* (no. 6, November-December 1966) Cipriano Mera made his contribution to the debate in the form of an interview which unfortunately is much too short and superficial to be of great value. If anything, the interview gives one ideas for a further interview in depth. For Mera does appear to be interested in establishing the facts and drawing conclusions and not at all concerned with justifying his own role in the "popular army" in 1937 following the militarisation of the militias (see chapter XVI). He recognises that "we all had our fair share of responsibility" so far as the CNT's collaborationist policy was concerned, and adds that the time has passed for a confrontation with the guilty men, but nevertheless "I wish to state that the politics of the fait accompli and executive decisions began right at the beginning of the war."

The other journal I would like to include in this postscript is *Noir et Rouge* (Paris). The last issue, no. 46, appeared in June 1970. It is undoubtedly one of the most important anarchist journals of the post-war years, and the critical material on the Spanish revolution is well worth consulting. In issues 36 and 38 one finds French translations of the Peirats and Mera contributions to *Presencia*, as well as the editors' comments on the former's article and an interesting reply by Peirats. The student will also find valuable contributions on the subject of self-management with special references to the experience of Algeria and the French "revolution" of May 1968.

Finally, I would refer the reader to the special issue of the journal *Government & Opposition* on the subject of "Anarchism

Today" (vol. 5, no. 4, Autumn 1970) which includes a well-documented contribution by J. Romero Maura on "The Spanish Case." What the author seeks to do is to "formulate a hypothetical explanation of how it happened that the anarchist movement only in Spain should have been so successful in building up a *mass* organization, largely based on industrial workers with such powerful and sustained revolutionary drive." Mr. Maura gives the five main explanations generally advanced for this phenomenon. The first "seeks the answer in the specificity of the Spanish character," but Mr. Maura rightly rejects this "romantic view," pointing out that "the indigenous middle classes in Spain have never turned anarchist and do not seem to have been less attached to their worldly goods and interests than middle classes elsewhere." The second "rests on the backwardness of the Spanish economy"; the third is based on the idea "that there must be some sort of causal relationship between the fact that industrial working-class anarchism was strongest in Catalonia and the emergence there of a powerful middle-class nationalist movement." The fourth explanation "alleges that anarchism was the explosive result of a lack of political freedom." And, finally, the Spanish anarchist phenomenon is ascribed to "the disillusionment of the workers with a liberal-democratic constitution which gave the workers no real power."

Mr. Maura has no difficulty in discounting these explanations. The true explanation he feels should, in the first place, be sought "in the very nature of the anarchist conception of society and of how to achieve revolution." And in his essay he attempts to explain how this conception was generated, and "last but by no means least, how strict adherence to the original conceptions in matters of organization allowed the movement to retain its drive over a long period of time." I should point out that in this essay Mr. Maura is not concerned with the events of 1936–1939, and it is therefore a pity that he should mar this well-documented study with a concluding paragraph which makes a number of generalisations about those events which cannot be taken seriously, any more than the quotation from "one of the FAI leaders." Perhaps Mr. Maura's "hypothetical explanation" can only be considered seriously in the context of the "Origins and Background" *plus* the events of 1936–1939, and that his final words on the latter, "But that is another story," may not be so!

Having said this I must add that I find Mr. Maura's essay refreshing, his theses controversial and stimulating (though I am not sure where he stands), and am most interested in some of his conclusions. For instance: "Although too little is known as yet of the growth and decay of French and Italian syndicalism, one thing is plain enough, namely that their conception of the revolutionary general strike was a dangerous myth." Mr. Maura enlarges on this when he adds that "the idea of the general strike was conceived as an alternative to armed insurrection," which after the Paris Commune was considered to have been defeated "once and for all . . . by the armies of the bourgeois state. French and Italian syndicalists thought that the general strike, by atomizing violence and preventing through sabotage the coordination of the state's effort, would make use of conventional armies against the workers impossible." I agree when Mr. Maura states that "this was an illusion," and he cites the case of "the anarcho-communists in the Italian USI (Italian Syndicalist Union) who realised the dangers of this mistake" and adds that "but for all Armando Borghi's efforts they could not impose their views on a movement they did not control." But he considers that in Spain

> this misjudgement never gained ground. . . . The found-
> ers of *Solidaridad Obrera* and of the CNT had an anarcho-
> communist background, so much so that—contrary to the
> programme of revolutionary syndicalism elsewhere—their
> avowed aim was to the end *comunismo libertario*. They never
> relinquished the anarcho-communist conception of the final
> battle as one which would be decided by sheer force.

I would find myself in agreement with Mr. Maura but for his last sentence, which seems to me to be crude and unimaginative and, anyway, in contradiction with what he writes about the Italian movement quoted above. What I think is imaginative in his "hypothesis" and deserves further research is that the CNT "success story," compared with the rest of Europe, was more deeply influenced by anarchist rather than Marxist or reformist influences; that "its avowed aim was to the end comunismo libertario."

VIII

Readers of *Malatesta: Life and Ideas* (London: Freedom Press, 1965) will not need to be reminded of the general strike versus the insurrection issues raised at some length in Part III of the volume, in which I discuss "Malatesta's Relevance for Anarchists Today" (271–309). I quote Malatesta as suggesting that the idea of the general strike was launched and "welcomed enthusiastically by those who had no faith in parliamentary action, and saw in it a new and promising road leading to popular action." But the trouble was that most of them viewed the general strike as "a substitute for the insurrection, a way of 'starving the bourgeoisie' and obliging it to capitulate without a blow being struck." To such views Malatesta's cryptic comment was that far from starving the bourgeoisie "we should starve ourselves first."

I think that Mr. Maura draws the wrong conclusions from the Monatte-Malatesta confrontation at the Amsterdam anarchist congress because he does not distinguish between the general strike, which is basically an authoritarian action by a section of society—the organised productive workers—and an insurrection, which is an uprising of the people against the ruling class and is only possible, let alone successful, if it embraces an overwhelming cross section of the community. I submit that the former—the general strike concept—is "a final battle . . . decided by sheer force" the outcome of which will largely depend on the number of organised workers and the nature of their work. The insurrection by definition is "a rising in open resistance to established authority" *by the people* and relies for its success not on holding society to ransom but on being the expression of society and therefore being welcomed. The idea of anarchism being decided "by sheer force" as Mr. Maura suggests is alien to all that anarchists stand for.

Mr. Maura, as a student of the Spanish struggle, will surely have observed that whereas the revolutionary elements in Spain, in spite of innumerable general strikes between February and July 1936, *could not* launch a revolution to overthrow the Popular Front government and its institutions (which included the armed forces), they were however the vanguard which inspired others to resist and defeat Franco's military uprising in two-thirds of the peninsula and set in motion a social revolution that radically modified the existing economic system and involved several million workers and peasants.

IX

I think one can expect a growing volume of material on different aspects of the Spanish Civil War, mainly coming from Spain. And as one writer has pointed out there is a tendency for more detailed accounts of specific events, such as, for instance, Manuel Cruells on *Els fets de Maig* (Barcelona: Juventut, 1970), which is a 140-page volume on the May Days of 1937 by a Barcelona journalist who actually witnessed the events. And the other source I think will be in reprints of contemporary material, much of which has long been out of print. One such reprint is Camillo Berneri's *Guerra di Classe (1936–1937)* (Pistoia: Ed. RL, 1971), a collection of twelve articles published in *Guerra di Classe*, the Italian newspaper he edited in Barcelona in 1936–1937, which includes such controversial and important pieces as his "Open Letter to Comrade Federica Montseny," "War and Revolution," and "Counter-Revolution Underway" (the latter appeared the day before he was murdered by the Stalinists).

Clearly the more material that appears the better, and from all quarters on the left (for instance Felix Morrow's *Revolution & Counter-Revolution in Spain* (New York: Pathfinder, 1938) has reappeared, as has also Franz Borkenau's *Spanish Cockpit* (London: Faber and Faber, 1937). But for anarchists already more than enough material has been published for the lessons of that epic struggle to emerge clearly and unequivocally.

FOOTNOTES TO THE BIBLIOGRAPHICAL POSTSCRIPT (1983)

These footnotes are limited to drawing readers' attention to any new editions of the books mentioned in the "Bibliographical Postscript," and any relevant new titles that have appeared during the ten years since writing the "Postscript." The same section numbers have been retained.

II

Background books. Three useful works have appeared. Murray Bookchin's *The Spanish Anarchists: The Heroic Years 1868–1936* (New York: Free Life Editions, 1977). Though it is an interesting and valuable book, it really deals with the syndicalist movement rather than with the anarchists, and by not seriously asking himself the basic question "Who in fact were the Spanish anarchists?" he obviously has difficulties when it comes to categorising some of his subjects. Juan Peiró who always declared himself an anarchist in his writings and has few critics among the Spanish revolutionaries is variously described by Bookchin as a "centrist," as a "moderate *cenetista*," and as a "syndicalist right-winger." Federica Montseny is described as one of the "FAI's luminaries" and as "the best known woman *faista*" in spite of the fact that she has publicly declared that the only organisation she belonged to was the CNT. And had the author consulted her considerable writings in the *Revista Blanca* (which first her father and then she edited in Barcelona from 1923–1936) he would surely have come to the conclusion that she was an out and out individualist anarchist, if not a Stirnerite.

Obviously, the author posed the question but warns the reader that he includes its solution as one of his "unorthodoxies" in the writing of this book. What he has done is to use the terms "anarchist" and "anarcho-syndicalist" "almost intuitively, ordinarily combining libertarians of all persuasions under the 'anarchist' rubric when they seemed to confront the Marxists, the state power, and their class opponents as a fairly unified tendency in Spanish society and singling out 'anarcho-syndicalists' when they were functioning largely from a syndicalist point of view."

By so doing, I think he has contributed to the existing political confusion, though it has not prevented him from writing a worthwhile book. Had he accepted the conclusions of a respected Spanish anarchist writing in 1945 about those years of "collaboration," that they had revealed "what a very few of us had suspected for some time: that there were a few, not many, hundred anarchists in Spain," he might have been dissuaded from writing this book. And that would have been a pity.

José Peirats's *Los anarquistas en la crisis politica Española* is now available in translation with the title *Anarchists in the Spanish Revolution* (Toronto: Solidarity Books, 1977). This edition, unlike the original, includes a thirty-five-page glossary of names and an index, which one assumes has been compiled by the publishing group and not by Peirats. I cannot imagine Peirats describing Armando Borghi as "Italian writer dedicated to propaganda journalism" or Colonel Casado as "famous for having concocted the *junta* which bore his name and unseated the dictator Negrín, at the end of the war."

The third deals entirely with what was in a sense a minor incident in the turbulent 1930s in Spain. Just as every self-respecting historian writing of the First International in Spain invariably includes a reference to Giuseppe Fanelli, generally as a subject for ridicule (Bookchin is an exception, and even includes two photographs of him), so all historians dealing with the Republic of the 1930s invariably refer to the Casas Viejas massacre at the end of 1933, and to old Seisdedos (Six Fingers) who was supposed to be the anarchist ringleader of the local insurrection which led to the "massacre." Well, they have all got it wrong, because Brenan and Hobsbawm got it wrong, and since all the other historians borrowed and embellished their accounts, they also will have to eat humble pie. *The Anarchists of Casas Viejas* by Jerome R. Mintz (Chicago: University of Chicago Press, 1982) is about the development of the anarchist movement in a town in Andalusia (not very far from Gibraltar), from its beginnings in 1914 and the uprising in 1933 to the personal experiences of the survivors in the troubled times that followed, as recounted to the author over a period of two years in the late 1960s. Apart from establishing the facts of the uprising and the role played by "Seisdedos," Professor Mintz exposes the use of religion as the key for conceptualising Spanish anarchism. As he points out in the introduction, "At first glance the religious model seems to make anarchism easier to understand, particularly in the absence of detailed observation and intimate contact. The model was, however, also used to serve the political ends of anarchism's opponents. Here use of the terms 'religious' and 'millenarian' stamp anarchist goals as unrealistic and unattainable. Anarchism is thus dismissed as a viable solution to social ills.

"The oversimplification posited became serious distortions of anarchist belief and practice. Gerald Brenan, Eric Hobsbawm, and Raymond Carr, for example, all maintained that there was a connection between anarchist strikes and sexual practices." And he quotes the most recent description, from Raymond Carr's *Spain*, in which they are presented thus: "Austere puritans, they sought to impose vegetarianism, sexual abstinence, and atheism on one of the most backward peasantries of Europe. . . . Thus strikes were moments of exaltation as well as demands for better conditions." Professor Mintz comments that "the level-headed anarchists were astonished by such descriptions of supposed Spanish puritanism by over-enthusiastic historians." The "religious" myth was due largely to the influence of Juan Díaz del Moral, a lawyer and historian who was also a landowner and who produced a massive history of the Andalusian peasant uprisings. The English historians beginning with Brenan adopted del Moral as their authority. Thus, in *The Spanish Labyrinth* in the chapter on "The Anarcho-Syndicalists" Brenan writes: "At this point it will be necessary to pause in our account of the development of anarcho-syndicalism in the industrial towns in order to say something of what was happening in the country. The principal areas of rural anarchism in Spain are Andalusia and the Levante. With the help of Díaz del Moral's admirably objective and detailed history of the movement in the province of Cordova it should be possible to obtain a fairly exact idea of this" (p. 173). Later, Professor Mintz points out, Raymond Carr, Hobsbawm, and Joll "accepted Díaz del Moral's characterization and even identified an age and people whom they judged to be comparable—seventeenth century England with its Anabaptists and Fifth Monarchy men." Franz Borkenau went further in *The Spanish Cockpit* when he declared that "anarchism is a religion," but George Woodcock in his history of anarchism also fell for the del Moral via Hobsbawm interpretation. Not only does he quote from del Moral via Hobsbawm in his *Primitive Rebels,* and from Brenan's *Spanish Labyrinth* in order to illustrate his view that "all anarchism has, of course, a moral-religious element which distinguishes it from ordinary political movements, and this element is far more strongly developed in Spain than elsewhere," but on facing pages he refers to "anarchist millenarianism" sweeping over the countryside "like a great religious revival" and of the "extremists led by fanatics like Durruti and his inseparable companion Ascaso, who were willing to use every means to speed the revolutionary millennium" (pp. 354–55).

Professor Mintz has done more than establish the facts about the rising in Casas Viejas. As he puts it in his preface:

This study of anarchist rebellion is itself part of a revolution in historical research, one aspect of which is the reexamination of history, using data from those in a despised station—personal narratives and life histories of slaves and sharecroppers in the American South, for example, and, in this instance, campesino accounts of circumstances in Andalusia. The new data are primarily oral; the narrators are uneducated, often illiterate. These oral versions challenge histories that have been based too often almost solely on the views of the educated and elitist classes. The introduction of these new sources in the study of social and political history can evoke a change in perception as radical as that stirred by the Impressionist movement in painting—now as then, the image of the world bathed in fresh light, which lends to scenes a dimension and scope previously unrealized.

IV

In 1975, Freedom Press published my translation of Gaston Leval's monumental work *Espagne Libertaire 1936–39* with the title *Collectives in the Spanish Revolution*, including a foreword and twelve pages of bibliographical notes by the translator.

Frank Mintz's original study of 1970 has since been published in a much expanded Spanish edition with the title *La autogestion en la Espana revolucionaria* (Madrid: La Piqueta, 1977). In his introduction the author refers to those reviewers who praised the French original for its thoroughness but criticised it for being indigestible so far as the average reader is concerned. Since I was one such critic and admirer I quote my friend's reply: "I don't know what an average reader is, and I prefer that people should think before they swallow a cat believing it to be a hare (even when the cat has been cooked by me)." The Spanish edition includes new appendices and new material uncovered by the author in the military archives in Salamance in July–August 1975. This new edition is an invaluable source work, and includes a thirty-six-page bibliography but, alas, no index.

In Ronald Fraser's *Blood of Spain: The Experience of Civil War 1936–1939* (London: Allen Lane, 1979), an oral history, there are a number of sections dealing with rural and urban collectivization. The author interviewed men and women who had actually taken an active part in the struggle and who were still living thirty-five years later in the villages where they had participated in the social revolution. In the case of Mas de las Matas (Tereul) one can compare what some of its inhabitants are thinking and saying about collectivization now with Gaston Leval's account of what happened at the time, and it makes fascinating reading. One witness told the author, "I was so enthusiastic, so fanatic, that I took everything in my parents' house—all the grain stocks, the dozen head of sheep, even the silver coins—and handed them into the collective." He came from a prosperous peasant family which owned two houses and more land than they could work with family labour alone. "So you see I wasn't in the CNT to defend my daily wage; I was in it for idealistic reasons. My parents weren't as convinced as I, that's for sure." Such youthful idealism reminds one of Malatesta's recollections of the life of a militant in those days of "enthusiasm" when the internationalists were "ever ready for any sacrifice for the cause and were inspired by the rosiest hopes." He wrote many years later "everyone gave to propaganda all they could, as well as what they could not afford; and when money was short we gladly sold household objects; facing in a resigned way the reprimands from our respective families."

V

As already noted, the 1968 London reprint of Bolloten's *The Spanish Civil War and Revolution 1936–1939* has vanished from the publishers lists, but a new and enlarged American edition was published by the University of North Carolina Press in 1979. The title has again been changed, this time to *The Spanish Revolution: The Left and the Struggle for Power during the Civil War*, and Trevor-Roper's politically naive introduction has been replaced by a short inoffensive foreword by Raymond Carr, which the publishers presumably hope will help to sell a few more copies.

I would be failing in my advocacy of Bolloten for all students of the Spanish revolution, were I not to refer in some detail to the editorial reorganisation of this new edition. The text runs to 477 pages of very readable source material, followed by 100 pages of notes with running heads referring to the pages in the text, thus making it an easy matter to consult the important notes at the time of reading the text; then there is a 30-page bibliography, which unfortunately in a number of cases has not been updated so far as new editions or English translations are concerned; and last, and most importantly, an invaluable 50-page index. Many of the footnotes in the original edition have rightly been incorporated into the text. Two chapters on "Catalonia: Revolution and Counter-Revolution" and "Barcelona: The May Events" have been added as well as an "Epilogue: The Demise of the Revolution" which covers the rise of Juan Negrín after the May Days of 1937 to the end of the Civil War in March 1939, which obviously cannot be adequately dealt with in a mere 20 pages. But the author is right in concentrating on events up to the May Days of 1937.

One chapter from the original edition has been omitted, though it hardly filled a page. Yet it seemed to me at the time that it was one of the most important statements in the book and endeared the author to me from the start. The first paragraph read:

> Although the outbreak of the Spanish Civil War in July, 1936, was followed by a far-reaching social revolution in the anti-Franco camp—more profound in some respects than the Bolshevik Revolution in its early stages—millions of discerning people outside Spain were kept in ignorance, not only of its depth and range, but even of its existence, by virtue of a policy of duplicity and dissimulation of which there is no parallel in history.

To my protests at the exclusion of this brief chapter the author generously replied, "I am in total agreement with you that it was a mistake on my part to eliminate the opening paragraphs that appeared in *The Grand Camouflage*. Whenever I get a chance to revise the book again I shall restore those passages." And his reason for wishing to do so is significant: "for I have since learned that even though they were written twenty years ago people, on the whole, are still unaware of the unparalleled revolution that took place in Spain."[1]

The new material I think presents the socialist/trade union leader Largo Caballero in too favourable a light—as a victim of intrigues—whereas he was an old fox, as are all trade union leaders—not least the anarcho-syndicalist variety, such as Juan López, Peiró, and Pestaña. I also disagree with the importance he attaches to Lorenzo's book, for the reasons given in my bibliographical postscript. But these are minor criticisms. Bolloten's *The Spanish Revolution* is surely the most important account and source book available in English and deserves wider distribution in this country.

Two further source books are now available in English. *Durruti: The People Armed* by Abel Paz (Montréal: Black Rose Books, 1976), badly translated from the French, is specially useful for the material he presents on Durruti and his group, which cannot be found elsewhere. It suffers by being a completely uncritical study of the man. Perhaps as an antidote the reader should see what García Oliver has to say of Durruti in his memoirs, *El Eco de les Pasos* (Barcelona: Ruedo Iberico, 1978). After all they were both members of "Los Solidarios" direct-action group. His comments are far from adulatory. But how reliable are such memoirs written nearly forty years after the events? A number of other leading figures in the Spanish anarcho-syndicalist and anarchist movement, including Juan López and Cipriano Mera, have published their memoirs in the past decade.

For English readers Ronald Fraser's *Blood of Spain*, briefly referred to in the previous footnote, is really important, because, as the blurb on the dust jacket puts it, you have a "mosaic" of more than three hundred personal accounts recorded between 1973 and 1975, 95 per cent of which were recorded in Spain, the rest in France. And the author declares, "No problems were put in my way. Apart from caution in rural areas, especially in Andalusia where there was still fear, people talked openly." (My own experience, limited

---

1   In a letter dated July 31, 1980.

to Catalonia, and much earlier—from 1958—was that in the rural areas people talked openly, because they knew who could not be trusted in the community, whereas in Barcelona, for instance, you did not know your neighbour at the next cafe table, and therefore you only talked openly at home or outside away from the crowds.) For those who really want to draw conclusions, learn lessons from the Spanish revolution, as human beings trying to make some sense in their own lives today, in Britain, this book in each of its six hundred pages has some gem to provoke thought and for reflection. There are so many interviews I would wish to quote verbatim! Margarita Balaguer, an eighteen-year-old seamstress in a haute couture fashion house "which she had attempted unsuccessfully to collectivize found the liberation of women the most rewarding of all the revolutionary conquests. For as long as she could remember, she had fought the accepted notion that 'men and women could never be friends.' Now she found she had better friends among men than among women. A new comradeship had arisen." And the author quotes her own words: "It was like being brothers and sisters. It had always annoyed me that men in this country didn't consider women as beings with full human rights. But now there was this big change. I believe it arose spontaneously out of the revolutionary movement."

In 1939, Franco won the war. How many more like Margarita Balaguer had made *their* revolution by then and survived as human beings those thirty-six years of dictatorship and religious obscurantism. One will not find any answers in the major historical works, but one does get an idea of what can be positive for some individuals even from a revolt that failed in this moving and important work.

VI

Ten years ago, I remarked that "surprisingly few critical works" had been published in the fifteen years between the editions of my book. Such is still the case in spite of the fact that Franco has been dead for at least seven years and the political and trade union free-for-all battle has, at the time of writing, led to the overwhelming victory of González's Socialist Party on a typical British social democratic programme. Perhaps it is not necessary to draw lessons from the experience of 1936–1939: events speak for themselves. Where are the CNT and the FAI today?

Peirats's book is now available in English, and, apart from the background material (already referred to), it is a very harsh criticism of the hierarchy of the CNT-FAI, much more critical than anything I have written in my book. And the preface, written in 1974 before Franco's death, is pessimistic for the future of the movement. The short postscript written after Franco's death is understandably optimistic, but I would not think of quoting against him the remark that "a promising new stage is opening up to anarchism in Spain." What I do feel justified in noting for anarchists who want to seriously learn something from the Spanish experience is that even Peirats, when the 1953 edition of my *Lessons* was published, condescendingly referred to it in *CENIT* (Toulouse) as "*esta obrita*" (in spite of the fact that "this minor work" was inspired by the publication of his monumental history!), but that apart, he criticised the book for being too "*severo*" not only of the "movement" but also of "individuals." Obviously if one is putting over the idea that the anarcho-syndicalist unions differ from the socialist trade unions by being organised from below upwards instead of from above, there are no leaders to blame if things go wrong. But in practice the more successful anarcho-syndicalist organisations are the more liable are they to be very quickly faced with the kinds of problems that are endemic in the reformist trade unions. So long as anarcho-syndicalist propagandists fail to recognise these problems, the experience of the CNT in Spain in 1936–1939 is lost on them.

Peirats did say at the time (1954) that though only a small part of the documentation on the events of 1936–1939 had been published, "it can be said that the basic material for examination is available to the student. And it is time that the task of completing an objective analysis is carried out. It is of importance to anarchists to draw the lessons of the facts and actions of their own movement." And he declares that I did this, apart from being too "*severo*," and later he adds "*demasiado lateral*" (too biased) and selective. He concludes: "none of his statements will be contradicted by history. But when one writes for the general public it is the measure of justice, not of clemency, to give to facts their relative importance." I think that readers of Peirats's *Anarchists in the Spanish Revolution* may well agree with me that belatedly the historiographer of the CNT has spelt out the lessons with more "severity" and less "clemency" for the leaders than will be found in my *Lessons*. And the memoirs of López, Oliver and Mera, and Horacio Prieto (via his son Cesar Lorenzo) are as politically revealing of the writers (in demonstrating that power, office, not only corrupts the others but anarchist ministers, anarchist colonels too) as they are of the moral and political frailty of their erstwhile comrades.

The dearth of books seeking to draw conclusions from the Spanish experience (I am only referring to what is available in English; I am sure that it is not the case in Spain, though I suspect that the great post-Franco publishing boom has come to an end— in spite of the fact that more histories appear from time to time) is a confirmation of Bolloten's remark that people on the whole are still unaware of the unparalleled revolution that took place in Spain"—but obviously enjoy "a good read" about the *war* or about the Reds burning churches and killing priests. Where one does occasionally find material drawing the lessons from an anarchist/ revolutionary standpoint is in the alternative press. For instance, *Telos*, an "American quarterly journal of radical thought," (in no. 34, Winter 1977–1978) used the occasion of the publication of Murray Bookchin's history to publish a long critical review by Michael Scrivener of that book and Sam Dolgoff's on the collectives and my *Lessons. Social Alternatives* 2, no. 3 (February 1982), published in Australia, has a long essay by Gregg George on "Social Alternatives and the State: Some Lessons of the Spanish Revolution," which indicates how important that experience could be for anarchists whose thoughts and propaganda are directed to the twenty-first century and not to the nineteenth.

BIBLIOGRAPHIC ADDENDUM

Vernon Richards's prediction of a "growing volume of material on different aspects of the Spanish Civil War, mainly coming from Spain," has proved correct. An abundance of academic and popular histories and memoirs has been produced in the thirty-six years since the author's last update to his postscript. The growth of the internet has meant that interested persons now have at their fingertips a wealth of primary and secondary resources that would have enraptured Richards just as surely as the web's less wholesome aspects would have appalled him. Any short survey of this literature must necessarily be incomplete. In this case it is doubly so as I have restricted myself to what is available in English, save for a brief consideration of authors I consider particularly salient and deserving of the attention of publishers and translators.

In this period, our historical understanding of Spanish anarchism before and during the Civil War has—to my mind—been most enhanced by work relating to the defence committees and to the role of women. In the former category, the contributions of Agustín Guillamón and Chris Ealham have been transformative. In *Ready for Revolution: The CNT Defense Committees in Barcelona, 1933–1938* (Oakland: AK Press, 2014), translated by Paul Sharkey, Agustín Guillamón—probably the most prolific historian working on the Civil War today—foregrounds the composition, functioning, and role of the committees tasked with forming the shock troops of the CNT's longed-for revolution. In meticulous detail, Guillamón demonstrates the fundamental contribution of the committees to the defeat of the mutinous army in Barcelona in July 1936 and in the subsequent revolutionary transformation of the city. Meanwhile, Chris Ealham's *Anarchism and the City: Revolution and Counter-Revolution in Barcelona, 1898–1937* (Oakland: AK Press: 2010) is the best single-volume account of the anarchist movement during the republican period. Its absorbing depiction of the social and cultural universe of Barcelona anarchism is essential to understanding the context in which the defence committees operated. Interested readers should also seek out a copy of the volume that Ealham edited with Michael Richards, *The Splintering of Spain: Cultural History and the Spanish Civil War* (Cambridge: Cambridge University Press, 2009). Ealham's own contribution, "The Myth of the Maddened Crowd: Class, Culture and Space in the Revolutionary Urbanist Project in Barcelona, 1936–1937," is an insightful, sympathetic, and beautifully written interpretation of its subject.

On anarchist women, Martha Ackelsberg's study of the Mujeres Libres grouping, *Free Women of Spain: Anarchism and the Struggle for the Emancipation of Women* (Oakland: AK Press, 2004) is as inspiring as it is authoritative. Mujeres Libres was an autonomous organisation of anarchist women that grew into a federation thousands strong during the Civil War but was never recognised as an official branch of the Spanish Libertarian Movement. Ackelsberg, who was able to interview several former members in the course of her research, depicts the efforts made by women to struggle for equality both within the anarchist movement and in the wider society of Republican Spain. The ready availability of Ackelsberg's book in an affordable edition has unfortunately not prevented untenable comparisons being drawn between Mujeres Libres, an organisation operating in the rearguard, and women's battalions fighting on the front line in present-day conflicts. Beyond Ackelsberg's work, English-language readers might also consult the biographies of members of Mujeres Libres written by Nick Heath and hosted on libcom.org and Paul Sharkey's translation of an important article by one of the organisation's founders, Lucía Sánchez Saornil, included in Robert Graham, *Anarchism: A Documentary History of Libertarian Ideas: From Anarchy to Anarchism (300CE–1939)*, vol. 1 (Montréal: Black Rose Books, 2005).

Paul Sharkey will doubtless be familiar to readers as a tireless translator of valuable works of anarchist history. It is due to his efforts that several of the works mentioned by Vernon Richards in his bibliography are now available in English-language editions, alongside an enormous and growing list of shorter primary and secondary material available through the website of the Kate Sharpley Library—itself a mine of information and commentary. Notable examples of Sharkey's translation work include: Frank Mintz, *Anarchism and Workers' Self-Management in Revolutionary Spain* (Oakland: AK Press, 2012); Abel Paz, *Story of the Iron Column: Militant Anarchism in the Spanish Civil War* (Oakland: AK Press, 2014); and his contribution to the monumental three-volume José Peirats, *The CNT in the Spanish Revolution* (Oakland: PM Press, 2011–2012), in which endeavour he was joined by Chris Ealham. The bringing of this invaluable work to an Anglophone audience was also due to the efforts of Paul Preston and Stuart Christie, whose *We, the Anarchists!: A Study of the Iberian Anarchist Federation (FAI) 1927–1937* (London: Meltzer Press, 2002) and christiebooks website are further resources of enormous value for enthusiasts of anarchist history. Sharkey's admirable output is due to expand with the translated edition of *The Sons of Night: Antoine Gimenez's Memories of the War in Spain* (Oakland: AK Press: 2019), an intriguing and entertaining war memoir made essential by the additional notes and biographical material provided by the editors, the "Gimenologues." The detective work carried out by this historian affinity group proves that the passing of the final survivors of the "generation of 36" has not exhausted the possibility of new insights and avenues of investigation emerging through the exertions of committed historians.

Further vital translations of recent years include Chuck Morse's elegant treatment of the epic work by Abel Paz, *Durruti in the Spanish Revolution* (Oakland: AK Press, 2007)—previously only available in English in the abridged edition mentioned by Richards—and the useful, though less sympathetic, Julián Casanova, *Anarchism, the Republic and Civil War in Spain: 1931–1939* (London: Routledge, 2014), translated by Andrew Dowling and Graham

Pollok and revised by Paul Preston. Meanwhile, the anonymous contributor "Alias Recluse" has made innumerable short translations of important primary sources and historical commentary freely available to libcom.org. It is to be hoped that other works currently unavailable in English but replete with insight and information, such as those of Anna Monjo, Eulàlia Vega, Manel Aisa, and Miquel Amorós, among many others, are on the radar of publishers and translators.

To this brief survey we might add local studies of Spanish anarchism during the Republic and Civil War, such as Pamela Beth Radcliff, *From Mobilization to Civil War: The Politics of Polarization in the Spanish City of Gijón, 1900–1937* (Cambridge: Cambridge University Press, 2002), Richard Purkiss, *Democracy, Trade Unions and Political Violence in Spain: The Valencian Anarchist Movement, 1918–1936* (Brighton, UK: Sussex Academic Press, 2011), and Graham Kelsey, *Anarchosyndicalism, Libertarian Communism and the State: The CNT in Zaragoza and Aragon, 1930–1937* (Dordrecht, NL: Springer, 1992), a new edition of which is apparently in the pipeline. Furthermore, the movement's pre-war years have been treated in works that include the path-breaking and recently republished Temma Kaplan, *Anarchists of Andalusia, 1868–1903* (Princeton, NJ: Princeton University Press, 2015), George Esenwein, *Anarchist Ideology and the Working-Class Movement in Spain, 1868–1898* (Berkeley: University of California Press, 1989), Jason Garner, *Goals and Means: Anarchism, Syndicalism, and Internationalism in the Origins of the Federacion Anarquista Iberica* (Oakland: AK Press, 2016) and the indispensable contribution from James Michael Yeoman, *Print Culture and the Formation of the Anarchist Movement in Spain: 1890–1915* (London: Routledge, forthcoming). It would be remiss not to also mention the light shone on some of the movement's less well-known aspects by Richard Cleminson, *Anarchism, Science and Sex* (Oxford: Peter Lang, 2000) and *Anarchism and Eugenics: An Unlikely Convergence, 1890–1940* (Manchester, UK: Manchester University Press, 2019).

The examples of English-language scholarship on Spanish anarchism mentioned in this far from exhaustive overview allow for a nuanced appreciation of what was a heterogeneous movement. Nevertheless, they have not made much of a dent on mainstream narrative histories of the Spanish Civil War. The most widely read historian of the period, Paul Preston, has moved in the opposite direction to the drift of specialist historiography, providing increasingly caricatured depictions of Spanish anarchists in his later work, most notably *The Spanish Holocaust* (London: Harper Press, 2013). His treatment of Antonio Martín, an anarchist murdered by Catalan nationalists in April 1937, has been thoroughly debunked by a recent and as yet untranslated work by Agustín Guillamón and Antonio Gascón, *Nacionalistas contra anarquistas en la Cerdaña (1936–37)* (Barcelona: Descontrol, 2018). The scant likelihood of this important contribution causing any significant revision to common tropes in mainstream history about anarchist "uncontrollables" has been anticipated by the authors in a combative manifesto translated by Paul Sharkey and hosted on the christiebooks website.

Nevertheless, the temporal, topical, and geographical expansion of scholarship on Spanish anarchism, combined with the almost overwhelming amount of material available online, has vastly expanded the potential for Anglophone anarchists to revisit the "lessons" of the Spanish Revolution. In fact, the sheer volume may help to explain the evident and regrettable imbalance between the amount of material available and the debate and discussion proceeding from it in the broader left-libertarian milieu. The question of where the interested but busy and bewildered rookie might start is a justifiable one, and it is in the hope of suggesting a way that the present survey is offered. Meanwhile, it is up to historians to make the case that the excavation of a useable past remains imperative for projects seeking to transform the present. The efforts being made to preserve the memory and enhance our understanding of libertarian Spain are hopeful contributions to that broader endeavour.

Danny Evans

INDEX

"Passim" (literally "scattered") indicates intermittent discussion of a topic over a cluster of pages.

ABOUT THE AUTHORS

Vernon Richards was a presence in anarchist publishing in Britain from the early 1930s until his death in December 2001. His publishing activity encompassed both his work with Freedom Press and as an editor of the anarchist newspaper *Freedom*—including its pre-war and wartime variations—a relationship that lasted into the nineties. Richards, who was imprisoned for nine months in 1945 for conspiring to cause disaffection among members of the armed forces, also translated works by the Italian anarchist Errico Malatesta, and as an avid photographer took a rare collection of photos of George Orwell. Richards's central place in twentieth-century British anarchism cannot be overestimated.

David Goodway is a British social and cultural historian who for thirty years has written principally on anarchism and libertarian socialism. He is the author of *Anarchist Seeds beneath the Snow: Left-Libertarian Thought and British Writers from William Morris to Colin Ward* and editor of *For Anarchism, Herbert Read Reassessed, The Letters of John Cowper Powys and Emma Goldman*, and collections of the writings of Alex Comfort, Herbert Read, Maurice Brinton, and Nicolas Walter.

Danny Evans is the author of *Revolution and the State: Anarchism in the Spanish Civil War* (London: Routledge, 2018), which, too modestly, he has not included in his admirable addendum.

ABOUT PM PRESS

PM Press was founded at the end of 2007 by a small collection of folks with decades of publishing, media, and organizing experience. PM Press co-conspirators have published and distributed hundreds of books, pamphlets, CDs, and DVDs. Members of PM have founded enduring book fairs, spearheaded victorious tenant organizing campaigns, and worked closely with bookstores, academic conferences, and even rock bands to deliver political and challenging ideas to all walks of life. We're old enough to know what we're doing and young enough to know what's at stake.

We seek to create radical and stimulating fiction and non-fiction books, pamphlets, T-shirts, visual and audio materials to entertain, educate, and inspire you. We aim to distribute these through every available channel with every available technology—whether that means you are seeing anarchist classics at our bookfair stalls, reading our latest vegan cookbook at the café, downloading geeky fiction e-books, or digging new music and timely videos from our website.

PM Press is always on the lookout for talented and skilled volunteers, artists, activists, and writers to work with. If you have a great idea for a project or can contribute in some way, please get in touch.

PM Press
PO Box 23912
Oakland, CA 94623
www.pmpress.org

PM Press in Europe
europe@pmpress.org
www.pmpress.org.uk

FRIENDS OF PM PRESS

These are indisputably momentous times—the financial system is melting down globally and the Empire is stumbling. Now more than ever there is a vital need for radical ideas.

In the years since its founding—and on a mere shoestring—PM Press has risen to the formidable challenge of publishing and distributing knowledge and entertainment for the struggles ahead. With over 300 releases to date, we have published an impressive and stimulating array of literature, art, music, politics, and culture. Using every available medium, we've succeeded in connecting those hungry for ideas and information to those putting them into practice.

Friends of PM allows you to directly help impact, amplify, and revitalize the discourse and actions of radical writers, filmmakers, and artists. It provides us with a stable foundation from which we can build upon our early successes and provides a much-needed subsidy for the materials that can't necessarily pay their own way. You can help make that happen—and receive every new title automatically delivered to your door once a month—by joining as a Friend of PM Press. And, we'll throw in a free T-shirt when you sign up.

Here are your options:

- **$30 a month** Get all books and pamphlets plus 50% discount on all webstore purchases

- **$40 a month** Get all PM Press releases (including CDs and DVDs) plus 50% discount on all webstore purchases

- **$100 a month** Superstar—Everything plus PM merchandise, free downloads, and 50% discount on all webstore purchases

For those who can't afford $30 or more a month, we have **Sustainer Rates** at $15, $10 and $5. Sustainers get a free PM Press T-shirt and a 50% discount on all purchases from our website.

Your Visa or Mastercard will be billed once a month, until you tell us to stop. Or until our efforts succeed in bringing the revolution around. Or the financial meltdown of Capital makes plastic redundant. Whichever comes first.

FREEDOM

ABOUT FREEDOM PRESS

The oldest anarchist publishing house in the English-speaking world, Freedom Press was founded in London by a group of volunteers including Charlotte Wilson and Peter Kropotkin in 1886.

The Press has repeatedly been the target of state repression, from crackdowns in the 1890s to raids during World War I and most famously, at the end of World War II. The 1945 free speech case, which saw four editors of its journal *War Commentary* arrested for causing "disaffection in the armed forces," prompted support from many famous names including Herbert Read, George Orwell, Benjamin Britten, and E.M. Forster. Three were jailed.

Despite this and many other threats, from fascists to organised crime, for over a century Freedom has regularly published works on the philosophy and activities of anarchists, and produced its *Freedom Newspaper* for the best part of a century. Freedom now maintains an anarchist-focused news site, www.freedomnews.org.uk, and publishes a biannual free journal.

Freedom runs Britain's largest anarchist bookshop at its home of more than 50 years in Whitechapel, in the heart of London. The upper floors of the Freedom building are home to a number of anarchist organisations, and the venue regularly hosts talks, meetings, and events for the wider movement.

About the Freedom Press Library Series
Freedom Press has partnered with PM Press to republish titles from Freedom's back catalogue, bringing important works back into circulation with new introductions and additional commentary. *Lessons of the Spanish Revolution* is part of this series.

Freedom Press
84b Whitechapel High St
London, E1 7QX

www.freedompress.org.uk
www.freedomnews.org.uk

The CNT in the Spanish Revolution Vols. 1–3

José Peirats

Introduction by Chris Ealham

Vol. 1 **ISBN: 978-1-60486-207-2**
$28.00   432 pages

Vol. 2 **ISBN: 978-1-60486-208-9**
$22.95   312 pages

Vol. 3 **ISBN: 978-1-60486-209-6**
$22.95   296 pages

The CNT in the Spanish Revolution is the history
of one of the most original and audacious, and
arguably also the most far-reaching, of all the
twentieth-century revolutions. It is the history
of the giddy years of political change and hope
in 1930s Spain, when the so-called 'Generation
of '36', Peirats' own generation, rose up against
the oppressive structures of Spanish society. It is
also a history of a revolution that failed, crushed
in the jaws of its enemies on both the reformist
left and the reactionary right. José Peirats' account
is effectively the official CNT history of the war,
passionate, partisan but, above all, intelligent.
Its huge sweeping canvas covers all areas of the
anarchist experience—the spontaneous militias,
the revolutionary collectives, the moral dilemmas
occasioned by the clash of revolutionary ideals and
the stark reality of the war effort against Franco and
his German Nazi and Italian Fascist allies.

This new edition is carefully indexed in a way that
converts the work into a usable tool for historians and makes it much easier
for the general reader to dip in with greater purpose and pleasure.

"*José Peirats' The CNT in the Spanish Revolution is a landmark in the
historiography of the Spanish Civil War. . . . Originally published in Toulouse in
the early 1950s, it was a rarity anxiously searched for by historians and others
who gleefully pillaged its wealth of documentation. Even its republication in Paris
in 1971 by the exiled Spanish publishing house, Ruedo Ibérico, though welcome,
still left the book in the territory of specialists. For that reason alone, the present
project to publish the entire work in English is to be applauded.*"
—Professor Paul Preston, London School of Economics

Collectives in the Spanish Revolution

Gaston Leval
Translation and Foreword by Vernon Richards
Introduction by Pedro García-Guirao

ISBN: 978-1-62963-447-0
$27.95   416 pages

Revolutionary Spain came about with an explosion of social change so advanced and sweeping that it remains widely studied as one of the foremost experiments in worker self-management in history. At the heart of this vast foray into toppling entrenched forms of domination and centralised control was the flourishing of an array of worker-run collectives in industry, agriculture, public services, and beyond.

Collectives in the Spanish Revolution is a unique account of this transformative process—a work combining impeccable research and analysis with lucid reportage. Its author, Gaston Leval, was not only a participant in the Revolution and a dedicated anarcho-syndicalist but an especially knowledgeable eyewitness to the many industrial and agrarian collectives. In documenting the collectives' organisation and how they improved working conditions and increased output, Leval also gave voice to the workers who made them, recording their stories and experiences. At the same time, Leval did not shy away from exploring some of the collectives' failings, often ignored in other accounts of the period, opening space for readers today to critically draw lessons from the Spanish experience with self-managed collectives.

This classic translation of the French original by Vernon Richards is presented in this edition for the first time with an index. A new introduction by Pedro García-Guirao and a preface by Stuart Christie offer a précis of Leval's life and methods, placing his landmark study in the context of more recent writing on the Spanish collectives—eloquently positing that Leval's account of collectivism and his assessments of their achievements and failings still have a great deal to teach us today.

Life and Ideas: The Anarchist Writings of Errico Malatesta

Errico Malatesta
Edited by Vernon Richards
Foreword by Carl Levy

ISBN: 978-1-62963-032-8
$21.95   320 pages

With the timely reprinting of this selection of
Malatesta's writings, first published in 1965
by Freedom Press, the full range of this great
anarchist activist's ideas are once again in
circulation. *Life and Ideas* gathers excerpts from Malatesta's writings over a
lifetime of revolutionary activity.

The editor, Vernon Richards, has translated hundreds of articles by Malatesta,
taken from the journals Malatesta either edited himself or contributed to,
from the earliest, *L'En Dehors* of 1892, through to *Pensiero e Volontà*, which
was forced to close by Mussolini's fascists in 1926, and the bilingual *Il
Risveglio/Le Réveil*, which published most of his writings after that date.
These articles have been pruned down to their essentials and collected under
subheadings ranging from "Ends and Means" to "Anarchist Propaganda."
Through the selections Malatesta's classical anarchism emerges: a
revolutionary, nonpacifist, nonreformist vision informed by decades of
engagement in struggle and study. In addition there is a short biographical
piece and an essay by the editor.

"*The first thing that strikes the reader about Malatesta is his lucidity and
straightforwardness. For him anarchism was not a philosophy for a future
utopia which would come about one day as if by magic, or simply through
the destruction of the state without any prior preparation. On the contrary,
Malatesta was, throughout his life, concerned with a practical idea. His
anarchism was something concrete, to be fought for and put into practice, not in
some distant future but now. It is in this aspect of practical anarchism that gives
him a special place amongst anarchist theorists and propagandists.*"
—Cienfuegos Press Anarchist Review

Anarchist Seeds beneath the Snow: Left-Libertarian Thought and British Writers from William Morris to Colin Ward

David Goodway

ISBN: 978-1-60486-221-8
$24.95   448 pages

From William Morris to Oscar Wilde to George Orwell, left-libertarian thought has long been an important but neglected part of British cultural and political history. In *Anarchist Seeds beneath the Snow*, David Goodway seeks to recover and revitalize that indigenous anarchist tradition. This book succeeds as simultaneously a cultural history of left-libertarian thought in Britain and a demonstration of the applicability of that history to current politics. Goodway argues that a recovered anarchist tradition could—and should—be a touchstone for contemporary political radicals. Moving seamlessly from Aldous Huxley and Colin Ward to the war in Iraq, this challenging volume will energize leftist movements throughout the world.

"*Anarchist Seeds beneath the Snow is an impressive achievement for its rigorous scholarship across a wide range of sources, for collating this diverse material in a cogent and systematic narrative-cum-argument, and for elucidating it with clarity and flair . . . It is a book that needed to be written and now deserves to be read.*"
—*Journal of William Morris Studies*

"*Goodway outlines with admirable clarity the many variations in anarchist thought. By extending outwards to left-libertarians he takes on even greater diversity.*"
—Sheila Rowbotham, *Red Pepper*

"*A splendid survey of 'left-libertarian thought' in this country, it has given me hours of delight and interest. Though it is very learned, it isn't dry. Goodway's friends in the awkward squad (especially William Blake) are both stimulating and comforting companions in today's political climate.*"
—A.N. Wilson, *Daily Telegraph*

Damned Fools in Utopia: And Other Writings on Anarchism and War Resistance

Nicolas Walter
Edited by David Goodway

ISBN: 978-1-60486-222-5
$22.95   304 pages

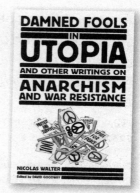

Nicolas Walter was the son of the neurologist, W. Grey Walter, and both his grandfathers had known Peter Kropotkin and Edward Carpenter. However, it was the twin jolts of Suez and the Hungarian Revolution while still a student, followed by participation in the resulting New Left and nuclear disarmament movement, that led him to anarchism himself. His personal history is recounted in two autobiographical pieces in this collection as well as the editor's introduction.

During the 1960s he was a militant in the British nuclear disarmament movement—especially its direct-action wing, the Committee of 100—he was one of the Spies for Peace (who revealed the State's preparations for the governance of Britain after a nuclear war), he was close to the innovative Solidarity Group and was a participant in the homelessness agitation. Concurrently with his impressive activism he was analyzing acutely and lucidly the history, practice, and theory of these intertwined movements; and it is such writings—including "Non-violent Resistance" and "The Spies for Peace and After"—that form the core of this book. But there are also memorable pieces on various libertarians, including the writers George Orwell, Herbert Read, and Alan Sillitoe, the publisher C.W. Daniel and the maverick Guy A. Aldred. "The Right to be Wrong" is a notable polemic against laws limiting the freedom of expression. Other than anarchism, the passion of Walter's intellectual life was the dual cause of atheism and rationalism; and the selection concludes appropriately with a fine essay on "Anarchism and Religion" and his moving reflections, "Facing Death."

Nicolas Walter scorned the pomp and frequent ignorance of the powerful and detested the obfuscatory prose and intellectual limitations of academia. He himself wrote straightforwardly and always accessibly, almost exclusively for the anarchist and freethought movements. The items collected in this volume display him at his considerable best.

About Anarchism

Nicolas Walter
Introduction by Natasha Walter

ISBN: 978-1-62963-640-5
$14.95   96 pages

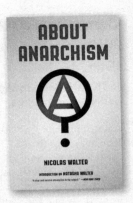

Today the word "anarchism" inspires both fear and fascination. But few people understand what anarchists believe, what anarchists want, and what anarchists do. This incisive book puts forward the case for anarchism as a pragmatic philosophy.

Originally written in 1969 and updated for the twenty-first century, *About Anarchism* is an uncluttered, precise, and urgently necessary expression of practical anarchism. Crafted in deliberately simple prose and without constant reference to other writers or past events, it can be understood without difficulty and without any prior knowledge of political ideology.

As one of the finest short introductions to the basic concepts, theories, and applications of anarchism, *About Anarchism* has been translated into many languages, including French, Spanish, Japanese, Chinese, Polish, and Russian. This new edition includes an updated introduction from Natasha Walter and an expanded biographical sketch of the author, Nicolas Walter, who was a respected writer, journalist, and an active protester against the powers of both the church and the state.

"A clear and incisive introduction to the subject."
—*New York Times*

"Walter's anarchism incorporates a wealth of influences and the best of both old and new anarchism. Almost every paragraph in this book contains examples of his subversive thinking, and many of his observations push contemporary anarchists to think harder about the nature of politics."
—Andrej Grubačić, coauthor of *Living at the Edges of Capitalism: Adventures in Exile and Mutual Aid*

"Nicolas Walter was a writer and lecturer of deep secular humanist and anarchist convictions—his book About Anarchism *is known round the world."*
—*Guardian*

Demanding the Impossible: A History of Anarchism

Peter Marshall

ISBN: 978-1-60486-064-1
$28.95   840 pages

Navigating the broad "river of anarchy," from Taoism to Situationism, from Ranters to Punk rockers, from individualists to communists, from anarcho-syndicalists to anarcha-feminists, *Demanding the Impossible* is an authoritative and lively study of a widely misunderstood subject. It explores the key anarchist concepts of society and the state, freedom and equality, authority and power, and investigates the successes and failure of the anarchist movements throughout the world. While remaining sympathetic to anarchism, it presents a balanced and critical account. It covers not only the classic anarchist thinkers, such as Godwin, Proudhon, Bakunin, Kropotkin, Reclus and Emma Goldman, but also other libertarian figures, such as Nietzsche, Camus, Gandhi, Foucault and Chomsky. No other book on anarchism covers so much so incisively.

In this updated edition, a new epilogue examines the most recent developments, including "post-anarchism" and "anarcho-primitivism" as well as the anarchist contribution to the peace, green and Global Justice movements.

Demanding the Impossible is essential reading for anyone wishing to understand what anarchists stand for and what they have achieved. It will also appeal to those who want to discover how anarchism offers an inspiring and original body of ideas and practices which is more relevant than ever in the twenty-first century.

"Demanding the Impossible *is the book I always recommend when asked—as I often am—for something on the history and ideas of anarchism.*"
—Noam Chomsky

"*Attractively written and fully referenced… bound to be the standard history.*"
—Colin Ward, *Times Educational Supplement*

"*Large, labyrinthine, tentative: for me these are all adjectives of praise when applied to works of history, and* Demanding the Impossible *meets all of them.*"
—George Woodcock, *Independent*

Anarchy, Geography, Modernity: Selected Writings of Elisée Reclus

Elisée Reclus
Edited by John P. Clark and Camille Martin
ISBN: 978-1-60486-429-8
$22.95   304 pages

Anarchy, Geography, Modernity is the first comprehensive introduction to the thought of Elisée Reclus, the great anarchist geographer and political theorist. It shows him to be an extraordinary figure for his age. Not only an anarchist but also a radical feminist, anti-racist, ecologist, animal rights advocate, cultural radical, nudist, and vegetarian. Not only a major social thinker but also a dedicated revolutionary.

The work analyzes Reclus' greatest achievement, a sweeping historical and theoretical synthesis recounting the story of the earth and humanity as an epochal struggle between freedom and domination. It presents his groundbreaking critique of all forms of domination: not only capitalism, the state, and authoritarian religion, but also patriarchy, racism, technological domination, and the domination of nature. His crucial insights on the interrelation between personal and small-group transformation, broader cultural change, and large-scale social organization are explored. Reclus' ideas are presented both through detailed exposition and analysis, and in extensive translations of key texts, most appearing in English for the first time.

"For far too long Elisée Reclus has stood in the shadow of Godwin, Proudhon, Bakunin, Kropotkin, and Emma Goldman. Now John Clark has pulled Reclus forward to stand shoulder to shoulder with Anarchism's cynosures. Reclus' light brought into anarchism's compass not only a focus on ecology, but a struggle against both patriarchy and racism. No serious reader can afford to neglect this book."
—Dana Ward, Pitzer College

"Finally! A century after his death, the great French geographer and anarchist Elisée Reclus has been honored by a vibrant selection of his writings expertly translated into English."
—Kent Mathewson, Louisiana State University

All Power to the Councils!
A Documentary History of the
German Revolution of 1918–1919

Edited and translated by Gabriel Kuhn

ISBN: 978-1-60486-111-2
$26.95   352 pages

The German Revolution erupted out of the ashes of World War I, triggered by mutinying sailors refusing to be sacrificed in the final carnage of the war. While the Social Democrats grabbed power, radicals across the country rallied to establish a communist society under the slogan "All Power to the Councils!" The Spartacus League launched an uprising in Berlin, council republics were proclaimed in Bremen and Bavaria, and workers' revolts shook numerous German towns. Yet in an act that would tragically shape the course of history, the Social Democratic government crushed the rebellions with the help of right-wing militias, paving the way for the ill-fated Weimar Republic—and ultimately the ascension of the Nazis.

This definitive documentary history collects manifestos, speeches, articles, and letters from the German Revolution—Rosa Luxemburg, the Revolutionary Stewards, and Gustav Landauer amongst others—introduced and annotated by the editor. Many documents, such as the anarchist Erich Mühsam's comprehensive account of the Bavarian Council Republic, are presented here in English for the first time. The volume also includes materials from the Red Ruhr Army that repelled the reactionary Kapp Putsch in 1920 and the communist bandits that roamed Eastern Germany until 1921. *All Power to the Councils!* provides a dynamic and vivid picture of a time of great hope and devastating betrayal.

"*Gabriel Kuhn's excellent volume illuminates a profound global revolutionary moment, in which brilliant ideas and debates lit the sky.*"
—Marcus Rediker, author of *Villains of All Nations* and *The Slave Ship*

"*This remarkable collection, skillfully edited by Gabriel Kuhn, brings to life that most pivotal of revolutions, crackling with the acrid odor of street fighting, insurgent hopes, and ultimately defeat… In an era brimming with anticapitalist aspirations, these pages ring with that still unmet revolutionary promise of a better world: I was, I am, I shall be.*"
—Sasha Lilley, author of *Capital and Its Discontents* and coauthor of *Catastrophism*